OTHER BOOKS BY RICHARD OFSHE AND ETHAN WATTERS

MAKING MONSTERS
False Memories, Psychotherapy, and Sexual Hysteria

THERAPY'S DELUSIONS

THE MYTH OF THE UNCONSCIOUS
AND THE EXPLOITATION OF TODAY'S
WALKING WORRIED

ETHAN WATTERS
AND RICHARD OFSHE

SCRIBNER

SCRIBNER
1230 Avenue of the Americas
New York, NY 10020

SCRIBNER and design are trademarks of Simon & Schuster Inc.

DESIGNED BY ERICH HOBBING

Set in Sabon

Manufactured in the United States of America

1   3   5   7   9   10   8   6   4   2

Library of Congress Cataloging-in-Publication Data
Watters, Ethan.
Therapy's delusions : the myth of the
unconscious and the exploitation of today's
walking worried / Ethan Watters and Richard Ofshe.
p.   cm.
Includes bibliographical references and index.
1. Antipsychiatry. 2. Psychodynamic psychotherapy.
3. Psychoanalysis. I. Ofshe, Richard. II. Title.
RC437.5.W39   1999
616.89'14—dc21   98-53528
CIP

ISBN 0-684-83584-3

To Frank Watters,
for his moral support
and contribution to this book.

Contents

Preface and
Acknowledgments

The order of the authors' names has been reversed from their first book collaboration (*Making Monsters,* 1994). This is to indicate that both books were a partnership in the best sense of the word.

Throughout this book the authors have relied on the Herculean effort of the historians, medical researchers, and scholars who are responsible for generating the original research that has revealed the fatal flaws of the psychodynamic conception of the mind. Our purpose has been to synthesize this information and to explain the social significance of this broad body of work.

The authors would like to thank Professor Frank Watters for his tireless research and other help in support of this project. Grateful thanks are due as well to Po Bronson for his careful reads and brutal deadlines.

Others in need of recognition for their work and support include Susie Marino, Rob Riddell, Cathy Chestnut, Olen Creech, and Vikki Kratz. Support from Ethan Canin and the other kind members of the San Francisco Writers' Grotto has also been invaluable to one of the authors. From the other author, special gratitude goes to Keri Ofshe. Thanks again to our agent, Bonnie Nadell. At Scribner, appreciation goes to Gillian Blake and her assistant, Joy Jacobs, who gracefully and thoughtfully finished this project, which the authors thank Hamilton Cain for having signed on.

Introduction

But there are always some men who cling to one or another of the older views, and they are simply read out of the profession, which thereafter ignores their work. The new paradigm implies a new and more rigid definition of the field. Those unwilling or unable to accommodate their work to it must proceed in isolation or attach themselves to some other group.

—Thomas Kuhn,
The Structure of Scientific Revolutions

There is no doubt we can be mysterious creatures to ourselves and that we can be troubled by the question of why our lives, which seem under our control, can go so badly. Although our brains are pattern-recognizing machines, they are sometimes no match for the amount of information and the immense number of possible patterns our lives generate. As a result, we can sometimes lose a coherent understanding of how we got here, who we are, and where we are going. Americans have long relied on the benevolent help of therapists to explain and ameliorate the twists and turns of mental life. Each day, hundreds of thousands receive talk therapy under a bewildering variety of names. The money spent on therapy each year adds up into the billions of dollars, but this outlay pales in comparison to the investment of human trust at stake in these encounters. Americans look to sincere and well-intentioned therapists when they are most disoriented and most deeply troubled.

While we hire these caring practitioners in the hopes of learning about ourselves, this role is just the beginning of their influence. Psychological theories about mind and human behavior do not simply leak into popular culture, they flood it— through television talk shows, magazines, and pop-psychology books. The ways that we, as a society, think about our behavior and the ways we describe the architecture of our minds are molded by therapists.

The case we intend to make in this book is that many, if not most, of the more than two hundred types of talk therapy currently being practiced share a lineage of mistakes. This means not only that generations of therapy patients have been misled, but that we all share cultural notions about the workings of our minds that are fundamentally incorrect. In particular, many forms of talk therapy have long advanced the idea of the psychodynamic mind. This theory, broadly defined, suggests that we are each largely at the mercy of unconscious mental forces outside of our awareness that we cannot by ourselves name or tame. These forces, the theory also holds, influence everything from the choices we make in our everyday lives to the form and function of mental illness, as well as explain the personal and collective social arrangements that define society.

As originator of the theory of the psychodynamic mind, Sigmund Freud claimed that professionals trained in certain methods could read the vectors, strengths, and sources of these unconscious forces in such a way as to explain and ameliorate mental illness and our troubling behaviors. Tens of thousands of psychotherapists rely on the axioms of the psychodynamic theory of the mind. While many pieces of Freud's conceptual machine have been replaced in the multitude of different schools of psychodynamic therapy that have bloomed over the last century, the essential axioms and the basic architecture of Freud's theory remains fundamentally unaltered in these treatments. In essence, these treatments propose that social or developmental anomalies cause mental illness, and that talking to a patient and persuading the patient to reinterpret his or her history can cure or effectively treat those illnesses. Further, these treatments follow Freud's belief that a practitioner has to be trained to employ special methods that allow him or her to see past a patient's mental defenses and expose drives, memories, or influences that are hidden from awareness yet rule the person's everyday behavior.

If one set out to design a nostrum for this troubled century, it would be hard to imagine a more appealing promise than that offered by the psychodynamic psychotherapist. Therapy promises an exploration of the self that has the stamp of science while supposedly avoiding its reductionism. At the same time, it offers a somewhat mystical journey, sans religious dogma. It is a secular attempt to explain the nature and experience of being human. Over the last century, hundreds of thousands of patients have been convinced that through therapy they have glimpsed the secret underworld of their minds.

The premise of this book is that the psychodynamic theory of the mind that has informed and shaped the current practice of so much psychotherapy is wrong. As compelling as the idea of the psychodynamic mind is, its principal axioms have either failed to be confirmed or have been exposed as arbitrary or incorrect. We will, in this book, peel away at the theory and practice of psychodynamic psychotherapy. We will show how each successive generation of talk therapists panders to voguish thinking; we will examine the belief-building leverage the therapist has over the patient; we will lay bare the process by which the patient and therapist can be mutually fooled; we will expose the lack of evidence for the assumptions common to most schools of psychotherapy; and then we will take stock of what is left.

In this book we define psychodynamic psychotherapy as any talk therapy that claims to have the power to cure mental illness or derives its status from that claim or from its relation to the theory of the mind promoted by Freud. Further, psychodynamic psychotherapy, as we define it, presumes a social/developmental cause for mental illness, alleging that it often stems from social interactions that took place in the patient's childhood, which the patient has forgotten or hidden in his or her unconscious. These therapists claim that they can cure mental illness by exposing the causes that set these unconscious forces in motion and then by redirecting or lessening the power of these currents. To seek out therapy today is to stick your hand into a grab bag of theories that often utterly contradict each other in their specific assumptions but that agree on a more general unproved assertion that the therapist has the knowledge and techniques allowing him or her to see into the most fundamental and hidden motivations of the mind.

Most important, but perhaps least controversial, we will show how talk therapy, in most of its forms, can make little claim to effectively cure major mental illnesses. While this conclusion may be a surprise to the general public, it has been largely accepted within the relevant professions. Yet despite this broad acknowledgment, there are still many seriously mentally ill patients who are being subjected to forms of talk therapy that have no realistic likelihood of ameliorating their symptoms.

Of course, the practice of psychotherapy has not limited itself to the attempt to cure the mentally ill. Talk therapy has largely retreated to a more amorphous calling of treating the mildly demoralized, often called the walking worried. On this front, it is necessary to make a clear distinction between counseling and the treatment of these non-mentally-ill that continues in the psychodynamic tradition.

The treatment some clients receive in talk therapy settings is not psychodynamic psychotherapy at all but rather a form of well-intended counseling and advice. The central elements of psychotherapy—its pretense as a cure of mental illness and its claim to expose the mental forces that are unseen to the patient—are not employed. Instead, clients receive encouragement and pragmatic advice regarding difficult decisions, troubled relationships, loss, or other of life's many trials. The advice given can be valuable or misguided or amount to nothing more or less than ineffectual hand-holding. Such counseling does not depend on the existence of any theory of psychological development, or on its ability to explain or cure mental illness. The counselor need not even claim to have special training or methods that give him or her privileged access to mental forces or motivations. For these reasons, these sorts of counseling services fall largely outside our critique of psychotherapy.*

There are, however, many therapists who specialize in treating the demoralized walking worried who continue to operate under the assumptions common to the psychodynamic tradition of psychotherapy. They apply the assumption of the psychodynamic mind to explain why a patient's life is troubled with failure and distress or why a patient is prone to deviant conduct such as drug or alcohol abuse. The therapist offers (and the patient expects) much more from the encounter than good advice and counsel. The relatively high social status of such therapists, which increases their influence over their patients, relies on the idea that they are the mental health equivalents of doctors and that they possess techniques that can expose and dissect the true influences operating on a patient's mental life and behavior. Their claim to such expertise gives them a dangerous degree of influence over the non-mentally-ill patient.

Patients often look to these therapists to help them piece through their developmental backgrounds and create life narratives that supposedly explain their current distress. The claim that psychotherapists can discover the true-life cause-and-effect stories in their patients' lives has created entrée for an increasingly bizarre collection of "zealots and charlatans" into the therapy profession, according to psychiatrist Paul McHugh of Johns Hopkins Medical School. "There have been Marxist therapists, feminist therapists, and socio-biological therapists—all attempting to write their presumptions into an explanation for mental disorders without a comprehensive study of the conditions themselves," writes McHugh. "In the last few years . . .

---

*While we will not critique this type of advice giving, we will question whether such practice deserves status as a mental health discipline as well as whether it warrants our shared investment through health care dollars. We will also question whether such counseling requires special training and certification.

patients have been told by therapists that their mental ailments were expressions of (you name it) infantile sexual assaults, satanic cult abuse, space alien abduction, or even irritating remnants of problems 'unsolved' in some prior life in other centuries. This is story explanation gone wild, with immeasurable damage to public confidence in the standards of practice represented by psychiatry and psychotherapy."

Many believe, particularly those in the educated strata of American society, that engaging in some sort of narrative creation with a psychodynamic psychotherapist is the best available path to self-knowledge. To the extent that we have accepted the claim that psychotherapy offers the high road to such wisdom, we have paid a cost in the partial abdication of our individual responsibility to work to understand how we conduct our lives each new day and accomplish our goals over time. If these psychodynamic therapists have made good on their promise to lead us to that self-knowledge as well as to explain and cure mental illness, this abdication might indeed be worth the cost. If, on the other hand, theories underlying psychodynamic therapy are baseless, American society has been cheated. The reckoning has been quietly going on for the last twenty-five years, with evidence coming in from all quarters. We ask only a few hours to show the reader the balance sheet.

Freud created one of the twentieth century's most significant myths but presented it as a scientific theory, supposedly based on rationalism and empirical observation. He claimed to be opening up the complexity of the mind to the world, but in fact he created a convoluted and speculative system of assumptions that has misled thousands upon thousands of well-intentioned therapists and vulnerable patients over the last hundred years. A master at couching his theories in the language of scientific work, Freud began a tradition of presenting talk therapy as based on solid empirical evidence and judiciously considered explanations that has continued throughout this century. Although it has yet to be fully understood by the public (or fully acknowledged within the field of psychology), recent

Freud scholarship has effectively demoted Freud from a revered physician/scientist with a keen and insightful mind to a shameless self-promoter who committed scientific fraud and deliberately claimed his speculations were proven facts.

This new criticism of Freud, we believe, has more disturbing repercussions for today's practice of talk therapy than simply revealing its founder to be a calculating rhetorician who employed methods and reasoning utterly divorced from scientific inquiry. Much more important than this conclusion about the historical Freud is that talk therapists continue to make many of the same glaring intellectual mistakes Freud himself doggedly repeated throughout his years of writing and practice.

These mistakes include: a lack of appreciation of how dramatically the therapist influences the patient's beliefs; the acceptance of the client's belief in the conclusions of therapy as proof of the validity of those conclusions; and a failure to understand how interpretations of the causes of a patient's illness or troubles are often nothing more than reflections of cultural beliefs and biases. One final mistake has remained more or less constant since Freud's time: the emphasis on early childhood social/developmental experience (whether it be some traumatic moment or a clash of the child's instincts or fantasies) as the root of psychopathology and the accompanying assumption that the methods of therapy are an effective way to unearth and neutralize the consequences of those experiences.

Like Freud, therapists continue to offer the idea that a patient's behavior is rooted in an underworld of psychological forces—forces patients cannot perceive and only therapists, with their special training and procedures, can explain. This is not to argue that we do not often feel carried along by internal currents that feel as if they are out of our control. Indeed, it is our knowledge that we are not transparent to ourselves that produces a desire to seek out people who profess the ability to see the source of our confused desires and who claim to be able to help us restore calm and meaning to our lives.

While it is clear that therapists cater to these often pressing needs, the important question is whether the psychodynamic theory of the mind as it is employed in therapy can offer a valid explanation for mental life and properly satisfy the patient's desire for understanding and aid. It is our contention that the psychodynamic approach has yielded little useful understanding of the forces that drive our behavior. Instead, it has given rise to hundreds of different schools of talk therapy and theories of behavior that take their authority not from their proven explanatory power but from consensus among practitioners and the undeserved deference and status accorded to psychotherapists as applied scientists.

Looked at from a distance, the theories and methods that have been the legacy of Freud's theories appear much like the mythological Gordian knot, which is said to be so complex as to be impossible to untie. True to the character of the Gordian knot, those who try to carefully unravel the snarl only add a new layer of twists and tangles to it. The only way to defeat a Gordian knot is not to try to untie it but to slice it through the center. This solution also works for disentangling the psychodynamic theory of the mind. It's not necessary to examine and weigh the value of each of the proposed mental mechanisms or therapeutic methods to come to a conclusion about the theory's value. It can, in fact, be sliced through with only two firm strokes.

At the heart of the psychodynamic approach is the assumption that there exists the idea of the powerful unconscious that oversees a variety of mental defenses including repression, dissociation, sublimation, and projection so that the human brain can supposedly hide disturbing information from the conscious self. Maintaining these defensive barriers, according to the psychodynamic theory, is what the unconscious mind spends its working day primarily engaged with. This is no small task, for it means hiding away sexual instincts, memories of childhood sexual traumas, and infantile and childhood sexual fantasies. The cumulative effect of all the defenses is supposedly the removal from awareness of knowledge of all manner of motivations, desires, and fears by corralling this information into the unconscious, where, although hidden, it still manages to be the central influence on our lives.

As we will show, there is no credible evidence that the mind purposefully hides memories of crucial events, fantasies, desires, or instincts, much less evidence that psychotherapists have special techniques to unearth them. There is similarly no credible evidence for a powerful dynamic unconscious that secretly controls our behavior as the psychodynamic theory proposes. Reject the concept of the mind's manifold defenses against distressing thoughts, along with the proposition that we are controlled by a seething undercurrent of unconscious desires and impulses, and you are halfway through the knot.

But if the patient and therapist are not uncovering the hidden forces that control the patient's thoughts and behaviors, what is happening in psychotherapy? Why do patients often come to believe in the talk therapists' interpretations of their behavior? The answer constitutes our second swing at the psychodynamic Gordian knot: We propose that what happens in therapy is primarily a process of influence by which the patient learns to conform to and adopt the ideas the therapist brings to the encounter. The assumption that a patient's behavior, thoughts, and desires are inauthentic, until interpreted in therapy, allows the therapists to "discover" any life narrative or deeply hidden force presumed to exist in the patient. Psychodynamic psychotherapy can often be nothing more than an exercise in influence that changes the way a person perceives his or her history and motivations but has no connection to the effective cure or symptom relief of mental illness.

While the influence and belief-building process of therapy primarily affects the patient, it also feeds back to the therapist, increasing his faith in his theory and special skills. We will show how the speculative notions of the psychodynamic mind can, through the process of therapy, mislead both the patient and the therapist.

We need only scan the history of the psychodynamic movement to see compelling proof of this back-and-forth belief-building phenomenon. Every interpretation, from Freud's penis envy to the more recent notions of prenatal trauma, has been adopted by some patients and, at least for a time, enthusiastically promoted by a number of therapists. Over the course of the century, therapists have believed in (and their patients have become convinced of) the most bizarre theories to explain behavior. Freud, for example, was variously fond of discovering that patients' problems stemmed from witnessing their parents having sex or the trauma of fantasizing the death of one parent while experiencing an urge to mate with the other. As inventive and bold as such interpretations were, contemporary psychodynamic therapists have matched Freud at least in terms of bizarreness. The most aberrant of modern therapists have traced their clients' problems to abuse by imaginary satanic cults, or to dozens of personalities living in their unconscious, and even abuse by space aliens or traumas in past lives. While most psychodynamic therapists do not pursue these more outlandish narratives (often preferring the more conventional story of poor socialization by one's parents), they must now acknowledge the dilemma that these enthusiasms suggest: Either these wild interpretations were correct, as the convinced patients and these fringe therapists loudly attested, or powerful forces of influence were at work during the hours those therapists and patients came to believe these improbable explanations. In this book, we will expose the central elements of these other forces and suggest that they operate in a broad range of psychodynamic schools of therapy.

Over the recent decades, during which psychodynamic psychotherapy has shown its fatal flaws, the scientific study of mental illness has steadily advanced. The biogenetic approach, for example, has yielded remarkable new information and, in some cases, effective treatments for disorders of the brain. Scientists have discovered neural chemical systems in the brain that may prove to be the nexus of specific mental illnesses. Technology such as positron emission tomography (PET scan) has illuminated the mind's interconnections. Scientists have developed a whole range of psychopharmaceuticals to treat mental illnesses. New information about genetically influenced diseases has helped identify at-risk populations for Huntington's disease, panic disorder, and others.

As a corollary to the advances in medical research, the cognitive-behavioral approach to counseling the mentally ill relies on a half-century of scientifically gathered knowledge of how organisms learn and how behavioral patterns are maintained and/or modified by the environment. This approach assumes that unwanted behaviors (those not caused by biological or neurological malfunctions like frontal lobe epilepsy or chemical imbalances) are learned and maintained in the same manner as desirable behaviors. Rather than seeing problematic behaviors as symptoms of conflicting unconscious forces, the practitioner treats them as *learned* behaviors that can be unlearned. Many studies have shown the cognitive-behavioral approach, often augmented with the use of drugs, is helpful in the treatment of a long list of problems, including phobias, addictions, obsessive-compulsive disorders, sexual dysfunctions, anorexia nervosa, depression, and panic disorders. The cognitive-behavioral therapist attempts to challenge, and ultimately change, the patient's irrational or self-defeating behaviors and habits of thinking.

Cognitive-behavioral approaches, when used in the treatment of mental illness, can be helpful as rehabilitative counseling. While such counseling cannot effectively cure mental illnesses, it can be helpful in managing many complications and difficulties that invariably accompany such an illness. The medical parallel is with physical therapy, which, although it cannot cure an injury, can speed recovery and help the patient avoid complications that inhibit the body's ability to heal.

The biogenetic and cognitive-behavioral approaches combined have ushered in a promising era for psychiatry and clinical psychology. Throwing off the Freudian notions, this new generation of psychiatrists has focused on identifying the natural history of mental diseases, with the presumption that identifying telling characteristics and the etiologies of diseases is central to being able to treat them. Although psychological rehabilitative counseling has been a helpful ancillary tool in treating mental illness, it has primarily been through the bio-genetic approach that we have begun to explain the underpin-nings and sometimes effectively treat severe mental disorders. These scientists have amassed evidence showing that serious mental illness likely depends on abnormalities in the patient's constitution, including neurologically based problems, mental retardation, genetic predisposition, and bodily disease. The biogenetically focused research on brain dysfunction has steadily amassed scientific knowledge of mental disorders as well as practical experience in assisting those in crisis. These scientists have learned to treat and sometimes successfully defeat illnesses that the profession couldn't lay a glove on two decades ago. Pursuing advances in the genetic, biochemical, and neurological underpinnings of mental illness, the biologi-cal approach has opened up new avenues—or rather high-ways—of exploration.

The biogenetic approach is not synonymous with doling out medication, although it can take credit for great advances in the area of psychopharmacology. Nor does the medical approach dismiss as unimportant the influence of upbringing and envi-ronment. However, it does not assume that an exploration of one's life narrative necessarily holds the secret pathogen of a disorder, nor does it assume the therapist has some special win-dow into hidden forces in the unconscious. Finally, the bio-genetic approach attempts to make a distinction between mental illness and common emotional difficulties. It does not assume, for example, that clinical depression is simply an extension of everyday sadness.

Through the cunning promotion and empire-building of Freud and his immediate followers, the idea of the powerful uncon-scious became institutionalized in America for much of this century. In providing a language with which we could describe and seem to explain our behavior, the idea of the psychodynamic mind occupied a void in our increasingly science-based culture that religion had once filled. The unique qualities of the human mind and human feeling that were once simply assumed to be God-given were accounted for by Freud and his followers through an amalgam of simplistic evolutionary biology and theories about unconscious (most often sexual) impulses. Accepted in America as profound truths, these assumptions about the mind and behavior were incorporated in the middle of the century into university teaching and found wide reception in popular culture. Several generations of psychologists and psychiatrists built their careers on these premises.

The conflict between such psychodynamic conceptions and the biogenetic/cognitive-behavioral approaches to disorders of the brain has recently become increasingly clear. We believe that this conflict will play out much like the conflict between competing scientific paradigms described in Thomas Kuhn's seminal analysis of the development of science, *The Structure of Scientific Revolutions.* Freud's psychoanalysis, as it was introduced and practiced early this century, had two critical qualities that define, for Kuhn, the idea of a paradigm.* First, the theory of the psychodynamic mind was sufficiently interesting that it attracted a substantial group of adherents away from competing modes of inquiry into mental functioning. Second, the theory was open-ended enough as to offer all sorts of puzzles for adherents of the theory to attempt to solve. Psychoanalysis had this second element in abundance. Any communication, perception, thought, or action could be, for the alert psychoanalyst, an opportunity to speculate about the patient's unconscious motivations. Similarly, all art, literature, politics, dress, tradition, and mythology could be seen as expressions of unconscious forces playing out on a societal level. It is not surprising that this new psychodynamic paradigm was so attractive to so many mental health practitioners and intellectuals over this century. Sign on to

---

*While psychoanalysis should not be classified as a science, Kuhn's analysis can still be applied. Freud's claims that his theories were confirmed by his clinical findings set the stage for those who came after him to address psychoanalytic theories as scientific. While many of Freud's claims have proved fraudulent—as we will address in chapter two—the fact that psychoanalysis has long masqueraded as a science makes it appropriate to apply Kuhn's theory of shifting paradigms.

its thesis and all questions about the complexities of human behavior were born anew.

It is the nature of scientific disciplines, Kuhn argues, that they don't evolve but rather, periodically, undergo revolutions that form new paradigms. When these revolutions occur, the vast majority of the work inspired by the previous paradigm becomes irrelevant. It is the central feature of a new paradigm that it defines entirely new questions to be answered. Because the questions fundamentally change, the answers to the old questions lose their importance.

It is easy to see that the psychodynamic paradigm asks fundamentally different questions than does biogenetic research into brain dysfunction and the cognitive-behavioral approach to counseling. For the psychodynamic therapists, the central questions revolve around the patients' unconscious forces and the manipulation of their life narratives, with particular focus on childhood and sexual experiences. The psychodynamic therapist is intent on finding the pieces of the patient's social/developmental history that set in motion unconscious currents of which the patient is unaware. The belief in the importance of finding these missing pieces of the patient's life history (along with the belief that such discoveries will be curative) is not an assumption shared by those engaged in exploring the biogenetic paradigm. Indeed, many of the questions surrounding the psychodynamic conception of the mind (particularly the search for supposedly unconsciously repressed material) are as irrelevant to these new researchers and healers as are the phrenologist's questions about skull shape.

Scientific revolutions, according to Kuhn, do not happen simply because one paradigm has become useless. No paradigm is summarily abandoned; rather, new scientific perspectives emerge that hold promise for a more precise understanding of the nature of the thing being studied. This is what has happened in the last three decades with the study of the biogenetic and cognitive-behavioral approach to mental illness and mental functioning. If we are correct that we are at the end of the usefulness of the psychodynamic conception of the mind, thousands upon thousands of therapists and their patients will be affected. The sad truth is that there are many mental health healers who have studied hard in the belief that they were receiving a solid understanding of the mind and behavior. What they often received instead, through no fault of their own, was an education in the psychological equivalent of alchemy.

Because of the massive investment the field of psychotherapy has made in the psychodynamic approach, the dying convulsions of the paradigm will not be pretty. Some in the field have acted honorably, praising the new advances and even retraining themselves or making graceful exits into retirement. Others have managed to studiously ignore the information that points to the death of the psychodynamic conception of the mind. Still others have found alliances and refuge with social movements from feminism to New Age mysticism. These latter therapists have discovered new territory and markets, most recently setting themselves up as protectors and caretakers of the "soul." Many have continued to claim, in ever shriller tones, that the psychodynamic study of the mind remains the only truly revealing approach to the examination of mental life. Some of these therapists have even begun a counterassault on the empirical end of the profession, claiming that the biogenetic approach to understanding the brain is dehumanizing to the patient. These true believers seem intent on going down with the psychodynamic ship.

It is, of course, possible that the ship will refuse to sink. Although it has run conceptually aground, it may retain the appearance of buoyancy to the uninformed or unsophisticated. Astrology and astronomy, as Kuhn points out, were once one and the same thing. That no one now considers astrology a science does not mean that it can't, today, claim more devotees than the study of astronomy.

Although we are outsiders to the field of talk therapy, we share an interest in the social psychological forces that have formed the practice and molded it into its current state. These social forces influence the practice of psychotherapy at the level of the relationship between the therapist and patient but also include the larger cultural forces and trends in which that relationship is necessarily set. The reason this perspective is so important right now is that the mental health professions are undergoing a transformation as dramatic as the one medicine went through at the beginning of the twentieth century. The treatment of mental illness is moving away from its pseudoscientific founding and toward becoming a scientifically based discipline. We will argue that the psychodynamic conception of mental illness is destined to fall from use. After a long season of dramatic growth, the mental health profession is moving into a hard winter during which many current practitioners and approaches will not survive. This is the story of the coming of age of the mental health field—written in the midst of its metamorphosis.

We will pursue four main goals. First, we will expose the gulf that exists between the scientific and psychodynamic conceptions of the mental health healer. Second, we will trace the lineage of the many current psychodynamic fallacies through the history of the discipline. Third, we will detail the trends and cultural shifts that are forcing a choice between two radically different sorts of mental health professions—one based on science and one on mythology. Finally, we will argue that the leadership of the mental health professions has the opportunity and responsibility to create disciplines that deserve the status and trust we now give the field of medicine.

We will explain the mistakes and excesses of psychodynamic forms of therapy both in terms of the history of the profession as well as in descriptions of the damage many of these theories have caused patients. The mistakes that these psychotherapists make today, for instance, cannot be understood without examining the rise of the quasi-spiritual human potential movement of the sixties and seventies, which, in turn, grew out of the rapid expansion of the profession after the Second World War. None of these movements can be understood without tracing their theories back to the source of the psychodynamic enterprise—the problematic and enormously influential ideas by which Freud claimed he could explain human behavior. Our

26

goal in tracing theoretical threads through the eras of this psychology-obsessed century is not to point out the individual mistakes of each enthusiasm but to explore the fallacies that they share.

There are some who have so closely linked therapy with the pursuit of self-understanding that they find the questioning of its premises offensive. In their eyes, to be a critic of psychodynamic therapy is to be against the very idea of introspection. These are the people who simply cannot fathom why someone, particularly a college-educated someone, would not have availed him- or herself of the benefits of therapy. Therapy is sacrosanct, end of discussion. This perspective is perhaps the most powerful reason to write a book like *Therapy's Delusions*. The fact that the idea of therapy has such a hold over certain individuals that they would defend it like religious dogma is exactly why it deserves close examination. It is when secular institutions become accepted with religious faith and fervor that great damage can be done.

There is no way to lessen the potential for harm by therapists unless their profession is forced to face the mistakes that have been repeated generation after generation. What would be left of psychodynamic therapists if we were to successfully strip away the unwarranted influence the therapist holds over the patient, as well as the cultural authority they gain by attaching their theories to the popular trends of the times? Could they maintain their status as seers into our hidden motivations? We think not. Much of what is practiced in the tradition of psychodynamic psychotherapy, and often paid for collectively as mental health care, is little more than modern mesmerism. Its power comes not from truth telling but from belief building.

CHAPTER ONE

A Profession in Crisis

Out in the rough-and-tumble psychotherapeutic marketplace, to which our mental health associations discreetly
turn their backs, Freudian clichés are breeding promiscu-
ously with those of religious zealots, self-help evangelists,
sociopolitical ideologues, and outright charlatans who trade
in the ever seductive currency of guilt and blame.
　　—FREDERICK CREWS,
　　　　The Memory Wars, Freud's Legacy in Dispute

Fifteen thousand therapists and scientific researchers descend on
Chicago for the annual convention of the American Psychological Association. Attendees fill a dozen hotels on both sides of
the Chicago River. Over one thousand seminars, lectures, and
discussions take place during the five-day conference in venues
spread over a three-square-mile area. In attendance are clinicians
of all types. Although many share the same credentials—mostly
Ph.D.s in psychology—they come from dramatically different
schools of thought. Hustling from conference room to conference room are thoughtful neo-Freudians, dreamy Jungians, and
pragmatic behaviorists, along with those from other schools of
psychotherapy, including existential, psychodrama, transactional, motivational, feminist, cognitive, and Gestalt. Also in
attendance, in greater force each year, are those therapists who
describe themselves as "eclectic." Adherents to no one school or
set of theories, these eclectics wander from seminar to discussion
group to lecture, picking and choosing from theories of behav-

ior and therapeutic methods like shoppers in an enormous department store of psychological notions and approaches.

While it's a diverse group, it's not hard to find one's favorite stereotype of a psychotherapist among the clinicians in the corridors and conference rooms of these hotels. There are the sincere-looking, Birkenstocked therapists with ponytails formed from thinning blond hair. There are the more severe types: East Coasters, bearded and wearing moderately well-tailored suits. There are also the bespectacled, late-thirties marriage, family, and child counselors, modestly accessorized, who sit attentively in seminars as one would imagine they sit when providing therapy: legs crossed, backs straight, with pens poised over leather-bound notebooks.

As a group, these clinicians are a sincere bunch whose desire to do good in this world is obvious. They take their work very seriously because, they seem to agree, the world outside the convention is a very sick place. In seminar after seminar one can hear therapists speaking in concerned tones about the state of the unenlightened population. What exactly the world is pronounced sick with depends on the particular interests and background of the therapist speaking. Some see racism at the root of most problems; others deplore the lack of connection individuals have with their spirituality and soul. The "media" takes a good bit of tongue-lashing for perpetuating negative stereotypes, promoting violence, and indoctrinating the public in the pursuit of shallow consumerism. However, it's the family, in particular poor parenting, that is most often condemned as the cause of poor mental health in adulthood. According to many of these clinical psychologists, the harsh socialization of boys is surpassed only by the constricted and abusive childhoods suffered by young women. While these professionals may disagree on the sickness, they all seem to agree that much of the population is gravely in need of their help.

"The field of modern psychology is as diverse as the people and personalities it studies," wrote a reporter for the *Chicago Tribune* about the convention. "So it's not surprising that this convention encompasses the whimsical and the serious, the theoretical and the real life." In the next few days, papers across the country would carry news from the convention on this year's crop of disorders and dysfunctions. Particular attention was being paid to those potentially "addicted" to on-line chat rooms.

While the majority of attendees are practicing clinicians and clinicians in training, there are also psychological researchers who study the human brain and behavior, including methods of teaching and ways of learning, memory, psychophysiology, neurology, social psychology, personality, and more. Although these researchers and academics who study the operation of the human brain and the way behavior is shaped give the profession its respectability and its claim to science, they are hugely outnumbered by those who work with clients.

Between the scientists and the clinicians, the conference addresses a breathtakingly diverse range of topics. The program, which is the size of a phone book, starts with a paper on "Holistic Health for Psychologists Approaching the Millennium" and ends, thousands of presentations and five days later, with a paper entitled "Evidence for Dysfunction of the Neo-cortical Systems in Autism." In the same afternoon one can find talks entitled "Functional Independent Coping Scale for Spinal Cord Injured Population," "When People Share: The Value of On-Line Support Groups," "Implicit Theories of Meaning," and "Developmental Triumphs and Troubles with Nonrelational Sex." Looking at all the seminar topics, one senses that the discipline of psychology claims every topic under the sun as its own. Because psychology deals with the mind, and the mind, by its nature, deals with the nearly infinitely complex world it perceives, psychologists act as if their realm of expertise should include everything the mind can comprehend.

The idea that the conference has something for everyone is given a cheerful spin by the organizers. When asked about the broad range of contradictory theories and treatments discussed at such conventions, a high-ranking member of the APA explained to us that the profession would "rather let a field of different treatments blossom than fight over the weeding-out of ineffective ones. The best will eventually win out."

Less often heard at this convention is any acknowledgment that the expansive scope of topics covered points to one of the profession's deepest-seated problems—namely, that it has no unified identity or clear sense of purpose.

"As a profession clinical psychology is suffering from an identity crisis," announced Richard Cox, president of the graduate school at Forest Institute of Professional Psychology. Speaking with rare frankness in a symposium entitled "Golden Opportunities for Psychology in the 21st Century," Cox initially sounded less than enthusiastic about therapy's future. "As a profession, we don't know who we are, we don't know what we do. We don't know where we are going or where we have been. We have dozens of different associations, professional groups, and specialties. Some of us want to be gurus, some want to be analysts, some want to be philosophers, some of us want to be diagnosticians. Our second problem is that the public doesn't understand who we are either."

This is a blunt but accurate assessment. If one wanted evidence for his conclusion, one would only need to flip through the meeting schedule. This convention is a megaclearinghouse for the ideas that feed our pop-psych culture and sustain the $67-billion-a-year mental health industry. Remarkably, Cox's solution to this identity crisis is not to pare back the profession's wide-ranging interests or to build a consensus among psychologists as to what methods are effective and efficacious. Cox's solution is to *expand* the role of the therapist.

"We need to get away from the idea of curing and into the idea of healing the mind, body, and soul," he declared. "We need to be able to use, without feeling guilty, all the tools for treating patients, including bio-feedback, meditation, guided imagery, hypnosis, relaxation training, homeopathic remedies, and prayer. We need to come back to a concept that spirituality is probably more important than prescription." Appropriately, Cox was followed by a massage therapist who, to prove the effectiveness of her treatment, showed an ultrasound picture of a developed fetus "smiling" after an in utero massage.

Although it is rarely acknowledged during the seminars,

there is a behind-the-scenes agreement that the clinical side of the profession is facing multiple crises, chief among them being the lack of cohesion within the field and lack of perceived cohesion by the public. Many, however, agree with Cox's paradoxical position that the profession should take an even more expansive role. Very few of these professionals are willing to publicly argue for a narrowing of the field. On this point most practicing therapists here are singing the same tune: a collective chorus of "Don't Fence Me In."

The APA convention illustrates a deeper problem than the fact that psychology continues to spread itself thinner and thinner. From room to room, the very language in which these professionals talk about human behavior and the mind shifts dramatically. In some meeting rooms one hears the language of science—presenters cite papers, display graphs on overhead projectors, and are careful not to make one remark or even inference that is not solidly grounded in hard data. In conference rooms catering to clinical practitioners, however, lecturers talk as if they were hybrids of philosophers and priests. These therapists discuss their calling not in the circumspect language of science but in the expansive rhetoric of myth and the spirit. Their theories do not focus on the alleviation of troubling behaviors, thoughts, or pathologies but rather on the more heady matter of human transcendence. "I personally like it when any therapist is willing to contemplate the therapeutic process in the spiritual dimension," pronounced one prominent therapist during her seminar. "I think that is where so much substantive change happens."

Although it is easy to agree that freedom from "mental illness" is a desirable notion, it is clear from the myriad treatments offered that there is no agreement in the profession over what constitutes the state of "mental health." At present, trends in treatments are less likely to begin at university research centers than they are to come out of suburban clinics or the pages of pop-psychology paperbacks. The careful observer can even watch the latest therapeutic trends develop live during the morning talk shows. Some treatments presume that mental health will be reached by healing our "inner child," while some feminist psychotherapies insist that patients can't truly progress unless they throw off the evil restraints of our patriarchal society. To be whole and happy, some treatments insist that we ferret out our past lives, while still others insist that we must "rebirth" or alternatively "reparent" ourselves. Even in the more mainstream therapies, much disagreement exists over the etiology of disorders and the correct path toward wellness. It is apparent that these schools are not only offering different routes to mental health but different destinations as well.

The various professional organizations make almost no effort to restrict the behavior of even the most bizarre pursuits of its practitioners. The profession has produced what Dr. Paul McHugh calls "a circus of psychotherapies." This parade has grown to include useless, sometimes harmful, and often simply ridiculous therapies.

The innocence, enthusiasm, and certainty of this generation of talk therapists represented at the APA is almost charming. They appear largely ignorant of (or unconcerned with) the misadventures of past treatments, for who has time for a strict accounting of the damage caused by the last trendy theory when the new crop of psychodynamic assumptions seems so promising? While the mistakes of past psychodynamic therapists are often left behind, unrectified and unatoned for, each new generation gladly accepts whatever cultural currency the previous generation of therapists has managed to preserve. Freud can, in this way, be hailed as a courageous healer despite the fact that his methods have failed to prove effective and his specific theories seem more and more bizarre and anachronistic with each passing year. Even feminist psychodynamic therapists willingly accept Freud's aura of courageous and iconoclastic healer and pick and choose from his theories and techniques to find evidence for their current beliefs without ever fully acknowledging his deep misogyny and the damage that his legacy has caused needy and insecure female patients over the century.

The relationship of the field of psychology to our culture is a symbiotic one. The theories and mistakes incubated within the profession affect us all, whether we are patients or not. As a recent president of the APA proclaimed: "I would like to get away from the medical model entirely . . . we are teachers. We have taught the whole culture. Our job is to bring knowledge to the world." But as much as we look to these professionals to define ourselves, psychologists look to the culture to find new trends and niches. Often practitioners do not even bother to hide the fact that they actively mine current social trends for new therapy markets. The publication *Psychotherapy Finances* recently hired a group of business consultants to recommend the "most fertile niche markets" for therapists. The consultants came up with forty growth areas, including "Women's PMS, ethnic specialty, premarital testing, weight control, and Sports/motivational training and counseling." As the ultimate example of how crowded and desperate for new angles the profession has become, one of the forty new growth areas was "career counseling *for other therapists*." That most of the "niches" are not covered by insurance is not a problem. As the magazine points out: "While the diagnosis of PMS will not qualify for most insurance coverage, a diagnosis of depression or anxiety can generally be used."

Psychotherapists are more than happy to accept the ground American society has given them. They interpret history and works of art and claim to draw together threads from philosophy, mythology, and religion. They declare that they can see the subterranean movements and motivations of culture as deftly as they discern hidden forces in their client's unconscious. That psychodynamic premises continue to spread outside the discipline is compelling proof that we have collectively agreed that complex matters are best addressed from a psychological perspective.

Self-help bookshelves overflow with treatises by psychotherapists of one credential or another giving advice on every conceivable aspect of life, from achieving the ultimate orgasm to facing a terminal illness. These books have little to do with science; rather, they are written by psychologists who seem to want to be a hybrid of novelist and philosopher. Once launched onto this course, therapists often allow themselves to go even beyond the role of protector of the human spirit to become guardians of humanity. Their job, as Gloria Steinem told the APA membership during one of their convention's keynote speeches, is to be social activists who change the world by "removing the restrictions on the human spirit."

Taking this advice to heart, some therapists have come to feel that it is their job, as psychiatrist Paul McHugh writes, to "interpret literature, counsel the electorate, and prescribe for the millennium."

It is worth wondering, here at the end of the twentieth century, how the practitioners of talk therapy came to this inflated assessment of themselves. It is our contention that the over-reaching of the talk therapy profession stems from the idea, made popular by Freud, that talk therapists can read the unseen forces that drive human thought and behavior. Freud's belief that talk therapy is the most valid method for unearthing and under-standing hidden human motivations remains the defining ethos of many modern clinicians at the APA convention. Discovering the true forces acting upon a patient's life is still the central promise and expectation of those practicing, although what forces are discovered (and whether they are classically Freudian in nature) varies widely from one school of talk therapy to another. That the mind hides the basic forces that affect our choices and behavior, and that the therapist can uncover these forces by talking to patients, comprise the central conceptual inheritance of what we will call Freud's psychodynamic tradition.

Currently, talk therapists educated within this tradition dom-inate psychology's clinical wing and, through sheer numbers, hold disproportionate sway over the discipline as a whole. Psycho-dynamic therapists abound among the clinical doctorate-level psychologists and are even more plentiful among the less rigor-ously trained mental health providers (such as therapists with masters in social work or marriage and family counseling). They, of course, include psychoanalysts and appear in ample numbers among the many psychiatrists who don't practice psy-choanalysis but some psychodynamic-derived psychotherapy rather than medicine. While the mistakes made by different schools of psychodynamic therapists often appear peculiar to each group (theories such as primal scream, reparenting, and recovered memory certainly seem radically different from each other), we posit that all schools of talk therapy derived from the psychodynamic tradition share a set of fundamental errors. Briefly drawn, these are the five fallacies.

1. The Fallacy of Causation. This fallacy combines three mistakes into one. First, the psychodynamic schools have often limited their search for the cause of disorders to the patient's childhood, believing that adult mental disorders are only *symptoms* of trauma, fantasy, or bad socialization experienced early in life and then hidden in the patient's unconscious. The belief that the roots of mental distress can be found in the stories of people's lives often requires a willful blindness to the troubles in the patient's adult life as well as an ignorance of the growing scientific evidence showing that the root cause of mental illnesses can be found through biochemistry, genetics, and neurology. Second, they have assumed that psychotherapy is an effective way to find these historical pathogens. This assumes that patients, through such methods as free association, can identify the variables that shaped their behavior and accurately report their histories without being influenced by their therapists' expectations and beliefs. Third, these therapists have offered the proposition that once a cause is discovered, the symptom will disappear. That is, even if the cause of troubling behavior *does* lie in the patient's past and he or she *can* accurately report those events, the question remains: Does simply discovering that explanation ameliorate the patient's troubles or mental illness?

2. The Fallacy of Noninfluence. Psychodynamic therapists have consistently failed to fully appreciate the many subtle ways a disoriented and needy patient learns what to say and how to act in order to satisfy the therapist's expectations. These "demand characteristics" of the therapy encounter not only explain why a patient often willingly buys into the therapist's theory of the moment, but can also lead to the shaping of the symptoms. Just as Freud predicted and then consistently "discovered" falling and shaking in all his patients suffering from hysteria, so, too, do today's specialists in multiple personality disorder predict and then consistently find their clients acting out child-like alter-personalities.

3. *The Fallacy of Confirmation.* This fallacy comes from the mistaken conception that a client's belief in a therapist's theory is proof of the validity of that theory. This anecdotal approach to knowledge has plagued the field since Freud and can be found as often in the professional journals as in mass-market paperbacks. Simply put, the patient's eventual certainty that his or her problems derive from oedipal rivalries, birth trauma, repressed abuse, a rejecting mother, witnessing parental sex, space alien abduction, or satanic cult abuse should not be considered as prima facie evidence of the truth of a causal relationship. Far from being the source of the patient's problems, these beliefs often arise out of the coercive power of the therapy setting.

4. *The Cultural Feedback Loop.* Psychodynamic therapists have long lacked an understanding of how their theories derive from passing cultural fears and interests. Although we can easily look back and see the influence of popular culture on a previous generation of psychodynamic practitioners—we can now see, for instance, how Freud's theories about sex and masturbation were influenced by Victorian society's fears and inhibitions—it is harder to see that influence as it happens. Today, this problem is compounded by the fact that ideas that emanate from inside the discipline of therapy influence our culture at large. A massive, self-confirming information loop is created when the profession broadcasts ideas about mental illness and then takes as proof of those ideas the patients who come to therapy, pop-psychology book in hand, predisposed to believe the therapist's theories.

5. *The Fallacy of the Freudian Dynamic Unconscious.* While it is clear that we all engage in out-of-awareness mental processes,

the idea of the dynamic unconscious proposes a powerful shadow mind that, unknown to its host, willfully influences the most minor thought and behavior. There is no scientific evidence of this sort of purposeful unconscious, nor is there evidence that psychotherapists have special methods for laying bare our out-of-awareness mental processes. Nevertheless, the therapist's claim to be able to expose and reshape the unconscious mind continues to be the seductive promise of many talk therapies.

These mistakes are not incidental to the psychodynamic approach to mental illness and healing; rather, they comprise its very foundation. In large part, they answer one of the most puzzling questions about the practice of therapy: Why do patients of the most absurd and demonstrably useless talk therapies report that they value the experience and admire their therapists? The answer can be found in an examination of how these fallacies play out during therapy. Far from being impartial observers, therapists hold and exert great influence over their patients, who are often desperate for approval. The patients' confirmation of the theory du jour builds the therapists' confidence in their assumptions and treatment methods. In deciding which windmills are actually dangerous monsters, both the therapist and patient are swayed by the culture's popular fears and phobias of the moment. Together they create a situation in which they are mutually misled.

Those who come to therapy for help are those most vulnerable to these fallacies. The so-called walking worried are often in need of exactly the sort of certainty about the world that these sorts of talk therapy settings offer. As outrageous as some of the beliefs to come out of talk therapy have been—from patients believing they were driven, since infancy, by sexual desire for their parents to those who believe their unconscious had a death instinct or that they suffered from multiple personality disorder—this sort of dramatic and singular explanation for one's inchoate feelings of uncertainty can have the marginal effect of relieving the anxiety of not having a ready explanation for one's troubles.

As a result of these fallacies, current and past schools of psychodynamic therapy have often promoted phantom "mental illnesses," for which they offer equally insubstantial cures. As cultural beliefs change, such theories are exposed as groundless. Masturbation and homosexuality have come and gone as mental health problems. Hysteria, penis envy, nymphomania, and draptomania (the "mental illness" once attributed to slaves who attempted to escape) have all been exposed as nothing more than psychotherapeutic labels for culturally held prejudices. In our day, the list of questionable or overdiagnosed disorders goes on and on, including "low self-esteem," "codependency," "self-defeating personality disorder," and the ever-present "dysfunctional family." Other legitimate problems such as depression and anxiety disorders are so vague and poorly defined that for some therapists they have become little more than catch-all phrases, principally useful for filling out health insurance reimbursement forms. In a more troubling example, many psychologists currently detect in their clients the subtle signs of multiple personality disorder—a diagnosis they then believe is confirmed when, after months or years of therapy and persuasion, their patients begin acting out self-destructive alter-personalities.

To find help for these and other in-vogue disorders, the prospective patient can select from dozens of impressive-sounding schools of treatment, from the mainstream schools to a menagerie of lesser-known procedures. A San Francisco newspaper recently ran ads for "core energetics," "transpersonal counseling," "body-oriented psychotherapy," "alchemical hypnotherapy," "intuitive counseling," "bonding therapy," "holotropic breathwork," and something called "Penumbra-Work," among others. One licensed marriage and family counselor advertised, "I shall bring you my gifts: body oriented psychotherapy, spiritual healing and a rich background in eastern and western spiritual mysticism and shamanic wisdom. . . . Using sharing, ritual, invocation, visualization, and dreams we empower your life." The pitch for most of these therapies ended with two particularly important words: "Insurance accepted."

Of course, no one should be barred from looking for help

wherever they please, nor should anyone be restricted from giving their money to whomever they feel adds value to their lives. However, a burden should be placed on the therapy profession to provide legitimate information to the prospective patient. Because patients are seldom informed of the soundness or shortcomings of the treatments they enter, they often assume that the treatment in which they are engaging is based on legitimate and current knowledge of mind and behavior, and is more effective than simply waiting for their troubling symptoms to go away on their own. These are in fact exactly the beliefs that all therapy schools explicitly or implicitly promote. Prospective clients have the right to know that these assumptions are not borne out by research.

What the history of the discipline shows is not only that psychodynamic therapy has proven ineffective in treating mental illnesses, but that practitioners have often done their patients great harm. As Frederick Crews, a critic of psychoanalysis, writes, because of Freud's legacy "people harboring disease or genetic conditions have deferred effective treatment while scouring their infantile past for the sources of their trouble. Parents have agonized about having caused their children's homosexuality, and gays have been told that their sexual preference is a mental disorder. And women have accepted a view of themselves as inherently envious, passive, and amoral." It is time that these professions find mechanisms for weeding out potentially damaging "cures."

Writing a decade ago about psychoanalysis, Hans Eysenck wrote that "all sciences have to pass through an ordeal by quackery." We contend that the general public is just beginning to be let in on what social scientists and the leadership of psychiatry and scientific psychology have known for years: The psychodynamic theory of the mind is the quackery the mental health profession is burdened with surviving.

Because there have been such dramatic advances through the bio-medical approach in the knowledge and treatment of mental disorders, distinctions between demonstrably effective practices and those based on myth and pseudoscience beg to be made. To offer someone in need a treatment known to be harmful is unconscionable. To knowingly offer a suffering person ineffective intervention when an effective one exists is no less cruel.

Because we assume a high level of expertise in scientific disciplines, we often defer to scientists' statements about things we do not ourselves understand because of their complexity. When an applied scientist, such as a doctor, explains a dark shadow on an X-ray, we assume that he or she is making the diagnosis on the basis of having studied hundreds of such X-rays, having kept up-to-date on the relevant research, and having gone through an intensive training that backs up the conclusion. While we may have the wherewithal to get a second opinion, we know we do not have the knowledge to provide our own interpretation of that shadow.

Our belief in and respect for such a science-based approach could not be more dramatic. On the basis of our faith in modern medical science and our respect for the doctor's authority, we may undergo a painful medical procedure such as a surgery. We allow them to make us much sicker for a time because of our belief that they understand how to make us well in the long term. Our outrage when this trust is betrayed—when doctors make mistakes because they were not well trained or because they went outside of the accepted norms of care—is an expression of how deep our trust is. Our anger is an acknowledgment that to accord someone such power is to make ourselves deeply vulnerable.

It is important to distinguish between the science and pseudoscience elements of modern mental health treatments precisely because patients' deep belief in the conclusions of their therapists often come from the appearance of scientific validity. The influence of the therapist and the therapeutic setting, combined with the cultural influences of the moment, are a powerful and volatile mixture.

Unfortunately, to the person in need, all psychotherapists may appear to share the authority and status of physicians.

The professional-looking manuals, the diagnostic jargon, the health insurance forms—all combine to inspire to have confidence in the therapist's legitimacy. Because it is difficult to know at a glance what set of theories and methods lies behind an impressively scripted and tastefully framed diploma, it is often impossible for the patient to discern the difference between the empiricists who base their treatments on scientific knowledge about the human mind and the talk therapists who offer treatments founded on little more than intuition and tradition. Patients, who do not understand that the interpretations and theories offered by the therapist are culturally based and fungible, will often hold to them as if they were scientifically proven fact. Patients in therapy can be, by nature, particularly vulnerable to influence. Unfortunately, the depth of the patient's loyalty to his or her therapist has shown no direct relation to the efficacy or demonstrable value of the treatment.

The mental health profession is suffering from a split between increasingly incompatible ways of thinking about human behavior and mental illness. This split between the psychodynamic and biogenetic approaches does not pit psychologists against psychiatrists who prescribe drugs, but rather juxtaposes two different ways of gathering and understanding information about the mind. The problem both groups face is the same: the monumentally complex workings of the human mind. The psychodynamic response to this complexity, as we will show, is to focus on creating a narrative that seemingly explains the patient's current problems. The patient's eventual acceptance of the narrative is seen as confirmation of the practitioner's ability to read the patient's unconscious.

Those who pursue the biomedical model of treatment know that simply because our behavior and feelings are breathtakingly complex does not put them out of reach of careful study. Indeed, they know that it's precisely the strength of the scientific method that makes it possible to chip away at the edges of what at first may seem hopelessly complex. The fears, hopes, fantasies, memories, and emotions that make up the patient's inner landscape are extremely difficult to delineate and predict, but that difficulty means that the effort should be redoubled, not abandoned. When asked whether the mental health profession should aspire to the same commitment to empiricism held by medical doctors, these mental health healers are likely to answer "no." They understand that because of the vagaries of mental health disorders and the difficulties in assessing effective care, mistakes of diagnosis and treatment are much too easy to make. For these reasons they maintain that the mental health field should aspire to a much *greater* level of skepticism, caution, and scientific rigor than medicine.

Simply put, the core of the biomedical approach is accountability—that is, an acceptance of the idea that what is done to the patient should be demonstrably effective, not wasteful, and, most important, not harmful. Those who pursue the biomedical approach understand that consistency of clinical description, firm guidelines for diagnosis, and an understanding of the biological advances in treatment are central to their practice. They understand that credibility does not come from one's good intentions—no matter how true and deeply felt—but rather, as Carl Sagan put it, that "credibility is the consequence of method."

The advances on the biogenetic front have been dramatic. After decades of ineffective treatment through psychotherapy, the biogenetic approach to understanding and treating schizophrenia through an investigation of its biological components has resulted in substantial progress. Researchers not only demonstrated a genetic link to schizophrenia, they also discovered much about the biochemical and physiological mechanisms of the disease. These discoveries have led to the beginnings of drug treatments for its symptoms, and hold the future possibility of effective management of the disorder, as well as hope for a greater understanding of the illness through genetic research. While rehabilitative counseling can play an important role in a schizophrenic's treatment, its sights have been substantially lowered from those of the psychodynamic psychotherapist. No longer responsible for determining causation or for single-handedly effecting a cure, rehabilitative counselors can focus on more attainable goals, such as helping patients manage the consequences of their handicap and teaching them strategies that will help them avoid social isolation. While there is much the biogenetic approach can't explain and many illnesses its proponents can't yet treat effectively, their success to date signals a sea change from the psychodynamic conception of psychotherapy.

Sadly, pressures that will expose this untenable split within the profession largely come from outside the mental health field. The increasingly bitter fights over health insurance dollars have forced the question of efficacy. Several years into managed care, some psychodynamic therapists still appear startled to be asked by the companies that fund their procedures to show that what they do is both effective and not wasteful compared to other possible treatments.

A dramatic rise in the number of malpractice cases against therapists of all stripes is also likely to force a crisis. As there is little recourse for aggrieved patients within the various professional organizations, they have taken their complaints to the courts. In this way, juries and judges are more and more being put in the position of determining such critical issues as what constitutes an acceptable "standard of care" for different disorders. Determining standards of care based on the relative effectiveness of different treatments is a responsibility that those inside the profession have ignored at their peril. If the profession won't take the time to weed out ineffective and damaging treatments, the courts will. And along the way it will cost practitioners dearly in the skyrocketing costs of what they have to pay to insure themselves against such lawsuits.

There is also a small but growing number of professionals within the field willing to expose the pseudoscientific practices of their colleagues to protect the public. With the growing cost of insurance coverage, as well as the cost in terms of public status to the profession each time malpractice comes to light, we are likely to see an increasing number of those inside the profession willing to expose abuses and name names. For these reasons it is becoming increasingly clear that the discipline of psychology can no longer house these divergent biomedical and psychodynamic factions.

The shift in the treatment of the severely mentally ill from talk therapy to the biogenetic approach has already begun and appears irreversible. The clear evidence that the biogenetic approach to treating major mental illness will eventually win out, however, is not the end of the story. This shift in the treatment of the most desperate and marginalized among us will have broader consequences to those practitioners who treat the walking worried as well as to our broader socially shared conception of human behavior. Just as Freud's theories surrounding mental illness expanded outward and eventually informed our shared cultural view of mental life, the advances in biogenetic treatment of mental illness have the potential to unfold a new metatheory for human behavior. Currently, the battle between these two incompatible views is being played out not only within the relevant professions but in our culture at large.

There is a good deal of resistance to the idea that the primary advances in treating mental illness have come about not through self-introspection but through science. Arguments that our human troubles cannot be treated on some strict schedule and that they are not the sum of their chemistry are often compelling. Drug efficacy tests and carefully designed experiments in human behavior may be illuminating, but they rarely jibe with our sense of our mental lives. Science is not the language we use to describe our feelings, and it disturbs us to be separated into groups with likelihoods of certain behaviors or chemical reactions. Our feeling of the shifting and labyrinthine complexity of our thoughts defies the parsing of science, so it follows that scientists have a hard time painting a comprehensive picture of the human experience in which laypeople can find inspiration or solace. There are many things that can be said about an ocean by studying drops under a microscope, but such an approach (no matter how many drops you examine) will fail to communicate the sense of a whole. The desire to believe that we are more than the sum of our parts is profound.

The argument against the biomedical approach to mental health treatment has legs for other reasons as well. From the patient's perspective, mental disorders often don't feel like medical conditions. Depression, to take the prime example, does not feel like a specific malady or injury that should be attended to with the single-mindedness of a doctor repairing a broken leg. As with many mental disorders, depression's thick and pervasive dread constrains all other thoughts, expressions, and perceptions. Because of this, both healers and patients often believe that it is the patient's very spirit that needs tending to.

Some from the psychodynamic schools of talk therapy have taken this argument and run with it. They often dismiss the work of social scientists, memory researchers, behavior psychologists, as well as medical researchers, implying that in the search to quantify aspects of human thought and behavior these scientists have underappreciated the depth and complexity of the human mind. Those who limit their thinking to the strictly scientific are often portrayed as sadly close-minded to the deeper truths of the universe. Whenever the results of scientific research contradict or challenge the results of therapy, therapists inevitably point out that these scientists are not clinicians and therefore do not have the intuitive knowledge that is learned from dealing each day with troubled human beings. The scientific dissection of the human mind, they imply, is interesting but leaves us in the end with a lifeless cadaver.

To get the upper hand in this debate, psychodynamic therapists often try to pretend consumers are being offered a bipolar choice between drugs like Prozac and the deep self-knowledge they claim is available through talk therapy. Michael Roth, curator of a recent Freud exhibit at the Library of Congress, compares Prozac to psychoanalysis and finds the drug wanting. "Psychoanalysis gave us a vernacular, a vocabulary of repression and trauma and unconscious drives. Psychopharmacology has not given us such a vocabulary." The obvious answer to this criticism is that of course psychopharmacology has not given us such a vocabulary—drugs are mute on the topic of the human condition. However, Prozac can do much to relieve the crippling lethargy and cycling thoughts of someone who is clinically depressed. Perhaps science does fail at speaking to our sense of the human spirit, but science has never claimed to fill this void. This does not mean that drugs, genetics, or other scientific approaches are against the pursuit of self-knowledge, but rather that they are *neutral*. Scientifically based research and treatment are about relieving specific impediments that block the patient from engaging in all manner of human endeavors, including the thousands of ways we search for self-understanding.

Nevertheless, psychodynamic therapists insist that the over-all effect of their work has been positive, at least to the extent that they have encouraged us all to be more introspective. But have they expanded or narrowed the view patients have of the world around them? As all-embracing as these notions may sound, on examination they often show a draw toward totalizing thought. While many psychodynamic schools now pretend to be concerned with such broad mandates as reforming society or caring for the soul, they come from a mock-scientific tradition in which obviously simplistic explanations have been offered to explain extremely complex behaviors and feelings.

Does the psychodynamic approach to the human condition have the richness and respect for the vagaries of existence that it claims science lacks? The answer is most certainly no. It is a trick of narrow systems of thought that they cloak themselves in pretensions of grandeur. Most of these psychodynamic schools of talk therapy (particularly psychoanalysis), we will argue, have only the *appearance* of complexity. Psychodynamic therapists possess, as Freud admitted of himself, a "longing to be able to open all secrets with a single key."

Take, for example, one recent theory, promoted by one of the most aberrant schools of talk therapy, that patients' symptoms often come from having been abducted by aliens from another planet. Harvard psychiatrist John Mack, the leading proponent of this theory, constantly defends alien abduction therapy because of its expansive theories about existence and the universe. According to Mack, he and his patients are committed to challenging society's sad and misguided zeal to find "conventional" explanations. They are engaged, Mack says, in nothing less than a "hero's journey" to regain the "ability to know a world beyond the physical."

This sounds like heady stuff until one looks at the system of beliefs these unfortunate patients are left with at the end of therapy. Their "hero's journey" has brought them to the belief that their lives have turned on a few dramatic (and obviously imagined) events. It often seems as if these stories are grandiose in inverse proportion to their complexity, as if the mind, when it forms a worldview around a narrow set of ideas, trades off complexity for the comforting belief that the ideas adopted are of singular importance. The more monumental the ideas adopted in therapy, the less one need be worried about the vagaries and struggles of day-to-day life.

The practice of UFO abduction treatment is not a silver bullet in the heart of talk therapy, for it is rarely very harmful, nor does it make up a significant percentage of clinical practice. To point out that many of the proponents of these beliefs are trained therapists, therefore, is a criticism that is easily dismissed. Every profession has its oddballs—why should the mental health field be any different? While it may seem mean-spirited to start with this admittedly deviant example, we would argue that space alien abduction therapy is only grossly aberrant in its specific details. The fact that many abduction and past-life counselors attract clients because of their scientific-sounding credentials is telling, but less so than the similarities these enthusiasms share with more mainstream talk therapies.*

At play are the same fallacies that infect the other psychodynamic schools of talk therapy. They have taken needy clients, hungry for meaning, and put them in a situation where they are particularly susceptible to the overt and subtle and even unin-

---

*That this alien abduction therapy is often practiced by licensed therapists is not only a good example of how far off reality's map psychodynamic therapists can travel with their clients in tow, but is also illustrative of the lack of any controls the various professional bodies have on the types of therapy their respective memberships practice. While sleeping with your therapy patients may get you in all sorts of trouble, helping your clients come to believe that they have slept with creatures from another planet will not.

tentional suggestions of a healer. In that situation they have been introduced to an idea with some degree of cultural currency. In this way the patient may be primed for and then introduced to a belief in a manner that might be very hard for him to articulate. The belief-building petri dish that is the therapeutic encounter is then sealed up. As the client begins to believe in the counselor's theories, the counselor is buoyed by the client's growing certainty that the therapy is really on to something. The patient's eventual belief is taken as proof of the validity of the theories. As Mack attests, "the power and intensity with which something is felt" is proof of the belief's validity. He adds that these stories of alien abduction are "completely persuasive because of the emotional power of these experiences." Client and therapist bolster each other's beliefs. Subtle but powerful forces at work in such bizarre therapies are pervasive elements in a wide range of talk therapies, both historically and among those currently being practiced.

CHAPTER TWO

Freud's Forest
of Resemblances

Now listen to this. During an industrious night last week, when I was suffering from that degree of pain which brings about the optimal conditions for my mental activities, the barriers suddenly lifted, the veils dropped, and everything became transparent—from the details of the neuroses to the determinants of consciousness. Everything seemed to fall into place, the cogs meshed. . . . Naturally I can scarcely manage to contain my delight.

—FREUD in a letter to Wilhelm Fliess,
October 20, 1895

I no longer understand the state of mind in which I hatched the psychology; I cannot conceive how I could have inflicted it on you . . . it appears to have been a kind of madness.

—FREUD'S letter to Fliess,
November 29, 1895

Much anticipated and two years delayed, the "Sigmund Freud: Conflict and Culture" exhibit opened at the Library of Congress in the fall of 1998. The exhibit was going to be, depending on which side of this acrimonious debate one listened to, a celebration of Freud's contribution to our understanding of the "drives and conflicts within the individual psyche and in society," or a carefully staged and "federally sanctioned coup against history."

The controversy ignited in 1995 when plans for the upcoming exhibit (originally scheduled for the fall of 1996) were joyfully announced at a gathering of the International Psychoanalytic Association. Freud's portrait would hang in the great rotunda of the Library of Congress, Dr. Harold Blum, executive director of New York's Sigmund Freud Archives, told the crowd, where "so many of our presidents' portraits have also been placed." A display of what Blum has called Freud's "revolutionary genius" was particularly important, he said, in a time when we have had so much Freud denigration." While the psychoanalysts in attendance were pleased by the news, grumblings were soon heard from other quarters.

No one objected to the idea that an exhibit on Freud was worthwhile. Whether you agree or disagree with Freud's theories, the fact that he had a massive influence on the course of Western thought can hardly be challenged. To many of the historians and scholars who have recently challenged Freud's views, however, something about the plans for the exhibit looked amiss. Just exactly *how* was Freud to be presented to the public, they wanted to know, and on whose authority? It appeared that the critical scholars who had examined Freud's claims and found them wanting were not going to be invited to the party. Although the officials at the Library of Congress promised that the exhibit would include a "close critical examination" of the more recent Freudian scholarship, no prominent or even minor Freud dissenter had been named as a potential contributor to the exhibit's catalog copy. The list of advisers for the exhibit looked—to put it mildly—psychoanalytically inclined.

A prominent independent Freud scholar, Peter J. Swales, drafted a petition asking the library's staff to take a close look at the plans for the exhibit to ensure that they represented a "full spectrum of informed opinion about the status of Freud's contribution to modern intellectual history." Fifty Freud scholars and others signed the document. While the petition was endorsed by many of the most cutting critics of Freudian doctrine, it also garnered the signatures of many sympathetic to psychoanalytic thinking, including some practicing psychoanalysts as well as the president-elect of the psychoanalytic division of the American Psychological Society. Freud's own granddaughter put her name to the letter.

While the petition initially appeared to be received in the spirit of respectful scholarship in which it was written, the good faith of many Freud critics soon evaporated when the exhibit organizers announced that fund-raising for the exhibit had fallen short of goals and that the celebration of Freud's genius would have to be postponed. While the library denied that the petition had anything to do with the postponement, the petitioners soon became the focus of an international campaign of vilification. Advisers for the exhibit and those in prominent psychoanalytic posts claimed that the exhibit was sabotaged by "censors." The petitioners were publicly compared to "puritans" and "inquisitors." The modest request that a broader spectrum of views be presented at the exhibit was compared to the "Ayatollah's fatwa against Salman Rushdie." The attacks on the petition signers became so loud and venomous that it garnered a good amount of popular press coverage. It is always interesting copy, after all, when normally staid members of the intelligentsia reveal themselves to be as vindictive and spiteful as the rabble.

When enough money was finally gathered to reschedule the exhibit, relations between the organizers and anyone associated with the petition had so deteriorated that there was little possibility of good-faith collaboration. In the end, the exhibit planners decided to duck the most controversial legacies of Freud altogether. For example, they completely ignore the impact of Freud's ideas in the treatment of the mentally ill. Instead, the exhibit blandly idolizes Freud as an important thinker who pondered many deep questions. The exhibit avoids presenting his specific conclusions in a clear enough manner to give the visitor a basis with which to form an opinion as to their merit.

While many have watched this debate with interest, others

have also wondered: Why all the fuss? Is the question of how Freud is presented to the modern public really of such importance? To understand why this debate *is* significant, one must first grasp how deeply Freud's work forms the basis for many talk therapies today. While many current therapists would like to cast Freud as the man who tipped the first domino in a series of ideas that has led to modern therapy (in this way he can be honored from a safe distance), his modern influence is far greater and more troubling.

Although the pieces of Freud's psychodynamic puzzle of the mind may have changed, the fatal fallacy remains in place in many modern therapy offices: the idea that the therapist has some special access to the connections and strings of causation within the patient's mind that influence his or her behavior. That the process of therapy can reveal these connections where the patient is blind to them, and that revealing them can be curative, is still the central promise of the modern psychodynamic therapist whether practicing psychoanalysis or any one of the hundred of derivative psychotherapies.

It is the fate of Freud critics to be characterized as pathological by those still in his thrall. While most Freud supporters agree that to question his genius is to be sick in the head, the diagnoses vary. Some critics are accused of oedipal conflicts—that is, the desire to kill Freud-the-father-figure. Others are accused of suffering the intellectual whiplash of negative transference. Mostly, however, the underlying pathology pinned to Freud critics is that they are suffering from a deep phobia of the complex. Apparently, to reject Freud is not only to reject the specifics of his ideas but to fearfully dismiss the conception of the mind and human behavior as multidimensional and richly elaborate. To criticize Freud, it is often implied, is to argue for a view of human behavior that is both simplistic and transparent.

The one "prejudice that still deters most observers from gazing on the perfect nakedness of Emperor Freud," writes Frederick Crews, who has been at the forefront of Freud criticism, is "the belief that the intricacy of Freudian theory more or less matches that of the human mind. So long as that misunderstanding prevails, a wholesale rejection of Freud will look like an unthinkable throwback to behaviorism, positivism, associationism, or a primitive psychology of faculties and humors."

Of all the illnesses Freud critics are accused of suffering, this phobia of the complex is the most unfair, for it ignores the central point of the recent Freudian criticism: that it is *Freud* who invariably made the mistake of imposing overly deterministic, mechanistic theories of behavior and mental functioning. Looking at the sheer volume of Freud's writings, one might assume that they contain a level of depth and complexity that they do not. On examination, they reveal themselves to be bizarrely idiosyncratic, rigid, and often utterly lacking in cohesion.

Despite Freud supporters' penchant for diagnosing critics as pathologically deluded, the confluence of the criticism has been building. As Crews writes, recent "independent studies have begun to converge toward a verdict that was once considered a sign of extremism or even of neurosis: that there is literally nothing to be said, scientifically or therapeutically, to the advantage of the entire Freudian system or any of its component dogmas." Crews lists the central problems of Freudian theory in one long footnote:

> The movement's anti-empirical features are legion. They include its cult of the founder's personality; its casually anecdotal approach to corroboration; its cavalier dismissal of its most besetting epistemic problem, that of suggestion; its habitual confusion of speculation with fact; its penchant for generalizing from a small number of imperfectly examined instances; its lack of vigilance against self-contradiction; its selective reporting of raw data to fit the latest theoretical enthusiasm; its ambiguities and exit clauses, allowing negative results to be counted as positive ones; its indifference to rival explanations and to mainstream science; its insistence that only the initiated are entitled to criticize; its stigmatizing of disagreement as "resistance," along with the corollary that, as Freud put it, all such resistance constitutes "actual evi-

dence in favor of the correctness" of the theory; and its narcissistic faith that, again in Freud's words, "applications of analysis are always confirmation" of it as well.

Of all the books that have recently examined Freud's body of work, Malcolm Macmillan's *Freud Evaluated: The Completed Arc* takes the prize as the most comprehensive.* Macmillan, to his credit, does not slash at Freud's body of work but carefully dissects it with the precision of a pathologist. His strength is in illustrating how Freud's successive theories were not additions built on a solid foundation but speculative notions layered onto each other with only minimal connection—usually that connection being the new theory's attempt to cover over a hole in its predecessor.

Macmillan, as pathologist, does suggest one central mistake infecting all of Freud's theories. It is an error that is particularly telling for the practice of psychodynamic therapy throughout the century. That mistake is Freud's ascribing wishful but wholly false attributes to his primary therapeutic technique: free association.

Today's understanding of the term *free association* is misleading, Macmillan argues, partly due to its less than precise translation from the German words *Freier Einfall*. As *Freier Einfall* implied, Freud did not believe that his patients trained in this technique were skipping randomly from thought to thought but rather that they were allowing themselves to communicate preconscious thoughts that were not merely associative but *intrusive and uncontrollable* to them. "Clearly," writes another Freud scholar on this point, "Freud himself did not believe that anything at all was truly 'free' in the life of the mind."

Freud dogmatically insisted that free associations yielded a specific lineage of mental connections leading back to the original source of the symptom or neurosis under examination.

---

*While Macmillan's work is the most wide-ranging, it is certainly Frederick Crews who best summarizes the larger body of recent Freudian critiques. The conciseness of his case, made originally in the *New York Review of Books* (November 1993) and reprinted in *Memory Wars: Freud's Legacy in Dispute,* is unsurpassed.

These associations, Freud maintained, inevitably revealed their *preceding* idea—that is, associations revealed where thoughts were coming from, not where they were going. He could believe, in this way, that he was tracing the patient's thoughts ever deeper into the psyche (and usually ever farther back into the patient's childhood).

In Freud's envisioning, the forces that affect behavior were not difficult to discover, for underneath any symptom or thought could be found a one-to-one correlation with its source. Freud's conception of a mental life was that of billiard balls hitting each other. While there might be many balls on the table (and therefore many interactions to ponder), the reaction between a single ball and another was utterly predictable. Freud's claim was to be able to read the interactions of the balls *backwards,* from the last hit to the original moment of movement. His patients' associations, he believed, showed him each billiard ball interaction of thoughts in reverse motion. While the chain of associations that connected cause to effect might be a long one, the ultimate connection made in therapy between the symptom and the root cause was usually a distressingly simplistic story.

The linkage of this association chain that led back from a thought to the source of that thought was quite strong, according to Freud, and led invariably (if not quickly) to a beginning point that Freud had presupposed. For Freud, that terminus was likely some sexual fantasy or desire in the patient's earliest childhood. As Freud wrote, "[T]he etiological pretensions of the infantile scenes rest . . . above all, on the evidence of there being associative and logical ties between those scenes and the hysterical symptoms." Those "ties" were the associations he elicited from his patients.

In this way, Freud's postulates were outwardly Newtonian in form as he presumed cause and certain effect. What Freud proposed does not remotely resemble modern scientific theories, which assume complex interactions among many variables and outcomes. This is particularly true of the science of studying human behavior in which there is great respect for the idea of probabilities of outcomes. Not even experiences as intense as childhood sexual abuse, for example, have shown to have any certain connection to the creation of mental illness in adulthood.* Freud's simple billiard ball conception of psychic cause and outcome simply has no place in the modern understanding of behavior, for as social science has repeatedly demonstrated, few single events or life experiences can be counted on to have a certain effect.

Freud's belief in the strength of the connections between associations had some obvious advantages in deflecting criticism. In particular, this assumption allowed him to dismiss the thorny problem of suggestion. If the connections between these associations were strong, he could assure his colleagues and patients that the danger of the therapist influencing the chain was quite small. What he was tracing, he said, were "subtle but *strong* interconnections," which could not be easily created or colored by the therapist's communications.

Freud's insistence that free associations yielded their determinants and that his own associations were deeply meaningful rested on his belief in psychic determinism. No one—not even modern Freudians—now defends the argument that associations invariably follow a path to their beginnings. It is clear that patients' decisions of what to say next in describing their thoughts and memories are influenced by any number of possible sources. There is now broad acceptance that one of the most likely sources of associations is the assumptions that patients learn during, or read into, the therapy experience.

As Crews notes, " 'Free' associations aren't free at all, since they have been amply shown to lack the imperviousness to suggestibility that Freud rashly ascribed to them. Freudian therapists and patients come to share a causal outlook predetermining the kinds of factors that both parties will consider significant, and both the patients' verbal productions and the therapist's the-

---

*As two researchers who examined seven studies on this issue concluded: "Conclusions about a causal link between child sexual abuse and later psychological maladjustment in the general population cannot safely be made because of the reliable presence of confounding variables."

matically pointed selection among them cannot escape being influenced by that bias."

This fundamental problem with free associations is a black hole into which the entire Freudian theory gets inescapably pulled. For "free association" was not only the method with which Freud claimed to have divined his theories; it was his method *for confirming them as well.*

While Freud's theory of psychic determinism at least explained his willful blindness to the issue of suggestion, modern-day therapists, who have largely abandoned psychic determinism, have no such excuse. But as Macmillan writes, "[T]he tendency not to reply to the criticism that free association generates associations, not determinants, is well established in the psychoanalytic literature. . . . None of his followers . . . have probed any deeper than did Freud into the assumptions underlying their 'basic method'—free association. None question whether those assumptions hold in the therapeutic situation; none has attempted to break out of the circle."

Remarkably, even though modern-day psychodynamic therapists don't openly defend primitive psychic determinism, they continue to insist that they are discovering something deeply meaningful in their patients' associations surrounding dreams, memories, and emotions. In addition, therapists continue to present their own loose associations (as we will show) as helpful to the understanding of the client's distress or mental illness.

But even his grand mistake of psychic determinism does not explain the bizarre quality of many of Freud's conclusions. In his *Why Freud Was Wrong*, Richard Webster puts forth the truly frightening hypothesis that Freud believed that his own idiosyncratic associations, between, for example, a patient's symptom and some bit of a remembered dream, had a type of real-world legitimacy. Freud may have believed that his own free associations (which were being made while he listened to the patient's free associations) manifested the deepest truths about his clients' lives. In other words, the same quasimystical unconscious forces that determined the patient's utterances also caused Freud to correctly interpret them. Armed with this more than convenient assumption, Freud could delude himself and his followers into believing that he was always correct merely because he reached a certain notion in his mind.

As evidence for this possibility, take, for example, Freud's interpretation of the Wolfman's dream. The patient supposedly remembered a dream from an early age in which he saw six white dogs sitting motionless outside his bedroom window. In this fantasy Freud finds confirmation of his suspicion that the Wolfman witnessed his parents having sex years before that childhood dream, sometime in his infancy. As Crews and others have pointed out, the flips and turns of logic required to find the sexual scene in this dream are quite impressive. As Freud's reasoning goes: The six dogs were actually the two parents; their whiteness indicated the color of bedsheets; their *lack* of motion means the opposite—grinding sexual movement; that they are dogs means that the parents were engaged in sex dog-like, from behind; and finally, the dogs' big tails indicated the baby-Wolfman's assumption that his mother's genitals had been "castrated."

In the end, the loose structure of psychoanalytic theory was adhered to (i.e., that the patient's problem was traced to witnessing the primal scene), but the evidence for the conclusion requires that we believe Freud's interpretation of the scene to be more than an absurd series of unsubstantiated connections.* Given the ridiculous turns of logic in the interpretation of the Wolfman's dream, it is hard to imagine a dream that couldn't produce the expected scene. Freud's interpretation has more dream-logic than the dream itself. Does anyone believe that Freud's reasoning would not have been equally imaginative had the Wolfman reported a childhood dream of a runaway cart in the marketplace?

---

*To make matters worse for the explanatory power of Freud's interpretations, these symbols did not always mean the same thing. Six was not always two, white was not necessarily a substitute for bedsheets. While a cigar was sometimes just a cigar, Freud otherwise gave himself license to make any connection he pleased so long as these connections had a collective momentum toward one of his pet theories of psychopathology.

Freud's certainty in his wild interpretations gives weight to Webster's conclusion. "[Freud] assumes that since he is able to perceive or construct a link between two discrete phenomena, then this link has some kind of operative reality: Freud's own internal and idiosyncratic logic is treated as though it were a real, external chain of causality." The patient's dream or chain of consciousness provided the raw material for Freud's chain of consciousness—which he assumed to have an inherent validity. With this chain-of-consciousness-squared procedure, no conclusion is outside the therapist's reach.

"The most charitable observation we can make about this kind of reasoning is that it is neither odd nor abnormal," Webster writes. "For it is exactly the kind of reasoning habitually encountered in necromancy, astrology, phrenology and many other forms of investigation with which psychoanalysis is not normally associated."

It is equally disturbing to consider that Freud's self-flattering belief in the credibility of his own free associations was at work in his theory creation as well as in his interpretation of his patients. Webster follows Freud's threads of reasoning to illustrate just how fanciful yet dogmatic they could become. For instance, he traces Freud's theoretical gambit that began with the observation that children often mistakenly assume that babies are born through the anus. This observation led him to the conclusion that children made an "imaginative equation between babies and feces." Freud had to cover another bet on this topic because he had already made an organic parallel between penis and feces (both, he had previously noted, were "solid bodies" that stimulated an organ lined with a mucous membrane). He proposed that feces represented the first penis and the rectum represented the vagina. Combining these theories, Freud becomes lost in a forest of resemblances in which he connects feces, penis, and baby in multiple roundabout ways and assumes that they were all treated by the unconscious, as Webster concludes, "as if they were equivalent and could replace one another freely."

The extensions and interconnections of this theory are as remarkable as they are ridiculous. Because "penis" = "feces" and "feces" = "baby," a woman's desire to have babies was, therefore, a confirmation of her unconscious desire to have a penis.

It is about as challenging as shooting dead fish floating in a barrel to critique these formulations, for they presently have zero cultural currency, few adherents, and even fewer public defenders. We bring them up not to challenge these specific ideas (for they are already lifeless from lack of use) but to point to the style of reasoning by which they were wrought—a style that willfully extrapolates from a combination of commonplaces, hunches, and symptoms to find deep psychological meaning.

Modern-day therapists, particularly those not obviously of the psychoanalytic schools, understandably bridle at any connections drawn between Freud's conclusions and their own. They are rightly offended in the particular. As we have noted, few modern therapists publicly attribute much validity to the idea that females are inherently masochistic, that they have babies to make up for the lack of a penis, or that masturbation is at the heart of many disorders. (The seemingly endless list of abandoned Freudian concepts should be enough to give one pause. Could it be that all this misbegotten theory came from a method that held any validity at all?) But this attempted distancing ignores the most important point: It is not *in the particular* that Freud remains dangerous. The problem lies with the more general Freudian-psychodynamic game that remains in play—despite the fact that his self-declared theoretical home runs have been dismissed as lies, exaggerations, cultural artifacts, or self-deceptions.

Saving the legend of Freud while ignoring his obvious mistakes is the exact tack taken by current defenders of Freud's legacy, as seen in the responses to Crews's flaying of Freud in the *New York Review of Books*. No less than Harold Blum, the executive director of the Sigmund Freud Archives, and Bernard Pacella, the former president of the American Psychoanalytic Association, wrote in to praise Freud's "enduring discoveries," while in the next sentence noting that same work was "no longer vital for the validation of psychoanalytic formulation." Crews refers to this tricky maneuver (of claiming Freud as an ally while defending none of his specific conclusions) as a rhetorical "two-step." Blum and Pacella praise Freud's theories, Crews writes, while "assuring us that present-day psychoanalysis has left those same treasures safely behind where they will cause no further harm."

What is "enduring" about Freud's work? In the conclusion of the Blum/Pacella letter they maintain that "the encompassing explanatory reach of psychoanalytic theory . . . [has] endured the test of time." This is half true. We would suggest that the reason Freud's psychodynamic notions and methods stay in vogue has little to do with their explanatory power (for they have none) but with their all-encompassing reach—that is, in the broad license they give therapists to come to any conclusion they desire.

Defenders of Freud's legacy make this case implicitly. In *The Rise and Crisis of Psychoanalysis,* Nathan Hale writes: "Freud's ambiguity . . . made it possible to deduce from psychoanalysis the orgiastic flights of Wilhelm Reich or the ego psychology of Freud's daughter Anna, to reconcile psychoanalysis with Marxism or American liberal capitalism or European social democracy. Psychoanalysis could be seen in its early guise as an optimistic movement of sexual and cultural reform or, from the perspective of Freud's final papers, as a stoical and tragic vision of unending conflict. It could appeal to American optimism or to the lingering sense of tragedy tinctured with hope associated with elements of Judaism or survivals of Calvinism."

Freud's implicit encouragement of wild speculation has been, and remains, a large part of his intrinsic appeal to scholars and therapists alike. The belief on the part of many modern-day therapists that they are so thoughtful and so intuitive as to construct clear pictures out of the puzzle pieces the patient provides is simply too appealing a notion for some modern-day therapists to willingly give up. Even without psychic determinism as an excuse, modern-day psychodynamic psychotherapists still wander off into the same forests of resemblances that Freud found so enchanting. The free-ticket-to-any-conclusion inherent in Freud's methods (and the invitation to view speculation as fact) is the psychodynamic approach's most seductive and most dangerous trait.

There is a remarkably poignant document written by a well-known psychoanalyst that you won't find in any journal. The document is entitled "Where Will Psychoanalysis Survive?" and it was written by Alan Stone, a psychoanalyst and a professor both of law and medicine at Harvard University. In its full form, the essay has been presented only once, as an address to the American Academy of Psychoanalysis. The fact that it did not appear in any of the many academic journals devoted to the subject is not surprising, for in the essay Stone sadly tenders his resignation as a true believer in the curative power of psychoanalysis. This is not something practicing psychoanalysts particularly want to hear, especially from such an eminent source.

Stone has spent most of his life practicing psychoanalysis and teaching Freudian studies. He recently looked back over the history of the discipline that has so enthralled him and came to some rather devastating conclusions. He reports these conclusions not with the passion of a whistle-blower but with the sad wistfulness of a man looking through the rubble of his burned-down house, hoping there is something to be salvaged and wishing things could have worked out altogether differently.

In the essay, Stone writes nostalgically of a time when he believed that all psychoanalysts were engaged in a similar pursuit. As Stone tells it, he deeply wanted to think that psychoanalysts were similar to the laborers collectively working on a century-long construction of a great cathedral. As a young scholar, he hoped to see this intellectual monument far along in its construction in his lifetime. But after over forty years of labor, Stone took the time to look back and, in what was clearly a difficult essay to write, was forced to admit that there is no cathedral in sight. "Unfortunately I and many others in my generation have lost that sense of conviction and with it the feeling that we are part of a collective enterprise," Stone writes. "Those who stand on Freud's shoulders have not seen further, they have only seen differently. . . . Rather than building a cathedral, psychoanalysts have built their own churches."

Stone is right: The history of Freudian thought is not one of systematic advance on Freud's theories, only new theoretical gambits. Taken together, the theories do not appear to be an accumulation of knowledge so much as an accumulation of speculations. Stone points out that those who claimed to be advancing Freud's ideas were in fact offering thoughts as different from Freud's as those who were deemed to be radically diverging from Freudian orthodoxy. He quotes another psychoanalyst to describe the resulting "thicket of similar overlapping, or identical terms and concepts which, however, did not carry the same meaning and were not employed as a part of the same conceptual context."

Considering the Freudian structure with which these psychoanalysts began, it is not surprising that they ended up in such a tangle of theories. Freud's own work, Stone points out, is caught in the exact same conceptual thicket. "Freud did not even feel the need to build with consistency on his own ideas," Stone admits, and this doomed several generations of well-intentioned scholars to labor "in vain to bring some semblance of order to what I think were flashes of inspired speculation."

Stone recounts that he was in mid-career when he first discovered how untethered Freud was from science. Intensively studying Freud's correspondence and other biographical material, Stone found himself amazed by the paucity of evidence Freud needed to launch a theory. While Freud often portrayed himself as a careful scientist, the record clearly showed that he could spout a new hypothesis every day. "It is astonishing to see how little evidence he needed" as backing for these theories, Stone writes; "a single patient hour was enough to launch a whole new theory of mental illness." Freud always acknowledged that he had a strong attraction toward speculation, but he also claimed to possess the willpower to "ruthlessly check" that tendency. On examining the record, Stone concludes dryly: "This 'ruthless' suppression of speculation is seldom to be found in the collected works of Sigmund Freud."

Although troubling, this revelation did little to dampen Stone's ardor for Freud's ideas. Stone admits to having been under the spell of an "idealized transference to Sigmund Freud" for over four decades of his life. While he was able to overlook Freud's failures as a scientist, more recent revelations surrounding Freud's manipulation of the people around him were harder for Stone to ignore. What finally broke that thralldom were the details of the Horace Frink affair, which came to light only in the late 1980s.

Horace Frink was an American analyst and patient of Freud's. In an example of his most brazen selfishness, Freud encouraged Frink to marry a rich patient whom Frink had been simultaneously treating and romancing. To convince him, Freud told Frink that he was a latent homosexual and would likely become an overt one unless Frink divorced his wife and married the wealthy patient. Freud also lobbied Frink's patient/lover, urging her to divorce her husband and marry Frink. There is little doubt that Freud's selfish goal in the whole affair was to further his own career and the cause of psychoanalysis with the woman's money. In what reads like a forced half-joke, Freud wrote to Frink: "Your complaint that you cannot grasp your homosexuality implies that you are not yet aware of your phantasy of making me a rich man. If matters turn out all right let us change this imaginary gift into a real contribution. . . ." Things, however, did not turn out all right. Both abandoned spouses died soon after the two divorces and Frink's marriage to his patient. The marriage was short-lived, and Frink soon sank into a psychotic depression and was driven to repeated suicide attempts.

It is a compliment to Stone's character that the revelations of this case troubled him so. Freud's abuse of his authority and power, along with his willingness to encourage a client to pursue such a drastic course of action, should give more Freud devotees pause. "My reading about the Frink affair was to some extent a mutative experience," Stone writes. "It certainly made me question Freud's moral authority. Am I alone in feeling this sense of disillusionment, or am I correct in thinking that others do as well and that [it] is part of our current predicament? Everywhere I go and talk to other analysts there is the scent of scandal hanging over our idealized leaders."

The balance sheet at the end of the twentieth century, Stone concludes, is not good for the whole enterprise of psychoanalysis. The scientific studies of the brain have devastated many fundamental psychoanalytic tenets, and our understanding of memory and influence in the therapy setting have given rise to a new understanding that patients' believed-in narratives of their psychological histories might be nothing more than just that. The basic premises of psychoanalysis "may all be incorrect," he writes. "Our critics might be right. Developmental experience may have very little to do with most forms of psychopathology, and we have no reason to assume that a careful historical reconstruction of those developmental events will have a therapeutic effect. . . . All of this makes the task of constructing meaningful histories of desire in the individual more daunting."

What makes Stone's argument so devastating is that in his essay he is clearly not out to destroy Freud but to rescue him from intellectual oblivion. His conclusion that Freud was no more a scientist than Marx is said "not in disrespect," for "both men were geniuses." To this day, Stone reads Freud in respectful awe of his "revolutionary reconception of the human condition." Referring to Freud's *Three Essays on the Theory of Sexuality*, Stone writes with reverence that he knows of "no other work in psychiatry or psychology so powerful, so lucid, and so immediately convincing." Convincing, that is, on a purely rhetorical level, for Stone admits in the next breath that these essays were in fact *too* convincing, and that the work is in fact "filled with what we now recognize as horrifying mistakes . . . about female sexuality that were taken as scientific truth by psychoanalysts. As a result we made several generations of educated women feel sexually inadequate and misled them about the possibilities of sexual gratification."

Stone's hope is to help Freud make a graceful exit from the stage of science and install him in the pantheon of literary greats. If Freud is seen as an "artist/subjectivist/philosopher," you can immediately step around the question of why no one has been able to systematically advance his work. No one, after all, tries to scientifically advance Shakespeare's vision of the world. As Stone notes, "Plato, Hegel, Kant, Michelangelo, DaVinci, Shakespeare, Dostoevsky and Sartre helped to shape Western Civilization and its conception of the human condition without any systematic proofs of their contentions."

While one appreciates Stone's anguish over his misplaced intellectual faith in Freud, it's impossible to ignore the illogic of proclaiming Freud a genius for work that was shot through with horrifying mistakes that resulted in the mistreatment of thousands upon thousands of vulnerable patients. Freud was not an artist or an academic philosopher. He claimed, at times, to be a scientist whose work would ameliorate the suffering of mental illness. How are we to divorce Freud's supposed genius from the validity and usefulness of his ideas? That he got so much wrong yet presented all his results as carefully observed facts begs a deeply troubling question: How many of the trappings surrounding these theories were a conscious con and how much was self-deception? One's reverence for the genius in such self-proclaimed messiahs as Marx and Freud should at least in part be based on the answer to the question: Would the world be better off without them? To laud Freud for his ability to write convincingly of falsehoods is strange praise if one has any faith in a rational-empirical approach to the world. On this topic Stone appears to have thrown his hands up in defeat: "This is a post modern world where everything is a paradox and hermeneutic uncertainty."

Undoubtedly, Freud would have refused Stone's rescue mission, for he was clearly not out to create a fiction or a set of theories subject to endless interpretation and reinterpretation. His goal was to find the Rosetta stone that could be used to decode the forces acting on human thought, behavior, and mental illness. He not only failed in his quest, but he caused a great deal of damage and consternation in the process. By admitting that Freud has no claim on science, we must face the fact that his work, *because it makes such repeated claims to science,* is either the confidence trick of the century or a monumental self-deception or some combination of the two. To take away from Freud his scientific pretension is to take away his work's persuasive power.

What is left for psychoanalysis in Stone's view? Not much as far as treatment. Stone mentions that there is still a possibility of helping the patient change destructive behaviors if the therapist is willing to leverage the "idealized transference" that the patient often develops toward the therapist. "The analyst is loved, admired, gains power over the patient, is accepted as [an] authority in the moral adventure of life, and that is one of the most important aspects of how the patient is changed," Stone writes. "[This] produces the power of suggestion which is the catalyst of change."

We would go farther. We would say that this "idealized transference" is the *essential* ingredient of the encounter. It is what keeps patients coming back and attesting to the importance of therapy in their lives.* But Stone's endorsement of such strong transference is troubling. Is this the same "idealized transference" that kept him blind to Freud's pseudoscience and led him intellectually astray for four decades? Stone makes himself a cautionary tale for such "idealized transference," and then, strangely, recommends it as a way to leverage change in others.

There is only one line toward the end of the essay that tries to rescue psychoanalysis as a practice: "I still believe that a traditional psychoanalytic experience is the best way to explore the mysterious otherness of one's self." With the problems Stone has pointed out—the fungible nature of the narratives, the speculative character of psychodynamic theories, the dangers of idealized transference—we wonder how he came to this

---

*Attributing this phenomenon to the Freudian conception of "transference," however, is wishful thinking on the part of Stone. That needy people quickly idealize those who claim to be healers is not a phenomenon limited to talk therapy.

conclusion. Psychoanalysis at its core speaks to the mysterious otherness of the self only in its prayerful and groundless claim to explain it.

The credo of the psychodynamic therapist is that truth telling about the most troubling moments in a patient's past is curative. In what appears at first to be an untenable paradox, much of the psychotherapy profession has continually obfuscated the historical facts surrounding Freud and his "discoveries." The story of Freud and the creation of psychodynamic therapy, as told by its adherents, is a self-serving myth.

On second look, this is not much of a paradox after all, considering that the credo of truth telling within the therapy setting is a myth itself. The story a patient learns to tell about his life during psychodynamic therapy is not necessarily the truth at all. As we argue elsewhere, what actually happens in the psychodynamic therapy setting is a molding of pieces of the patient's life into preexisting theories of behavior. What we have, then, is not a paradox but a telling parallel between the practice of therapy and the telling of its history. The willingness of talk therapists to create self-serving myths out of their movement's own intellectual history is quite similar to the sort of belief building psychodynamic therapists do with their patients. Bits of evidence from the history of the discipline are not puzzle pieces that shape a whole, but malleable things to be molded, or discretely disregarded.

CHAPTER THREE

Rise and Fall
of the Psychodynamic Mind

We stand at the threshold of many more psychoanalytic discoveries that are bound to have a far-reaching effect on our lives during the next century. The psychoanalytic revolution may yet prove to be more important than the atomic bomb.

—G. B. LEVITAS,
The World of Psychoanalysis, 1965

Freud's psychodynamic conception of the mind has had a particularly tenacious hold over Americans largely due to the enduring myth that Freud's followers told of the man. This myth, more or less successfully promoted during the middle of the century, held that Freud was the first to cross into unexplored mental landscapes. One historian of psychoanalysis describes this as the belief that "before Freud there had been mostly darkness, inhumanity, a narrow constraint which ignored sexuality and childhood." But the myth that Freud brought light, which we addressed in the last chapter, cannot fully explain the success of his theories in America. Despite the recent decline of his brainchild, psychoanalysis, his success continues to this day in a proliferation of Freudian-inspired psychotherapies, as well as through the use of psychoanalytic notions in many "eclectic" forms of therapies.

The influence of Freud's ideas about the mind throughout

the century leads many of the uninitiated to assume that there must be *something* to them. It just seems unlikely that they were so widely popular for no good reason. This is not a foolish assumption. Those reasons, however, lie largely outside the issue of his theories' validity, as well as outside the question of psychoanalysis or psychodynamic therapy's effectiveness in curing patients. The causes for the rise of Freud's star, and the popular acceptance of many of his theories, can be found in the social trends of the century, in particular: the openness of American culture to notions of progress and change; our seemingly insatiable appetite for cure-alls and nostrums; and our unshakable faith that all problems can be easily solved through sincere effort. These factors, in combination with the cunning self-promotion of psychoanalysts and psychodynamic psychotherapists alike, led to the wide acceptance of the psychodynamic conception of the mind after the Second World War.

While from 1910 to the 1930s psychoanalytic associations sprang up in major cities with some regularity, their major impact on America's mental health profession. It wasn't until the influx of European analysts fleeing fascism and anti-Semitism in Europe that the relatively small number of enthusiasts for Freudian psychoanalysis began to affect psychiatry in America. The immigrant analysts played a central role in promoting a strict Freudian doctrine, which had the odd result that American psychoanalysis became much more orthodox than its European counterpart. As one analyst noted, "These analysts formed a kind of bodyguard around an imaginary Freud." Instead of the "relaxed and free debating atmosphere of the psychoanalytic coffeehouses in Berlin [American psychoanalysis was] frighteningly standardized. . . .They tried to keep psychoanalytic theory, technique, therapy and training unchanged for years to come." Over the next decades, psychoanalysis became something it had never been in Europe: a doctrinaire and accepted standard of practice.

That these immigrant analysts would promote a stricter Freudian doctrine than they had adhered to in their homelands is easy to understand. The commodity they had to sell in America was being a European, and therefore having a supposedly more profound, understanding of Freud. Americans assumed that these analysts had closer ties to the master himself. The immigrants responded to their assumption by accepting the role of Freudian fundamentalists. By setting themselves up as transmitters of the sacrosanct Freudian theories, these analysts made themselves valuable in the marketplace. If they had treated Freud's ideas as they had in Europe—simply as a starting point for further speculation—they would have devalued the most valuable commodity they had to sell in America.

Starting in the 1940s, the psychoanalytic movement used its flood of European talent to launch a campaign to take over or establish prestigious psychiatry chairs at university departments and medical schools across the United States. Beginning in New York and spreading steadily outward to Philadelphia, New Haven, Boston, Washington, D.C., and Baltimore, psychoanalysts successfully established themselves as holders of prestigious chairmanships in major universities.

"The émigré analysts, with memories still alive of their craft being spurned in the European professoriate, were astonished at these developments," writes Edward Shorter in *A History of Psychiatry*. Analyst Edith Weigert, who had been a resident physician in a sanitarium in Berlin in the early 1930s, was elevated to the chair of the Washington Psychoanalytic Institute after her arrival in the United States. Writing at the time, she reported: "Psychoanalysis in the United States has not descended to the status of serving maid of psychiatry, as Freud feared it might . . . but instead has tended to become psychiatry's highly respected pathfinder."

By the early 1950s, the reach of psychoanalysts went even farther, capturing crucial positions, including the presidency of the American Psychiatric Association. In a presidential address to the American Psychoanalytic Association in 1954, one can still hear the surprise of Ives Hendrick at the victory of psychoanalysis in America. "Our success . . . hugely magnified by our growth in numbers and by the esteem of other medical groups, has given us unsought and unexpected powers, the equivalent of powers of faculty appointment, selection of students, and the curriculum policies of universities." By the 1960s, the post of presidency of the American Psychiatric Association was repeatedly held by analysts or psychiatrists intellectually affiliated with analysts.

America, it was noted at the time, had become the first country in the world to adopt psychodynamic psychiatry as its leading psychiatric trend. The postwar years were described by one psychoanalyst as "something of a gold rush" for psychoanalytic training and services. At the center of all the excitement was a remarkably small group of actual psychoanalysts. In the mid-1950s, there were only 1,400 practicing psychoanalysts in the world—approximately 1,000 of whom were in the United States—and perhaps only ten times that number of patients in treatment worldwide. Fewer than 100,000 patients had completed treatment. The interest in psychoanalysis by potential patients far outweighed the possible supply of services by these professionals.

The acceptance of psychoanalysis was helped immeasurably by American journalists and writers eager to write about this new treatment from Europe. Many popular magazines ran stories overstating and glamorizing the work of psychoanalysis in combating soldiers' war neurosis in the closing years of the war. In October of 1945, John Hersey wrote of a soldier who received treatment from a psychoanalyst after suffering hysterical paralysis. Once uncovering and reliving the battlefield trauma (the death of a friend by mortar fire), the therapist plumbed the patient's unconscious to find a whole host of psychoanalytic forces, including oedipal hatreds, feelings of inadequacy, and, of course, transference. Finally the therapist uncovered the childhood source of the paralysis: The patient's father had made him work unnecessarily hard by complaining of pain in his leg. Tying it all together, the therapist was said to pronounce: "You don't have to be afraid of dying anymore, the way you think your father was afraid of working." After that pronouncement the patient was supposedly able to walk, unaided.

The published accounts of psychoanalysis over the next ten years were mostly positive, often attesting to what now seem to be suspiciously miraculous cures for everything from depression and phobias to rapid heartbeat, difficulty breathing, severe colitis, and homosexuality. Freud was lionized, as in a *Saturday Review* article that praised him as a heroic healer who "labored tirelessly to cure men and women who were suffering horribly." Many of the first-person accounts were written by journalists, notes one historian, and they were "eager to convert others by the story of their own cure. And they were finding a wide audience."

Writers sympathetic to the ideas of psychoanalysis now look back at this period and claim to bemoan that psychoanalysis was presented as a proven cure at a time when it still might have been making headway in research and theory. In his book *The Rise and Crisis of Psychoanalysis in the United States,* Nathan Hale writes that "popularization further inflated the already optimistic claims of some psychoanalysts. . . . That the hopes and claims of a popularized psychoanalysis were dangerously overextended soon became abundantly clear."

It would be wrong, however, to lay too much blame for this turn of events on popular accounts and press reports. Psychoanalysts themselves were eager to report dramatic and enduring cures both to the press and to one another within their professional journals. William Menninger declared at the time that "any doubts about the efficacy of psychiatric treatments have been dissipated in the heat of war. Thousands of men have been returned to normal life and even to combat life by uses of the new therapy." Menninger pressed his case whenever he could, insisting that psychoanalysis was the only basis for "valid mental hygiene," and promoted its spread into other mental health fields as well as into the examination of other cultures, art, and literature.

Both professionally and in the public mind, psychoanalysis was becoming the accepted treatment for mental illness. Though it proposed that the cause of mental illness lay in the developmental experience of the sufferer, it implied that it was fixable. As long as medical science lacked the knowledge to even conceptualize the biochemical interactions that regulated normal and abnormal brain function, all that could be noted was that some major disorders ran in families and were largely incurable. Relative to other treatments of the time, Freud's methods seemed progressive, in that they offered hope for the mentally ill.

In 1953, at the height of the fervor over psychoanalysis, the first volume of Ernest Jones's three-volume biography of Freud appeared. Although some praised these volumes for their "warts and all" honesty because the work noted some of Freud's many personal quirks and anxieties, taken together the biography was a promotional piece for psychoanalysis and a one-man cheerleading routine for Freud as the genius healer of our time. Supposedly, Freud had "in the highest degree . . . the capacity to know instinctively what is true . . . he had a high and serious respect for the reality of psychological facts. They were as real and concrete to him as metals are to a metallurgist." If the popular press was overstating the case for psychoanalysis, it was understandable: They were taking their cues from the practitioners themselves.

Indeed, if one wanted to look for the central figure in the zealous overselling of psychoanalysis, one need look no farther than the writings of Freud himself, who was suddenly a bestselling author in America. Throughout the 1950s, New American Library published printing after printing of Sigmund Freud's *Psychopathology of Everyday Life*. "According to Sigmund Freud," the back cover of this fifty-cent paperback reads, "most common slips of the tongue or annoying errors are reflections of disturbances in our personalities, some of which may be buried so deep that we ourselves are hardly aware of them." The jacket copy goes on to attest that "one of the great thinkers of our times" will "show that there is nothing accidental in psychic life." This promise is repeated in the preface by esteemed analyst A. A. Brill: "By discarding the old methods of treatment and strictly applying himself to a study of the patient's life [Freud] discovered . . . that there was nothing arbitrary in any morbid manifestations. Psychoanalysis always showed that they referred to some definite problem or conflict of the person concerned."

To prove that there was "nothing arbitrary" and "nothing accidental" in the systems of mental illness or in our often troubled mental lives is the core promise of psychoanalysis, and one Freud was not shy of stating. More than anything else, it is this daring and unsupported guarantee that made his theories so immensely popular and influential. Freud's writings, along with the psychoanalysts who promoted this treatment, exploited the secular hope that through reason and study we might face the intricate nature of our thoughts, and that one could adopt a system of thinking about the mind and behavior that would be able to explain (if not globally, then piece by piece) how we think about our lives, behave in the world we encounter, and arrive at a comprehensive understanding of ourselves.

Before psychoanalysis, American psychiatry was an unglamorous medical specialty that was limited mainly to the care of the severely mentally ill in isolated asylums. The profession had no cures to offer its patients and was confined mostly to their stewardship, which it managed with widely varying degrees of humaneness. If patients got better, it was generally only because their symptoms went into remission (often temporarily) of their own accord. Psychiatry had even less to offer the non-mentally-ill general public. Psychoanalysis, however, was a method that could be said to be applicable to the non-mentally-ill: the neurotics and even those who suffered from common trials of living. For psychiatrists who adopted psychoanalysis, it had the advantage of expanding their practice beyond the mental asylums where they had previously found work. As one historian writes, "Psychoanalysis was the caisson on which American psychiatry rode triumphantly into private practice." Early on, other psychiatrists identified this trend. "The flood of patients seeking salvation through psychoanalysis is explainable," wrote one physician, "partly from the publicity, partly from the receptiveness of our time to introversion and introspection." It was a prescient remark, for that interest in personal introspection would only grow throughout the century.

As if to further fuel this trend toward treating the relatively healthy, some prominent psychoanalysts promoted the idea that what separated the mentally ill from the healthy were only degrees of severity. It is hard not to see this trend as self-serving, since the corollary proposition was clearly that everyone could use at least a little bit of psychoanalytic therapy. Karl Menninger was clearly out front with this argument. In his book *The Vital Balance,* he argued that "most people have some degree of mental illness at some time." In good Freudian fashion, he drove his point home with the threat that those who did not believe him were more prone to serious psychiatric illness than those who did.

The question of who was to control this market and how led to bitter debate both within the discipline of psychoanalysis and among the other mental health professions. The debate focused mainly on the question of who could carry what title or claim membership to which professional organization. The practice of psychoanalysis itself, and the ideas that surrounded it, however, were impossible to control. Indeed, they were difficult to even define. Shortly after the war, the American Psychoanalytic Association set up a committee to write an acceptable definition of what psychoanalysis entailed. It worked for six and a half years but could not come up with a definition that the members of the organization could agree upon.

With a huge, burgeoning new market of wealthy and relatively healthy clients, nonanalysts, from psychiatrists to psychologists, were quickly adopting and even advertising psychodynamic approaches. William Menninger, who became the president of the American Psychoanalytic Association in 1946, was a central figure in this trend. Noting that many nonpsychoanalytically trained professionals were applying Freudian concepts, he argued for assimilation of these therapists into the professional organizations.

Most of Menninger's proposals in this vein were defeated by those intent on jealously guarding the practice of psychoanalysis. Ernest Jones argued that the major threat to Freud's ideas was that they would be accepted as true by society and other therapists but deprived of their real value or meaning. In the mid-1950s, psychoanalysts were attempting to stem the rapid growth of lay psychotherapists and their rampant appropriation of psychoanalytic notions. In 1954, the American Medical Association, the American Psychiatric Association, and the American Psychoanalytic Association issued a joint statement about the dangers of lay psychotherapy. Two years later, the president of the American Psychoanalytic Association wrote that he was "committed to the ultimate liquidation of lay therapy in the United States." As ominous-sounding as this may be, this threat may never have been a serious one. This was the same organization, remember, that could not achieve a consensus to *define* its practice. Psychoanalysts were in the awkward and untenable position, as another psychoanalytic historian writes, of defending and "demanding strict adherence to a doctrine [they could] define only approximately."

In retrospect, the hope to defend the psychodynamic enterprise and restrict it to psychoanalysts was doomed from the start. If the Freudian stalwarts had taken Menninger's assimilationist approach early on, they may have had some hope of building a large enough base of clinicians to hold sway over the mental health profession at large. As it was, they were too small a group to block other practitioners from feeding the growing public demand for their glamorous and mysterious type of therapy. And while psychoanalysts heatedly debated whether to accept interlopers into the fold, they did not hope to stop the flow of their theories into other modes of talk therapy. In the end, little was actually required of a therapist who advertised himself as "psychodynamically oriented."

Critics and defenders alike recognize that it was the upper-middle-class enthusiasm for Freud's psychoanalysis, along with the acceptance of those theories within wide-ranging intellectual circles, that ensured the reliance on his ideas in clinical psychology and psychiatry, and later in other clinical branches such as social work. This sort of spillover can clearly be seen in Benjamin Spock's *Common Sense Book of Baby and Child Care,* which borrowed heavily from Freud's ideas. "A boy loves his mother much more than he loves any little girl," Spock wrote, for example. "He feels much more rivalrous with his father and more in awe of him than he feels towards any boy. So the sight of his mother [undressed] may be a little too stimulating and the chance to compare himself so unfavorably with his father every day may make him feel like doing something violent to his old man." The book sold more than 19 million copies by 1965.

Despite similarities in credentials, psychoanalysts themselves were all over the map in terms of the actual techniques they were using in their individual therapy settings. While they tried to present a united front to the public, psychoanalytic institutions had the habit of splitting into ever-smaller warring factions. "Training was inextricably linked with an ideology and subculture apparently unable to tolerate or resolve fundamental disputes without creating separate organizations," writes Hale in *The Rise and Crisis of Psychoanalysis in the United States.* "These clashes of opinion could be likened to the disputes of religious sects, to the dismay or amusement of some analysts and the delight of their opponents."

"We are laughed at by the profession because of our intramural squabbles and split-offs," one disgruntled analyst wrote to the president of the American Psychoanalytic Association in 1945, "and our prestige is not enhanced thereby."

In 1947, when the American Psychoanalytic Association appointed another committee to evaluate the therapeutic results of the treatment, that committee immediately reported back that its efforts might "come to grief" because of the lack of agreement over just what constituted psychoanalytic therapy. The report of this evaluation project, finally begun in 1952, wasn't published *until 1967,* after three committees worked over its content. Although it claimed a 97 percent rate of "improvement in total functioning" in the three thousand cases it examined, the therapy claimed a cure of the patient's presenting problems (which were largely not mental illnesses) only 27 percent of the time. For example, the report was less than impressive for a variety of other reasons as well. The study had no semblance of control groups and therefore no ability to determine what percentage of patients might have had an "improvement in total functioning" with the passage of time (much less with a believable placebo treatment). In addition, it relied entirely on reports of success by the therapists and patients.

In one final, embarrassing note, the code identifying which therapist reported which case was lost over the fifteen years the report bounced from committee to committee. There was no way to tell, therefore, whether better-trained or more experienced psychoanalysts reported better results. After this fiasco, the American Psychoanalytic Association, perhaps wisely, got out of the business of conducting large-scale outcome studies.

At the end of his life, even Freud hinted at a growing pessimism about his therapy's effectiveness in curing the mentally ill. This is perhaps why in the latter part of his career Freud's writing broadened out from the issues of mental health to those of history and culture. His pessimism (as well as his penchant for relabeling failure as victory) can be heard in a letter to a colleague: "I often console myself with the idea that, even though we achieve so little therapeutically, at least we understand why more cannot be achieved. In this sense our therapy seems to me to be the only rational one." To believe the diary of Freud's longtime associate Sándor Ferenczi, Freud made even darker admissions. "I remember certain statements Freud made to me. . . ." Ferenczi writes. "He said that patients are only riffraff. The only thing patients were good for is to help the analyst make a living and to provide material for theory. It is clear we cannot help them." Freud appeared to recognize, at least in private moments, that his method did little actual good even for the most devoted patients, and had little hope of curing major mental illnesses such as schizophrenia, depression, and mood disorders.

Not surprisingly, there is little evidence that this pessimism was shared with patients or by the enthusiastic American psychoanalysts. Emboldened by their cultural influence and acceptance, American analysts, in fact, were claiming that they could quickly retake the ground of major mental illness largely abandoned by Freud. Because many of these analysts held influential positions in American medical schools, their renewed assertion that psychoanalysis *could* cure mental illness was taken seriously. Even as most psychoanalysts chose private practice, their influence over mental hospitals and asylums grew through their dominant roles as directors or consultants and teachers. In Boston in 1961, for example, psychoanalysts held 70 percent of the teaching positions in schools of social work and 75 percent of professorial posts in psychiatry in the area's numerous medical schools.

The theories surrounding the cause and treatment of asthma in the postwar years is a prime example of psychoanalytic overreach and the inflated self-regard of these practitioners. It had long been observed that psychological factors, such as stress or strong emotions, could bring on asthmatic attacks, but it was much more than this observation that psychoanalysts wanted to document. Building, as usual, on the accumulation of case reports and conjecture, psychoanalysts developed the theory that asthmatics were reacting to a pathologically overprotective (or, alternatively, ambivalent or rejecting) "asthmatogenic mother." The eminent analyst Franz Alexander, the onetime president of the American Psychoanalytic Association, promoted the idea that asthmatics suffered from "excessive, unresolved dependence" on their mothers. As proof, he claimed that asthmatics dreamed more frequently of intrauterine symbols such as water, caves, and enclosed spaces than nonasthmatic analytic patients.

Behind the psychoanalytic theory of etiology lay, of course, the promise of the psychoanalytic cure. Working through the patient's feelings toward the mother—or even possibly removing the child from the home—was the obvious step once the "asthmatogenic mother" was identified. This cure, we now know, had little effect. The theory was simply wrong.

It is, however, an excellent example of psychoanalytic thinking, as it confuses effects with causes and requires a predisposition to Freudian thinking in order to see the evidence as proof of psychoanalytic theory. Take, for example, the observation that asthmatics dreamed more of enclosed spaces and water. One must first accept these images as "intrauterine symbols" in order to come anywhere near the conclusion that these dreams suggested troubles with the patient's mother. In addition, this line of logic requires the psychoanalyst to leap to the obvious. Even the youngest asthma sufferer might have been able to suggest to his esteemed analyst a more plausible reason why someone suffering from shortness of breath might sometimes dream of water or enclosed spaces.

But what of the theory that mothers of asthmatics were controlling, overly protective, or ambivalent? First of all, note that the possibilities are two ends of an entire range of parental attitudes, thus making it likely that a clinician might discover predicted behavior in the mother. But even if these mothers did possess these traits more than mothers of healthy children, we are likely looking at just another confusion of cause and effect. Is it possible that the difficulties of caring for a chronically sick and frightened child might provoke overprotectiveness or ambivalence?

The shaky evidentiary ground for such conclusions was spotted by other more thoughtful psychoanalytic researchers. In particular, psychoanalyst Peter Knapp challenged Alexander's theory as being too simplistic, noting that no single trait factor "predicted asthma or its absence with conspicuous success." He went on to develop a more complicated psychoanalytic theory for the onset of asthma, incorporating a whole range of Freudian and quasi-Freudian concepts such as regressive, primitive fantasies of destruction and guilt. These theories, though fatally flawed by their reliance on clinical observation for confirmation, had at least one advantage: The psychoanalyst who believed them was less likely to blame the mother outright for her child's suffering.

The psychoanalytic theory of schizophrenia shows this same overconfidence, in its most disastrous form. Several prominent psychoanalysts put forward the idea that the disorder was caused by perverse mothers who cruelly failed to meet their child's needs in their early infancy. This led to a search for cures through therapeutic examination of parental relationships and early trauma. Psychoanalytic psychiatrist John Rosen believed he could enter the patient's delusional world, find there the unconscious conflicts that were causing the disorder, and neutralize them. He reports this exchange between himself and a patient to illustrate his interpretation of his disturbed patient's communications:

> PATIENT: You are a son of a bitch. Cock-sucker. Your father put his cock in your mother's mouth, and that is how you were born. I had a feeling stronger than ever to throw myself under an elevated train.
>
> ROSEN: Father will fuck you in the ass. The train is a big powerful penis and you wish to lay under it.

Rosen's own published accounts reported such supposedly therapeutic badgering along with other techniques that included beating patients and threatening ever more severe physical abuse if they didn't stop acting "crazy." Rosen claimed his method was remarkably successful in bringing patients out of psychotic episodes.

Rosen was no marginalized figure. He was an extremely influential psychiatrist who used psychoanalytic methods and assumptions. He published widely and was loudly praised for his groundbreaking work. In 1971, he received the Man of the Year award of the American Academy of Psychotherapy.

His methods, however, proved more brutal than even his published reports indicated. Eventually he was implicated in the death of two of his patients (one who died in isolation and one who was beaten to death), as well as for a series of assaults on his patients in which he was said to have forced heterosexual and homosexual acts on them. Avoiding prosecution on these charges, he surrendered his medical license in 1983.

Rosen's treatment techniques are remarkable for two reasons entirely outside their brutality. First, it is critical to note that he was exposed, as Jeffrey Masson points out, not by other psychiatrists or by psychoanalysts (dozens of whom likely worked closely enough with Rosen to have seen his penchant for brutality), but by patients who came forward and reported him to law enforcement and the media.

Similarly, while his theories were published widely, his public downfall was seldom written about in psychoanalytic journals. This attempt to sweep Rosen under the rug can be seen ten years later. In *The Rise and Crisis of Psychoanalysis in the United States,* Hale recounts many of Rosen's methods but mentions none of his outrageous abuses, such as the deaths of the two patients and the alleged sexual assaults. Hale does point out that enthusiasm waned for Rosen's techniques, which he claimed "many psychoanalysts at the time opposed."

Perhaps Hale knows from private conversations that other psychoanalysts had concerns about Rosen's treatment. However, there is a distinct *absence* in the professional literature of criticism of his bizarre methods. Even the papers that challenged his inflated cure rates avoided criticizing his techniques. More common were comments such as this one written by Paul Federn, an associate of Freud, in the prestigious psychoanalytic journal *Quarterly*: "It is clear to me that this technique and its good results can be used by psychiatrists who are as fully convinced of Freud's interpretation of the unconscious as Rosen is. Rosen's findings are also another proof of the truth of Freud's tenets. . . . I pay my tribute to Dr. Rosen that, as a psychiatrist, he has incorporated Freud's work into his own mind, with great clarity combined with pioneer enthusiasm."

The second critical point about Rosen is that he arrived at his methods with the same lack of care by which Freud and many other psychoanalysts came to their conclusions. He simply asserted that his theories were valid on the basis of the material (and supposed success) he was finding during treatment. The hubris required for such a method of theory building is apparent in Rosen's own description of the qualities therapists should have in order to deal with the schizophrenic patient: "He must make up for the tremendous deficit of love experienced in the patient's life. Some people have this capacity for loving as a divine gift. But it is possible to acquire this the hard way—by psychoanalysis. It is the *sine qua non* for the application of this method in the treatment of schizophrenia."

Freud, of course, had an enormous impact outside the mental health profession. In the first and second decades of this century, artists and writers began to adopt psychoanalysis, often reading Freud as arguing for an overturning of Victorian sexual mores. "American artists and writers turned to psychoanalysis as a doctrine that would justify liberation from the previous generation. In its early years it achieved a type of jazz age currency," said Frederick Crews.* "Freud was seen as progressive, when in fact he was fatalistic, pessimistic, sardonic, and determinist in his orientation. It was a subject of amusement for Freud all his life that the country that welcomed psychoanalysis most warmly was the one that misunderstood it most thoroughly."

In the late twenties and thirties, Freud rode the coattails of Marx, who was the golden boy in artistic and intellectual circles. "Although American intellectuals were much more entranced by Marx, there were many who felt that Freud was a radical, Marx was a radical, and radicalism was good," Crews said. The Stalin-Hitler pact of 1939 was a tremendous blow to these American Marxists, and the news only worsened. With the revelations of Stalin's barbarity in the 1950s there was a growing disillusionment with Marx among American intellectuals. There was little left for them but to make an orderly retreat to Freudianism.

As the universities began to open up their doors to Jewish teachers and intellectuals after the Second World War, a good deal of Freudianism came in with them. For young literary critics like Crews, who learned his profession during the fifties, Freudianism still had a great deal of avant-garde appeal. Crews recalls: "Figures like Lionel Trilling gave young readers like me

---

*As a Freudian literary scholar during the late sixties and early seventies, and subsequently as a critic of Freud and psychoanalysis, Berkeley professor emeritus Frederick Crews was in a unique position to witness the triumph of Freudianism in academic areas outside the mental health profession. The authors interviewed Crews on the subject of Freud's influence on American intellectual trends during this century.

the impression that if you wanted to be both anti-establishment and intellectually astute, there was nowhere to go but to Freud."

It was in the later sixties that Freud got another boost, one that firmly established his presence in the humanities in American academia. This was the American intellectual infatuation with French structuralists, including Lacan, Foucault, and Lévi-Strauss, who all had Freudian leanings. With the subsequent evolution of poststructuralism—a.k.a. deconstructionism—Freud only grew in popularity. For poststructuralists, it was in poor taste to talk about "evidence" in a text and a breathtaking social gaffe to speak of something being closer to the "truth" than something else. (They, of course, exempted their own discourse from these dismissive assumptions.) In this environment, Freudian theory had the same appeal to scholars as it did to therapists: They could use it to make any verdict they liked.

"The fact that you can use the ideas of Freud and psychoanalysis to come to any conclusion you wanted wasn't even regarded as a criticism among many academics in the humanities," said Crews. "The very fact that they could do anything with it—that they could have discourse ad infinitum—was seen as a good thing. There was no longer any empirical friction between the would-be Freudian literary critic and his discourse. As a student of the history of Freudianism, I find this profoundly apt because from the very beginning, psychoanalysis was a way of reaching conclusions that you had already reached."

It was in the early 1970s that Crews began to question and then criticize Freudian premises. He eventually came, as he writes, "to the painful realization that Freudianism in its self-authenticating approach to knowledge constitutes not an exemplification of the rational-empirical ethos to which I felt loyal, and to which Freud himself had professed allegiance, but a seductive mythic alternative to it."

To this day, Freud remains a darling of literary critics and other intellectuals and academics. As English professors and the like are unbound by the needs of patients, Freud's influence in these areas may be a good deal more resilient than his influence on the treatment of the mentally ill.

"The fortunes of Freud in areas of the humanities do not seem to be declining," Crews said, admitting that this is one of the reasons he is glad to be retired from the fray. "Freudianism still gives the wielder of discourse the illusion that everything is up for grabs. It can give people the impression that they are on the cutting edge of the reorganization of the human personality and that the world is waiting for the answers they find. Of course, it is all a fantasy game, but it's a game that is immensely appealing to play."

The momentum of Freudian theories, once they have reached a certain self-sustaining threshold, appears to have the ability to go on and on despite the theories having fallen out of vogue in other areas. Freud's fortunes in areas such as literary criticism, for example, seem to rise and fall independent of his influence in the mental health profession. Because Freudian theories can thrive independently in different areas means that scholars in different fields will have to fight individual wars against Freud's self-confirming and anti-empirical mode of reasoning. Weeding Freudianism out of the modern academy may be a long process.

Of course, there might be a quicker end to the entire structuralist and poststructuralist enterprise into which Freud has been so welcome. Such quixotic notions as the dismissal of the idea of evidence and of the idea that it is the burden of the scholar to strive toward what is true could only have blossomed during a period of steady prosperity such as we've seen over the last forty years. As useless as they are, these ideas reveal themselves to be a by-product of a society that can afford to support such academic tail-chasing.

"If we were to have a good old-fashioned depression or even a long recession, attitudes toward literary questions might start to change," said Crews. "It's not something I'd look forward to, but it is clear that literary criticism as it is practiced today is a luxury in the sense that these critics have forgotten the real circumstances under which people live. If there was a large-scale social phenomenon that created pressure from the outside, it's likely that the whole insulated discourse might disappear."

*   *   *

Although the Freudian intellectual enthusiasm continues, by the early 1970s, there was a general acknowledgment that psychoanalysis, as a mental health treatment, was in decline. Fewer and fewer patients seemed interested in signing on for the rigors of classical Freudian technique. Unfortunately, this decline cannot be attributed to the falling out of vogue of the ideas of the psychodynamic mind. Rather, different types of talk therapy were crowding the market with cheaper, shorter, and allegedly less intensive forms of therapy that co-opted the essential ideas of the psychodynamic approach, including that of the powerful unconscious, free association, and the notion that childhood traumas formed psychic abscesses that could be pierced and drained by talking them through. These ideas had become institutionalized in American culture and became the basis of an endless stream of therapeutic approaches, each of which was promoted like the latest-model car, promising a smoother ride, better performance, and the social status of being on the cutting edge of fashion. During this time of the decline of psychoanalysis, the market for therapy was not falling—quite the opposite. Psychoanalysis was losing market share, while the market for talk therapy itself was growing. Between 1950 and 1980, the number of psychologists and social workers in the United States increased by 700 percent.

Psychoanalysis also precipitously lost the prestige it had during the 1950s and 1960s for other reasons. Prominent mental health professionals began, ever so respectfully, to point out problems that could no longer be ignored. The National Institute of Mental Health, for instance, began giving less and less research money to psychoanalysts because, as one researcher pointed out, all they could show for seventy-five years of work was a compilation of "observations, data collection and theory building." One of the founders of the NIMH's foundation for research into psychiatry noted that psychoanalysis had only yielded "glimpses and hunches, not really convincing facts."

As research money began to funnel toward more promising therapies and drug treatments, more papers and books came out challenging the notions held dear by psychoanalysts. Nonpsychoanalytically inclined scholars, as summarized in the previous chapter, began examining Freud and his premises in a critical light. Although many of the criticisms were already acknowledged within the profession, the collection and expansion of this Freud criticism by prominent scholars proved increasingly devastating. No less than British medical researcher and Nobel Prize winner Peter Medawar came forward to label doctrinaire psychoanalytic theory the "most stupendous intellectual confidence trick of the twentieth century."

The biological approach to mental illness was gaining momentum during these same years. By the late 1970s, the winds had significantly shifted. New drugs had been developed and many more were being tested for an increasing number of mental disorders. In addition, other, nonpsychoanalytically oriented treatments, such as behavioral therapy, were challenging the long and expensive process of psychodynamic psychotherapy. These new treatments (both pharmacological and behavioral) were proving, in a growing number of studies, that they had demonstrable beneficial effects.

In 1975, between 5 and 6 million Americans were spending more than a billion dollars a year for some sort of mental health treatment. Much of this money went to psychodynamic psychotherapy, which, by stealing the glamour and many psychodynamic concepts from psychoanalysis, had gained a position in American society. Clinical practitioners of all stripes, who once represented a subspecialty of the field of psychology, gained professional power over the researchers in their professional organizations as their numbers increased. In the 1970s, for the first time, clinical psychologists outnumbered scientific psychologists in the American Psychological Association. Even at the universities, the traditional home for psychological researchers, clinical training programs began to usurp resources because of the large number of students they attracted. Given these forces, it is perhaps inevitable that the clinicians would untether themselves from the field's scientific base. While the scientific psychologists continued to work to empirically establish small bits of truth about the human brain and behavior, the clinicians started making increasingly outlandish claims about their ability to change the human condition.

While more and more clinicians demurred from labeling themselves "Freudian" or "psychodynamically oriented," a growing number labeled themselves "eclectics." This made it possible for many practitioners to duck the growing criticism of Freud from feminist circles while still borrowing heavily from his concepts. Even those who labeled themselves "feminist psychotherapists" could, in this manner, criticize Freud while at the same time spending the social currency many of his theories, such as repression and transference, maintained in popular culture.

With the rise of the medical approach to mental illness, clinicians found themselves increasingly boxed out of the treatment of major mental diseases. Responding to this squeeze, practitioners and their professional organizations continued the trend of expanding the definition of what should be considered a mental health problem. Grief, trouble at work, sadness, a deteriorating relationship, the nagging sense of being unfulfilled or simply less than happy—these things became the stuff of clinical psychotherapy. The appeal of these expanded services was further fueled by the rapid spread of health insurance, which came to principally fund them. The message of this expansion was that even the most common forms of human distress or unhappiness were defects that required examination and fixing.

But even these broader promises proved limiting to the growing ranks of therapists. Underlying the so-called human potential movement of the 1970s was the idea that the purpose of therapy was not to fix something but to reach a more fulfilled state of being. Various fad treatments sprang up promoting the idea that everyone needs a fine-tuning of his or her internal gyroscope. No disorder or life-problem required—every person could use the wisdom of self-proclaimed life experts. With such a grand responsibility, it is not surprising that many psychotherapists had little time for the slow plodding of the university researchers who maintained their focus on the empirical study of major mental illness, human behavior, perception, learning, and a long list of other subjects with little marketability. During the 1970s, the American public became the greatest per capita consumer of therapy in the world.

With each new influx of ever more minimally trained therapists, the competition for clients grew stiffer. The decision as to what could and should be treated, along with the question of *how* it should be treated, often seemed to become progressively more an issue of marketability than of scientific or professional agreement. Not surprisingly, ideas about how to reach new and higher levels of existence sprang out of the social trends of a given moment. Sold like vacation packages, paths to nirvana appeared everywhere. Businesses like est and Lifespring appeared and utopias sprouted across the country.

In addition, encounter groups of all types flourished. Often run by therapists, these small groups proved to be an effective way of mobilizing the forces of peer pressure to produce conformity. This pressure wasn't necessarily harmful although it could be deadly. If the leader sought to produce conformity to the idea that the people in the group should be supportive of one another, the encounter session would likely be a pleasant, uplifting experience. Often, however, more radical belief changes were demanded and more coercive methods were employed. Many encounter groups became settings of high drama, producing in the members anxiety, extreme emotional arousal, psychotic breaks, and suicide attempts.

The human potential movement of the sixties and seventies brought an underlying message that those who failed to attempt this quasispiritual awakening were ill or deluded in ways they had not yet realized. In this way, many therapists promoted the mental health version of original sin. More and more they began offering up the myth that we are born perfect only to be corrupted in our upbringing. Degraded by our childhood, we would never achieve our true potential unless we received redemption through psychotherapy.

In the past twenty years, the paths to gaining a credential and proclaiming oneself a practitioner of psychotherapy have multiplied and shortened. Adding to the ranks of psychiatrists and

Ph.D. psychologists, various institutions have graduated thousands of practitioners holding psychology doctorate degrees that require no dissertation research and little methods training or a master's in clinical social work and marriage, family, and child counselor degrees. Between 1975 and 1990, the number of psychiatrists, clinical psychologists, MFCCs, and clinical social workers more than doubled, growing from 72,000 to 198,000. By far the greatest growth in the profession was among the category of therapists with the less rigorous degrees that incorporated little or no exposure to scientific method.

In all the excitement of this expansion the treatment of the truly mentally ill became a subdiscipline within the profession of talk therapy. This is undoubtedly due to the fact that talk therapy approaches showed no significant ability to cure severe disorders. In the end, the dissipation of theories such as the "asthmatogenic and psychophrenogenic mother" came about less through criticism from inside psychoanalytic circles than from advances in medical treatments and empirical exploration. Epidemiological research, for example, found that half the children suffering from asthma began suffering from the disease around the age of three, and that more than twice as many boys suffered from the disorder as girls. These facts did not, of course, fit well with the idea that asthma was caused by bad parenting. New discoveries indicating more likely causes for asthma made the question moot. By the 1970s, asthma symptoms could, in many cases, be effectively controlled and the psychoanalytic theory of cause and cure simply faded away.

The same arc can be seen with other psychoanalytic theories. At a symposium on schizophrenia in 1985, one psychoanalytic historian observed that "psychoanalysis was conspicuous by its absence." The theories and treatments of psychoanalysis were completely eclipsed by biological research, brain function studies, and genetic theories. Behavioral therapies still had a role in the patient's management, but not because they had any hope of curing or determining the etiology of the disease. By 1997, advances in genetic research pointed toward the interaction of multiple genes as the likely cause. Although some researchers continue to probe how such a genetic predisposition might be influenced by environmental factors such as drug abuse, psychodynamic theories of etiology had almost entirely vanished from the research landscape. Dr. Steven Molden and Irving Gottesman recently wrote in the *Schizophrenia Bulletin* that "no consistent evidence exists that the social environment, or any specific nongenetic factor, will induce schizophrenia in individuals who are not genetically predisposed to this condition."

The retreat of such psychoanalytic theories is rarely ever complete. Often the retreat from cause-and-effect notions is only into more archaic and complex theories, which are no more demonstrable. Regardless of ebbs and flows of confidence among psychoanalytic elites, it is worth wondering how long these ideas remained in play by ill-informed therapists long after they had been thoroughly discredited.

The case of Dr. Ray Osheroff illustrates the shift in the late 1970s away from psychoanalytic treatment for severe mental disorders. In 1976, when Dr. Osheroff learned that his ex-wife was remarrying and planning to take his two sons to live in Europe, he felt the black cloud of depression settling over him. Sadness at these events was, of course, natural. The finality of his former wife's new marriage coupled with the loss of contact with his sons made him feel deeply blue and he cried often in those months. But the downturn in his feelings didn't stop with sadness; as he reported later, his mood "switched to something else, unlike anything I could have imagined."

In the following months, Osheroff's mood didn't improve. "That melancholia," he described later, "was totally different and beyond my experience—an emptiness of feeling and bleakness. I had intense psychic pain, so overwhelming that death became one of the alternatives." Other troubling symptoms soon emerged. Osheroff found it more and more difficult to stay still and began pacing compulsively. Even when he would lie down at night, he could not get his legs to stop moving. He soon found he could not make it through a meal at a restaurant or a movie without feeling compelled to jump out of his seat and find a space to walk back and forth.

Over the course of his adulthood, Osheroff had often been troubled by periods of severe depression and anxiety. Nevertheless, until then he had managed to function well enough to complete medical school and his residency, specialize in nephrology, marry, and father three children. An ambitious and successful man, Osheroff was one of the first kidney specialists to establish a dialysis center away from a hospital. His symptoms now, however, became overwhelming, so Osheroff decided to check himself into a mental hospital.

Osheroff was forty-two when he walked through the doors of the Chestnut Lodge on the second day of 1979. Unwilling to take chances with his mental health, Osheroff had picked an institution with a world-class reputation. Chestnut Lodge had employed many of the nation's most well-recognized and -respected stars of psychoanalytic psychiatry. Freida Fromm-Reichmann, one of the leading psychoanalysts to emigrate from Germany, was a staff member at the Lodge. Harry Stack Sullivan, founder of "interpersonal psychiatry," was a consultant to the institution. Such luminaries attracted wealthy and famous patients. Heirs to America's largest fortunes, children of cabinet officers, and relatives of movie stars sought help here.

Opened in 1910 as a sanitarium for alcoholics, the Lodge, for its first twenty years of operation, had been mostly offering custodial care for the seriously mentally ill. In 1933, when Dexter Bullard took over from his father, the Lodge took a turn toward Freud. Introduced to psychoanalysis while living in Boston, Bullard decided that the key to mental illness lay not in the crude and often cruel biological treatments of the time but in the new "talking cure." Bullard encouraged a close and intense bond between patients and therapists. While orthodox Freudians were supposed to maintain an emotional distance, the doctors at the Lodge worked on regressing patients to the point of trauma in infancy and then "reparented" them from that point. By doing this, the doctors believed they could treat and cure even the most distressing mental illnesses, including schizophrenia. Drugs were viewed as an impediment to this process—at best only hiding the patient's symptoms.

In these early years, the commitment and compassion of the Lodge's doctors for their well-heeled patients was hard to doubt. While at other mental health institutions there was only one caretaker for dozens or even hundreds of patients, the Lodge made sure that each patient was under the care of two psychiatrists. The Lodge avoided making some of the profession's most grotesque mistakes—it did not medicate its patients into vegetative inactivity, as some hospitals were known to do, nor did it perform lobotomies or induce insulin comas. Aside from its mainstay treatment—four hours of psychotherapy each week—the Lodge tried many different methods such as art, music, and dance therapy. Although it disdained drugs, the Lodge did employ at least one harsh physical practice to calm agitated psychotic patients: the use of cold wet sheet packs. Patients were stripped to their underwear and wrapped in cold sheets in order to exhaust them. While most hospitals stopped the practice after Thorazine, a powerful antipsychotic drug, was introduced in the mid-1950s, the Lodge continued using cold wet sheet packs until 1987.

The treatment Osheroff received at Chestnut Lodge was a regime of intensive individual psychotherapy. Four days a week, the therapists at the Lodge explored his dreams, fantasies, and childhood memories in order to discover the causes of his current state of acute depression. The early results from Osheroff's psychoanalysis were not good. Despite his lack of improvement, the therapists at the Chestnut Lodge continued Osheroff's treatment four days a week *for seven months*. At the hospital he paced so compulsively that his feet had to be treated for blisters and swelling. He experienced severe insomnia and lost forty pounds. According to the summary of one prominent medical historian, who later wrote about the case, Osheroff's treatment did no more good than if he had been left to "vegetate" for more than half a year.

Being a doctor and having had depressive episodes in the past, Osheroff of course knew of the availability of antidepressive drugs.* Even through the fog of his illness Osheroff knew to ask for medication. He was refused. Mining his childhood for memories of trauma and evidence of unconscious pathogens took precedence.

Because the therapists at Chestnut Lodge were so devoted to the ideas of psychoanalysis, they were holdouts in the transition to the use of medications that were proving more and more effective in the treatment of major mental illnesses. Despite the clear trend away from psychoanalysis as a treatment for major mental illnesses, the doctors at the Lodge who failed to use these new medications were protected under what is called the "respectable minority rule," which argues that doctors are allowed to select from a number of treatment options as long as these options were advocated by a respectable minority of practitioners. This respectable minority rule is employed when legitimate questions remain about the best treatment for a disease and assumes that there will be good-faith differences of opinion even among the best-trained and most up-to-date doctors. The respectable minority rule protects doctors who often have to attempt treatments before all the answers are known.

Seeing no improvement, Osheroff's family became concerned with the length and ineffectiveness of his treatment. Not only was he not improving, but he seemed to be getting worse. They arranged to move him to Silver Hill Foundation in Connecticut, where he was immediately diagnosed as having a psychotic depressive reaction. The doctors at Silver Hill put him on a regimen of antidepressives and phenothiazine. Within a few weeks he showed significant improvement. He was out of the hospital within three months. His doctor at Silver Hill wrote that Osheroff had "a good response to appropriate treatment." The question implied in this statement—that is, what constitutes "appropriate" treatment for someone like Osheroff—was about to come into the spotlight.

---

*Before his hospitalization at Chestnut Lodge, he had sought help on an outpatient basis from a psychiatrist who prescribed tricyclic antidepressive medication. A tricyclic is a category of antidepressant medication. Although the drug produced moderate improvement for a time, Osheroff failed to stay on the doctor's recommended dosage.

Finally released, Osheroff discovered that not much was left of the life he had left ten months earlier. His medical partner (who had driven him to the Lodge for treatment) had dropped him from their joint practice, and Osheroff had lost his hospital accreditation. While he knew he had not been well served by Chestnut Lodge, he began to consider that he might have been the victim of malpractice.

In 1982, Osheroff brought a lawsuit against Chestnut Lodge, claiming that he had been the victim of malpractice because they had failed to diagnose and treat with appropriate medication what he believed was a "biological" depression. The Lodge defended itself by invoking the respectable minority rule. No one disputed that drugs to treat severe depression existed, and that they had been shown effective; however, they argued, psychoanalysis was still practiced by a respectable minority of the profession and therefore they could not be found at fault for violating an "acceptable standard of care."

The first hearing for the Osheroff suit was held in front of the Maryland Health Claims Arbitration Office. The list of Osheroff's advocates reads like a who's who of modern psychiatry. Testifying on his behalf was Gerald Klerman of Harvard Medical School, Donald Klein of Columbia University, and Bernard Carroll of Duke University. After hearing both sides, the board found that Chestnut Lodge had indeed ignored the recent advances in the field at its patient's peril. The standard of care for patients such as Osheroff was not a grab bag of "respectable minorities," the board decided; it definitely included drugs. They awarded Osheroff $250,000.

Both Chestnut Lodge and Osheroff appealed the ruling. Although Osheroff agreed with the decision, he felt the compensation was far too small for what he had suffered and lost. The interval between the hearing and the new jury trial could be characterized as an increasingly dramatic drum roll. Many people agreed that the outcome of the case could be pivotal for the course of mental health care. The executive editor of the *California Law Review* wrote that because the case had the potential to "indicate that a large enough consensus exists as to the particular effective treatment for a given mental disorder, a practitioner who fails to administer that treatment will have fallen below the acceptable standard of care and will not be protected by the respectable minority rule."

The public comments on the case by Chestnut Lodge's lawyer clearly show that both sides understood the potential implications of the case. A finding for the patient would "make a number of psychiatrists fearful of how they treat patients," he said. "It will make them gun shy and nervous."

No doubt with consideration of the case's possible implications, Chestnut Lodge settled out of court with Osheroff. As part of that agreement, Osheroff was contractually bound not to reveal the specifics of the settlement. In this way, the case failed to make the legal precedent that many proponents of psychoanalysis had feared. Although it did not establish a specific standard of care legally, the case was widely read as a cautionary tale for those who insist on ignoring the advances in the biological approaches to treating major mental illnesses.

The difficulties of applying the idea of respectable minority rule to the practice of talk therapy go to the very heart of our argument in this book. If the profession makes no effort to weed out ineffective treatments (and seems to have little desire to control even the most outrageous practices), what are the standards that would make one group of practitioners a "respectable minority"? "Respectable minority" cannot be the standard in a profession that does not take the time to make any minority opinion *dis*respectable. Surely the qualification for respectable minority cannot simply be that a significant number of practitioners make undocumented claims that a treatment helps patients, for anyone can gather adherents to a treatment and *claim* effectiveness. In a practice such as psychotherapy, the shield of respectable minority has become as hollow as the adolescent refrain "But everyone else is doing it."

CHAPTER FOUR

Three Cases from a Legacy of Intellectual Hubris

Psychodynamic psychotherapy is being rediscovered by a new generation of clinicians. . . . The patient must be taught, at the outset, to enter a dreamlike state, to let his or her thoughts drift where they will, and to report everything that comes to mind. What happens next—when the therapist intervenes to shape new understandings—is a complex art.
—MICHAEL NICHOLS AND THOMAS PAOLINO, JR.,
Basic Techniques of Psychodynamic Psychotherapy

In 1912, Ernest Jones, a Freud devotee and confidant, wrote a paper entitled "An Unusual Case of 'Dying Together,'" in which he psychoanalyzed the tragic death of a young couple who accidentally drowned in the Niagara River. In the essay, Jones recounts the primary facts he read in a newspaper story: A married couple in their late twenties were on vacation in Niagara when they ventured out with a small group onto an ice bridge that forms every winter near the falls. When the ice on which the group was walking began to crack and threaten to drift downstream, a local river man yelled to the group to make for the Canadian side of the river. Instead, the young couple headed for the American side and were stopped by open water. Trying to get back to the Canadian side of the river, the woman fell down fifty yards from the shore and cried, "I can't go on! Let us die here!" Dragged near shore by her husband, the woman refused to take the last few steps to the shore over smaller chunks of floating ice. The couple were soon swept downriver, where another attempted rescue (a rope lowered from a bridge) also failed. The couple soon drowned.

In his paper, Jones declares the man's conduct to be in need of no deep interpretation. He tried valiantly to save his wife and then died with her as, Jones concludes, any respectable man would. The woman's apparent unwillingness to be saved is more interesting to Jones, requiring the application of complex psychoanalytic theory.

"Her efforts to escape were either paralyzed or else actively hindering, and she did not respond even to the powerful motive of saving her husband," writes Jones. From her actions, Jones claims to perceive the workings of the woman's hidden wishes—wishes she not only hid from the world but from her own conscious mind. "Now it is known to psychoanalysts . . . that emotional paralysis is not so much a traumatic effect of fright as a manifestation of inhibition resulting from a conflict between a conscious and unconscious impulse. A familiar example is that of a woman who cannot protect herself with her whole strength against being raped, part of her energy being inhibited by the opposing unconscious impulse which is on the side of the assailant."

Jones proposes that the woman's unconscious desire, which kept her from safety that day, was her wish to commit suicide with her husband. In piecing together evidence for his conclusion that the woman was overwhelmed by this impulse, Jones claims to have known a good friend of the couple who revealed to him that the woman had been sad that the couple's seven-year marriage had yielded no children.

"It is known, through analysis," he writes, "not only that the ideas of sex, birth, and death are extensively associated with one another, but also that the idea of dying in the arms of a loved one symbolizes certain quite specific desires of the unconscious." The connection between the wish to have a child with one's love and to share a common suicide with that person, according to Jones, was "now well enough known to justify one in assuming an understanding of [this conception] in informed circles."

Everything is illuminated under psychoanalysis. Jones explains that the couple had been drawn to Niagara during the winter because the season's association with death and cold "was beginning to correspond with their attitude of hopelessness about ever getting a child." In the end, he interprets the events as he would a dream: "a childbirth fantasy of a sterile woman, the floating on a block of ice in a dangerous current of water, in company with a lover, in sight of all the world yet isolated from it, the threatened catastrophe of drowning, and the rapid movement of being passively swept to and fro—all of this forms a perfect picture." Let us be clear. Jones's purpose is not to find metaphorical meaning in the event, but rather to claim to understand the actual motivations of the woman in thwarting her own rescue. "We may thus imagine the woman in question," he writes, "as reacting to her frightful situation by rapidly transforming it in the unconscious and replacing reality by the fantasy of the gratification of her deepest desire."

To back up his conclusion, Jones footnotes himself, citing a previous chapter from the same book where he exhibits a truly remarkable string of a psychoanalytic thinking, connecting death, love, and childbirth. The unconscious wish to die together, he writes, comes from a combination of other psychoanalytically established longings, including the fantasy of sleeping or lying with one's mother; the desire to return to heaven, "i.e., to the mother's womb"; as well as one's deeper unconscious wish to make love to dead people. Necrophilic tendencies are further related to our preoccupation with feces (feces are dead material once part of a living body, he points out, like a corpse), which in turn are closely associated to birth fantasies. He credits Freud for establishing the connection between expelling feces and giving birth, noting that it has "been amply confirmed by most observers."

He does not stop here, but goes on to connect the wish to die with the desire to travel, for a "common expression for defecation is movement." At this point, we admit to being unable to summarize Jones's next psychoanalytic derivation. Lest the reader think we are attempting to make his theories appear more bizarre than they deserve, we will let him try to explain them on his own:

> ... when the act of defecation is especially pleasurable it is apt to acquire the significance of a sexual projecting, just as of urine and semen ... this connotation of sexual projecting, and of movement in general, is especially closely associated in the unconscious with the act of passing flatus [gas], and that this later act, on account of the idea of penetration to a distance, is sometimes conceived of by children as constituting the essential part of coitus. . . . The latter fantasy would, through its association with movement, be particularly well adapted to find expression, together with the other coprophilic [extreme interest in feces], sadistic, and incestuous tendencies referred to above, in the love condition of dying together. . . .

Jones, like many psychoanalysts of the time, believed himself a scientist. Egocentric and notoriously quick to quarrel, Jones wrote of himself that he craved "the sense of security that the pursuit of truth gives" and claimed a "curious intolerance of illusion." His belief that he was getting at the truth of this tragic situation is clear from the forceful tone of his argument.

With a few generations' distance, Jones's interpretation of these events seems more than a little troubling. Considering the changes in cultural assumptions during the last eighty years, we doubt even the most psychoanalytically inclined therapist would today rush to defend his "dying together" interpretation or many of the attendant associations. The blatant misogyny of the story now leaps off the page. The man acts completely rationally while the woman, with her hidden pathologies, thwarts him at every turn. And surely, most psychoanalysts today would question the conception of a woman's mental life revolving so tightly around the idea of childbirth (which in the psychoanalytic thinking of the time was only a reaction to her penis envy) that she would will her own death. Similarly, few of Jones's supporting assumptions remain in play today. The confident connection between giving birth and bowel movements (or with necrophilia) is not much heard anymore in psychoanalytic circles. Jones's confident assertion that a woman's unconscious often assists sexual attackers is also, to put it mildly, out of vogue.

There is another sign of hubris in Jones's willingness to run with questionable facts surrounding events and people of which he had no firsthand knowledge. Is there really enough information in the newspaper account to support the key assumption that the woman "actively hindered" her rescue? Neatly confirming details, such as the woman's cry "Let us die here," look particularly suspicious. Could the observers from shore hear this? But even regardless of their accuracy, the facts Jones reports to know seem far too few to give anything but the weakest support for his interpretation. Despite attesting to know a friend of the doomed couple, Jones claims no in-depth knowledge about their lives. Jones is so infatuated by the process of fitting the metaphorical symbols in the event to his interpretation that he never even acknowledges that the amount of information he has access to is paltry. One begins to suspect that it is his *lack* of access to more information that allows him to make such outlandish conclusions.

If modern readers are impressed by the interpretation at all, it is likely because they are intimidated by its scholarly presentation. We can be cowed like neophytes who are told in a modern art museum that a stick figure is actually an insightful portrait. We don't immediately object because Jones seems so confident.

On examination, however, his conclusion crumbles. Considering the imaginative leaps he makes from evidence to interpretation, how many other possible narratives might be created from the same material? There is no hint that Jones weighed and rejected other possible explanations. And given his turns of logic, it seems likely that Jones would have been able to come to similar conclusions given radically different facts. If the couple had drowned in springtime instead of winter and in a lake instead of a river, could Jones still have employed the same tautalogic reasoning to reach the same conclusion?

Let's consider a story that Jones rejects: that this couple, through a combination of bad fortune and run-of-the-mill panic, drowned in a tragic accident. This is a much more frightening version of these events, for it is harder for readers to distance themselves from the random and cruel world this story suggests. We all live under the constant threat of death through accident or misjudgment. How much easier is it to believe that the person drowned in the river (or hit by a bus) was actually fulfilling some deep-seated unconscious desire? Not only does this quell the anxiety that the threat of random tragedy can bring on, but it also offers the hope that we might be able to avoid similar fates if we hire a psychoanalyst to defuse these subterranean self-destructive tendencies.

Jones's recounting of the doomed lovers reads like nothing so much as parable: a simple and dramatic tale meant to illustrate larger truths about the dynamic unconscious forces at work in our lives. All facts in the story are brought into line and none are introduced that might throw doubt on the conclusion. It is for this exact reason that we would suggest that Jones's recounting is not trustworthy at all. Jones's interpretation requires, as parables do, that the reader be predisposed to the belief (in this case the belief of the dynamic unconscious) that the tale is created to illustrate.

No doubt many people might quickly object to our use of this case because it is not drawn from therapy. First, it should be noted that psychoanalysts and other romantic therapists have seldom held themselves back from making pronouncements based on similarly small sets of evidence. What emerges from a broad look at psychoanalytic writing over the course of this century is a group of men and women so taken with their own theories that they seem to have no compunction about making grand pronouncements about the motivations of historical figures and others they have never met, nor about characterizing whole races and populations about whom they have only thin knowledge.

Evidence that even the most esteemed therapists are trigger-happy when it comes to employing their favorite interpretations can be seen from their writings about the world outside of the therapy setting. Their willingness to apply their theories in any situation—given even the smallest amounts of information—should call into question their offhanded assurances that their interpretations in therapy are driven by a deep and careful hearing of the client's communications. The record of psychoanalytic writing about history, literature, society, and current events frequently reveals them to be not the careful connoisseurs of life's complexities but rather professionals so eager to find psychodynamic meaning in events that they often make fools of themselves in the process. As we will show, for many therapists, the facts of patients' lives don't seem to matter much at all except insofar as they give the psychodynamic therapist enough material to weave the interpretation du jour.

To the nonpsychoanalytically inclined, Jones's conclusion is plainly ridiculous. Because there is not enough evidence to convince even the credulous modern reader, the only apparent weight to Jones's conclusion is his constant reference to a larger body of psychoanalytic reasoning. "Most observers," Jones writes, have confirmed one bit of logic, while "informed circles" have accepted another. Who are these observers and informed people? They are other psychoanalysts who have engaged in exactly the same type of questionable connection-making that Jones has done here.

Modern-day apologists for the history of psychoanalytic thinking often resort to the justification that even when wrong, such interpretations as Jones's are richer than what one might otherwise surmise from a surface view of things. In this way, Jones's interpretation might be defended on the basis that it makes a better story than the newspaper account. Like painters who no longer strive to represent their subjects, some Freudians loose themselves from any obligation they have to the facts of their patients' lives. But is Jones's tale even a good story? It has nothing, we would suggest, of the depth or complexity of life; it is, rather, narrowly deterministic. Jones appears to have little or no appreciation of the complexity of life, except for the fact that such complexity is guaranteed to give him adequate grist for his narrow interpretation.

Jones's paper not only illustrates the brazenly misogynistic nature of early psychoanalytic reasoning, it is also a fine example of the arrogance that this system of thinking draws out of its practitioners. This prideful belief that the psychoanalyst can read other people's minds and explain their behavior through an examination of symbols and metaphoric happenstance remains in place today. While cultural shifts require that new generations of psychoanalysts dismiss the conclusions of their predecessors, those same psychoanalysts don't give up their penchant to author new conclusions based on the same sort of questionable reasoning. Groundless speculations about people's motivations, presented as deep and studied interpretations, are found in every generation of psychodynamic therapy.

• • •

Each generation of psychodynamic therapists dismisses the conclusions of past generations while at the same time praising and reusing the methods of their predecessors. Elisabeth Young-Bruehl, a professor at Haverford College and a practicing psychoanalyst in Philadelphia, illustrates this maneuver. She writes in her foreword to *What Freud Really Said* that we should ignore many of Freud's conclusions about women because they were "probably products of his resistances to his own discoveries." Freud could not see his mistakes, she concludes, because he "could not leap out of his own narcissism to say where the theoretical problem lay." By employing "resistance" and "narcissism," Young-Bruehl deftly shows not only how the psychodynamic mistakes of yesteryear can be explained away but also how they can be recycled into evidence of the correctness and explanatory power of the theory.

In *The Heart of Psychotherapy*, best-selling author and therapist George Weinberg takes a similar tack when he writes about early therapists. "Our forefathers who set down the principles in this field were loaded with biases," he writes. "Men who knew nothing about women's sexuality, for instance, presumed to know about healthy orgasms for women. Men who were grandiose and racist defined the less privileged as paranoid and schizophrenic as a way of keeping them at bay and avoiding dealing with them." Thankfully, he notes, modern therapists have been enlightened by the "new insights from feminists, from members of minority groups, from people in different economic brackets, from single parents, from gays, from celibates, [and] from other so-called 'deviants.'" With these new insights at hand, the challenge for the modern therapist was to separate the previous generations' misconceptions from "their real contributions," which was the psychodynamic mode of thinking.

The flaw in many modern psychoanalysts' theories is that what they were bequeathed was not a set of tools that could be distinguished from the ideas they created. They inherited instead a system of thinking that was incapable of separating wish from fact, a method that gives a scientific patina to whatever conclusion the therapist happens to intuit. In this way it is not the conclusions these therapists come to that are so troubling (although they are often troubling) but the method by which they have allowed their associative thought process to be confused with deep and meaningful insight.

But are therapists today as self-assured about their ability to see into the hidden motivations of clients? Are they as willing as Jones and Freud to base interpretations on similarly small bits of evidence?

In his book, Weinberg gives us an answer almost immediately, as he claims that he can tell from the posture of a child whether he or she is beaten at home. In another anecdote he tells the story of a phone call one of the therapists he supervises had with a prospective patient. Recounting the story of the phone call to Weinberg, the young therapist told of feeling mildly annoyed at the series of questions the patient asked at the end of the conversation. (She had wanted to know where the therapist's office was located as well as which subway stop and which subway train might be best for getting there.) To Weinberg's heightened senses, the rest of the patient's case file (including details about the patient's medical history, family background, disappointing professional life, and an unhappy marriage) were less informative than the fact that she had annoyed her prospective therapist by asking so many questions.

"[The case file] revealed less to me than did the dialogue over the phone," Weinberg states. Not only did it reveal a telling portrait of the patient, but Weinberg believes that the interchange exposed the problems of the therapist as well. "From this incident and how it was handled, we learn about both the patient and the therapist. It would not be wrong to speculate that the woman's obliviousness to boundaries, as shown in that phone call, might have much to do with why her life was going badly. And the therapist's decision not to react, to subdue the feelings he had at the time and forget them, had much to do with why his practice was going badly."

This is a virtuoso performance by a psychodynamic therapist. From one brief, barely remembered conversation recounted by another therapist, he quickly sees to the heart of the patient's personality, as well as claiming to perceive the fundamental failing of the therapist. To point out the obvious problems in this scenario (that he is claiming insight into a person he has never met based on a minute-long conversation he didn't hear) would be to misunderstand the nature of the treatments being offered in the psychodynamic therapy marketplace. If you have a problem with someone making such quick-draw interpretations from such limited evidential ground, you are not in the market for the treatment psychotherapists offer. It is precisely this sort of claim to great intuitive powers that draws patient to therapist.

Of course, everyone *thinks* they see behind the motivations of other people. We all make snap judgments about why someone might have cut us off in traffic or why a bank teller might treat us badly. We might even offer these interpretations to friends and debate them over coffee. However, if we have any understanding of the complexity of human behavior, we do not believe that our gut reactions are deep insights into other people's lives. Therapists have no legitimate claim to this ability either.

Let us examine a longer illustration of how a modern psychodynamically oriented therapist pieces together conclusions about his patients' lives from the recently published case of "Oedipus from Brooklyn." In an award-winning paper, psychoanalyst Arnold Wm. Rachman tells the story of Oedipus, who went to therapy in his mid-twenties when he felt depressed and isolated. After a successful college career at an elite school, he was living at home with his widowed mother and working at a job he felt was uncreative and deadening. Instead of focusing on these two facts, Rachman and Oedipus embark on an exploration of the patient's unconscious mind, trying to link up current feelings to experiences and emotions from childhood.

The pair quickly focus on Oedipus's relationship with his mother, whom the patient felt was overbearing and controlling. (This is perhaps not surprising considering that Oedipus was living alone with his mother as an adult. Apparently, however, Rachman never suggests the obvious—that Oedipus's relationship with his mother might feel less overbearing if he simply moved out.) Once focused in on his mother, Rachman and Oedipus begin to build a narrative in which they tie his current behavior and feelings to the way his mother supposedly stifled his creativity in early childhood.

Eventually, the therapy yields a critical piece of the psychodynamic narrative. Oedipus comes to believe he remembers a critical scene from when he was between four and six months old. Rachman describes the scene Oedipus supposedly remembers:

> One day, he was busily engaged in playing with building blocks. He was completely absorbed in building a structure, perhaps a building. He had his back to his mother, completely ignoring her, as he was totally involved in the adventure of creating a structure. He was enthralled. His mother, either intentionally or by accident, reached over his shoulder and knocked the blocks over. Oedipus was surprised, but picked the blocks up and proceeded to rebuild the structure. The blocks were knocked down again. This time he was frustrated and angry. He tried to stop the invasion by moving into a corner of his playpen and hovering over his building. Once again, he returned to his building construction. This time, when his

mother knocked down the blocks, he curled into a ball and gave up. . . . Apparently, the mother, resentful that her son was more interested in his own creation than in her, struck out at him and tried to force him to pay attention to her. . . . He never forgot and he never forgave it.

This scene, combined with a variety of other pieces of memory, dream interpretation, and free association, pieced together during *two decades* of private and group therapy, builds a narrative that Oedipus solidly believes explains his problems. So compact and focused is the eventual story, it can be summed up in four sentences in Rachman's account: "During his first year . . . Oedipus experienced a series of traumas when his emerging creative self was seriously thwarted, from which he did not begin to recover until recently. From the age of roughly 6 months to the present, Oedipus suffered intense emotional pain because he felt his mother had destroyed his natural desire to create. Instead of being a creative, happy individual, he was forced to work at an uncreative job he hated. Hopelessness, passivity, and resignation pervaded his existence."

The extent to which the mother is portrayed as the villain of this story is sometimes comical. She is blamed at some point for creating a "symbiotic-like connection" between herself and Oedipus's brother, which supposedly caused the brother's homosexuality. In Oedipus's dream of rodents his mother is interpreted to be the "giant mole," an animal-like creature who bored her way into "every cell of his body and mind." They also trace his inability to make any positive changes in his life back to his controlling mother.

Oedipus is not unswerving in his belief in the narrative he and Rachman are creating in therapy. At one point (it is unclear exactly how long into therapy), Oedipus admits to being unsatisfied with the exploration of his early childhood because he feels they have not pinpointed "the exact factors that caused his creative block." To clarify the story, Rachman offers to interview the mother in an "attempt to discern the locus of psychopathology."

On meeting Oedipus's mother, Rachman finds his initial impression of her one of "vitality, eagerness, and willingness to please and cooperate." Considering the caricature of her he helped paint in therapy, his own reaction must have been disorienting. Apparently, Rachman is troubled enough to ask another therapist to listen to a tape of his sessions with the mother. When this consultant listens to the tape, the two therapists discovered a much more sinister truth. "[The consultant] concluded that the mother's voice quality, manner of relating, thought processes, emotionality, and level of denial suggested a borderline adaptation. Although these personality characteristics were not as apparent in the face-to-face interviews, they were discernible when the therapist [as Rachman refers to himself] also listened to the tapes. What became clear in trying to reconcile the discrepancy between the consultant's and the therapist's assessments of the mother's functioning was that being in the mother's presence may have had a 'seductive' effect on the therapist." This is one mean mother. Not only does she sap the creative life of one son and cause the other to become homosexual, she is also able to use her seductive powers to blind the therapist to her "borderline" personality.

Not surprisingly, the mother does not remember having cruelly and repeatedly destroyed little Oedipus's first creative effort. "Do you think I would do something like that to my son? Never!" Rachman reports her as protesting. He concludes that "she practiced almost total denial when the therapist attempted to link two significant childhood experiences to Oedipus's adult personality problems." She also denies that she was the cause of the brother's homosexuality.

Although the sessions are a failure in their initial intent (they do not uncover any new locus of psychopathologies), the mother's adamant denials, along with the discovery of her "borderline adaptation," finally convinces Oedipus that his therapy is on the correct story line. After watching some films of negative mother-infant interaction (provided by the ever-helpful consulting therapist), Oedipus finally becomes "satisfied that the proper diagnosis had been made about his mother and that he was the victim of her intrusiveness and control. He was once a curious, adventurous, and potentially creative child who was thwarted."

The nonpsychodynamically inclined will likely have a great deal of sympathy for Oedipus's mother's shocked reaction to the role in which she was being cast. The way the story narrows around the idea that she was the source seems highly implausible. Even in the paper's account, several clear inconsistencies are never explained. For instance, Rachman mentions in his initial description of Oedipus that he was an "honors graduate from one of the most prestigious colleges in the United States." Although we don't learn what Oedipus studied, we can assume that this achievement indicates a good deal of creative ability, self-confidence, and a string of academic successes that stretched back through high school and grade school. Oedipus also manages to teach himself Greek during the early part of the therapy—not a trivial challenge for someone so beaten into submission by his evil mother. These facts seem to indicate a person who lacked creative *opportunity* in his mid-twenties life (a common enough state), not one who lacked ability. Can the mother take credit for encouraging his many accomplishments as she takes blame for his failures? We don't know, because Oedipus's achievements are never worked into the narrative.

But these inconsistencies are trivial next to the questionable pieces of data out of which the narrative is created. Take the dream interpretations, for example. The associations and metaphors are so loosely based on the dream content that any dream could be made to conform to the narrative in creation. If Oedipus had been in different hands, the giant rodents he dreamt of could have been identified as distorted images of the space aliens who abducted him, or, in recovered memory therapy, as symbols of the genitals of the uncle who sexually assaulted him as a child.* Because the patient and therapist

*Charlotte Prozan, in her book *The Techniques of Feminist Psychoanalysis,* interprets her patient's dream of rodents in just this manner.

often use strings of associations to connect the content of the dream to the narrative, it appears that the narrative molds the content found in the dream, not the other way around.

The story of the brother's homosexuality is another red flag. The idea that bad parenting causes people to become gay is a throwback to an antiquated idea—long promoted by psycho-analysis—that homosexuality is a mental illness that has its origins in upbringing. But without getting into the debate over the nature/nurture origins of homosexual preferences, the therapist's conclusion is telling. He confidently holds to this idea that the mother skewed the brother's sexual orientation despite the fact that he seems to have very little firsthand information about the mother, who apparently had only two consultation sessions with the therapist.

Finally, there is the dramatic scene Oedipus supposedly uncovers of his mother repeatedly destroying his first creative attempt. The entire story line rests heavily on this highly suspect memory* and provides the eventual breakthrough in therapy. After more than fifteen years of therapy, Rachman re-creates the damaging scene in group therapy so that Oedipus can reexperience and heal from it. Here is Rachman's account of what happened:

> The scene was set by excluding all outside stimuli; the shades were drawn, the lights were lowered, and an area was cleared for the encounter. The group surrounded Oedipus to form the walls of a symbolic playpen. He sat on the floor, playing with the pillows from the couch. The pillows functioned as symbolic building blocks. A group member role-played the intrusive mother. Each time Oedipus built a structure with the building blocks, the member came from behind without warning and knocked it down. This was repeated several times. With each interruption of his attempt to build a structure, Oedipus became more frustrated and withdrawn. Finally, he sat immo-

---

*Most studies dispute the notion that people are able to remember incidents that occurred when they were less than one year old.

bilized, unable to continue. The encounter ended. Oedipus and the group reported that a profoundly moving experience had occurred. He was convinced that he had re-experienced a basic event of his early childhood in which his mother intruded her presence into his physical and emotional space, forcing him to pay attention to her, rather than to be left free to create.

After this encounter Oedipus has a dream that he is an architect. Rachman, perhaps seeing the potential for a truly grand end to the therapeutic experience, prompts him to enroll in architecture school. Unfortunately, after enrolling in basic drafting classes, Oedipus finds he has neither the hand-eye coordination nor the artistic talent. This failure is clearly a disappointment for all involved. The symbolism of his becoming an architect after untangling the trauma of his mother toppling his first building would have been a perfect denouement to the tale of treatment.

Rachman has to look elsewhere for the proof that he has uncorked Oedipus's long-repressed creative impulses. Oedipus, being a participant in his narrative creation, was likely feeling a fair amount of pressure to come up with just such proof. Slowly, Oedipus develops an interest in photography. Not surprisingly, most of his photographs have something to do with his preoccupations in therapy. The reader, apparently, is supposed to see this interest as the culmination of therapy because Rachman attests that his photographs "demonstrated a warm, sensitive feeling." Would it be mean-spirited to wonder about the costs and benefits of all this work? Twenty years of individual and group therapy, during which he vilified his mother, yielded a new passion for photography.

• • •

As we have mentioned, every generation of romantic talk therapist claims to have overcome the mistakes of the past and renews its claim to legitimacy. Recently, Susan C. Vaughan, a young Manhattan psychoanalyst, has done exactly this for her generation. "I am a microsurgeon of the mind. I use words and symbols to explore and change the neural landscape of my patients' minds and brains the way a surgeon uses a scalpel to expose and excise problematic structures in the body. . . . I am not speaking metaphorically," she writes in the introduction to her recent book, *The Talking Cure: The Science Behind Psychotherapy*. For this statement alone she wins points for gumption. While many talk therapists have been retreating into the domain of spirituality and the soul, where they are unlikely to be dogged by questions of scientific legitimacy, Vaughan and others have charged into the breach, claiming that psychotherapy is, after all, scientifically valid. She wants, as she says, to put the "neuron back in neurosis." "We now have solid scientific evidence to suggest that the so-called 'talking cure,' originally devised by Freud, literally alters the way in which the neurons in the brain are connected to one another."

Despite her promise to deliver science, Vaughan's book begins with a story about her treatment of a client named Katie. Katie's need for Vaughan's "neurosurgery," the reader learns, does not come from any sort of mental illness (Katie is described as a functioning upwardly mobile businesswoman), but rather from "Katie's nagging feeling that she is hurting her mother as she grows up and becomes more independent." As with the half dozen other cases Vaughan presents in her book, she begins by quoting one of Katie's dreams:

> I dreamed I was at your office. I was sad that it was the end of our session, the last one before I go away on my trip. As I was leaving, I accidentally jarred a glass by the door. I saw the sheet of glass fall off the table—in slow motion. I wanted to catch the edge, but I couldn't move. The glass hit the ground and shattered into thousands of shards. I was afraid to look at you. I thought you would be very angry. When I finally looked up I saw that a gash on your right palm was bleeding. I felt scared and sad.

Later, in therapy, Katie also tells Vaughan of a childhood memory of breaking three of her mother's favorite dishes. In addition, she talks of anxieties about becoming independent from her mother as well as her wish that Vaughan could come with her on an upcoming business trip. After that, Vaughan decides "it's time to tie together these themes," and to offer an interpretation. " 'It's as if the relationship itself, the bond between you and your mother, was fragile and easy to shatter,' " she reports telling Katie. " 'And now, you're going off on your own, without me. . . . I think you're concerned about whether I can tolerate your capability and your independence. . . .' I feel certain that my interpretation has literally touched a nerve when Katie begins to cry."

In her book, Vaughan takes several tacks to try and prove that such interpretive treatments find a basis in science. Her first attempt to give psychoanalysis scientific standing is by association. She slips away from the story of Katie's treatment to give the reader a quick summary of some recent scientific research surrounding dreams. To explain dreams in terms of occipital cortexes, PGO waves, and rapid eye movement, Vaughan relies heavily on J. Allan Hobson's book *The Dreaming Brain*. She repeats his theory that the images of dreams are the brain's reaction to rapidly firing neurons from the brain stem during REM sleep. Vaughan's enthusiasm for Hobson's work is obvious, although it is far from clear how it supports her practice.

The psychoanalytic proposition about dreams is far different from the commonplace understanding that dreams reflect our waking world sometimes realistically and sometimes through a distorted fun-house mirror. The fact that we can find some meaning in dreams does not in any way cover Freud's or Vaughan's bet that they have *specific coded* meanings. The fascinating science that has begun to explain the neurology of dreaming offers no support for this psychodynamic proposition. Simply putting the Freudian style of dream interpretation next to neurological theories of the brain, as Vaughan does in her book, is akin to an astrologer pointing to the discovery of thousands of new galaxies and arguing that this new understanding of the grandeur and complexity of the universe is evidence for the validity of horoscopes. "You see," the astrologer might argue, "we always knew there was something really interesting going on up there."

To try to bring these Freudian views of the brain together with her claim to be a "neurosurgeon," Vaughan, in good Freudian tradition, postulates a new mechanism in the brain. "I believe the cerebral cortex houses a 'story synthesizer,'" she writes, "whose job it is to provide the plot-lines and the characters for the unique personal stories. . . . This thesis is rather radical. I am suggesting that a network of neurons in the association cortex functions as a story synthesizer, which fundamentally shapes our approach to relationships in daily life."

The audacity of this move might startle those who haven't read Freud. To connect the neurology of dreaming with her own interpretations, Vaughan simply creates a mental apparatus. What scientific evidence does Vaughan offer for the "story synthesizer"? None. Regardless, once she has declared a new mental mechanism, she can now claim her job as a therapist is to perform microsurgery on the "story synthesizer."

Let's for a moment ignore Vaughan's pseudoscientific coining of phrases and give her line of reasoning its due. That our minds create stories about our own lives and relationships and that those stories inform the way we act in the future is obvious, and there is no need to postulate a new mental mechanism. We live by the stories we tell ourselves about our lives and those stories are sometimes even reflected in our dreams. That we can, to some degree, change these narratives is also clear. So, given that how we think is a matter of brain chemistry, isn't changing the way we think a matter of changing our very brain chemistry, as Vaughan claims? Shouldn't that count as a scientific activity along the lines of brain surgery? And what of Vaughan's reports of her patients' improvements? Isn't that proof that she is doing something right?

There are a number of reasons to question Vaughan's conclusion. To begin with, she fails to make an empirical hurdle of a much lower sort than the one she pretends to leap. In none of the cases does she offer a rationale for favoring one interpretation of a dream or set of memories over thousands of possible others. This is critical, for it is out of this material that Vaughan says she is able to see how the neural networks are tangled. (After which she writes that she can, "like a good hair stylist," comb out these tangles and give those neural pathways just the right "lift and body.") Vaughan never truly addresses the problem that she has no rationale for one interpretation over another, nor does she attempt to make the case that two different psychoanalysts would, with a fair degree of accuracy, interpret a set of memories or dreams in the same manner.

Instead, she relies on the compelling nature of the story to convince us that her interpretation is accurate. The fact that all patients are said to reach epiphanies of insight and come to agree with Vaughan's interpretation is assumed to be enough to convince the reader that the interpretation was manifest.

In doing this, she avoids the question that her patients—and even the dreams and free associations they present—are being influenced by the therapy. Vaughan need look no farther than the first dream presented in her own book to find evidence that the dreams she interprets are influenced by the therapy itself, for Vaughan herself appears in the dream of Katie breaking the glass table. If Vaughan is a character in her clients' dreams, can we assume that her assumptions and ideas surrounding dream interpretation do not similarly pervade her clients' dreams? What could be more dramatic proof that Vaughan has created a feedback loop, where the interpretations in therapy are incorporated into the material the patient brings back to the next session, thus confirming the original theory?

Vaughan is a true believer in the most flattering assumption shared by many psychodynamic therapists—that is, that her own free associations can lead to the truth behind the material her patients suggest. She writes that sometimes "our neural networks seem to make contact on a level that I cannot describe in words. At these moments, I can listen to my own associations and they'll lead me in the right direction in terms of how things are laid out in my patient's neural networks."

The proof of Katie's recovery is Vaughan's interpretation of another dream in which Katie swims in a glass pool that doesn't break. The dream proves to Vaughan that after two years of therapy, "Katie and I have created a new narrative about who she is and how she came to be that way. I believe we have done so by carefully and systematically examining, challenging, and rewiring the story synthesizer her cortex contains."

Given Vaughan's own account of her methods, it is exceedingly difficult to see a compelling parallel between her practice and that of a neurosurgeon.

In the last chapter, Vaughan interprets one of her own dreams, which she describes in two quick sentences: "I bought stock in Johnson & Johnson that appreciated dramatically over time. I was about to sell it to buy a red Saab Turbo convertible, when I woke up." While this dream might not seem much for the interpretive mill, rest assured that for a trained therapist such as Vaughan it offers plenty of material for the next dozen pages. Hidden in it, she finds an array of meanings:

- The fact that Johnson & Johnson is a "buy and hold" blue-chip stock is for Vaughan a "metaphor for how I think about the process of psychotherapy." (She seems not to worry about the fact that she was about to get rid of the stock in the dream.)
- She remembers her mother washing her hair with Johnson & Johnson shampoo before church, where her mother often cried: "I realize with a start that 'Saab' is a homonym for 'sob.' "
- Perhaps, she muses at another point, the Johnson & Johnson stock is a sign of a burgeoning desire to have children: "Is that a baby seat I see in the back [of the Saab]?" she asks herself.
- The Saab, "curvaceous and rather sexy," is a reflection of her own body and personality, she also decides. "Being a bit off-beat and turbo-charged, mirrors something about me. . . ."
- She imagines driving the car over the George Washington Bridge and remembers the last scene from a vampire movie

where the characters also drive over a bridge, from which she deduces: "I guess it's a way of reminding myself that I have the Wolf Within onboard too."

- At the very end of her interpretation she remembers the Saab advertisement "Find your own road," and realizes happily that she has done just that with her own life.

This example rather nakedly shows how self-serving psychodynamic logic can become. To illustrate our point, let us offer another possible interpretation for Vaughan's dream of selling stock and buying an expensive sports car. Perhaps this dream expresses the shallow consumerism of a young and immature professional who has bought into the notion that buying a car (especially one so "offbeat" and "turbo-charged" as the Saab) is a way to express her personality. We offer this interpretation not from any knowledge of Vaughan's personality nor to suggest that we are certain that Vaughan's dream was a trite materialistic fantasy, for to make such a claim would be to enter the same shaky epistemological ground that these therapists inhabit. Our point, rather, is that there is no remotely scientific reason to choose our interpretation over hers.

If, as she claims, psychotherapy can have as much impact on a patient's life as neurosurgery might, it is truly frightening that Vaughan (like Freud) makes her interpretations based on speculative intuition and her own free associations. What Vaughan presents as her method of creating stories out of dreams and memories is to our eyes nothing more than an elaborate parlor game.

In the end, she doesn't give an adequate explanation for how she arrives at the interpretations that she believes alter the brain's "story synthesizer," nor does she provide much of an explanation for how the "neural network" changes when her treatment is done right or how it might be damaged if done wrong. Since the discrediting of lobotomy, brain surgeons have been discouraged from operating on hope and good intention. If Vaughan were really a neurosurgeon of the brain in any literal sense, "using words and symbols to . . . change the neural landscape," she would be stopped immediately until she could demonstrate some science behind her methods, just as a doctor is required to do.

If, as we maintain, many of the psychodynamic talk therapies lack even the semblance of legitimate structure to their treatments, one must ask: How could so many seemingly smart people get it wrong? Underlying all forms of psychodynamic therapy is a seductive notion: the idea that the world is revealing itself to the therapist through his or her most unlabored thoughts. Couched in the language of scientific observation, the romantic practice of perceiving connections between memories, symbols, and dreams is a method that allows the therapists to offer intuition in the form of certainties. It is a form of thinking that appeals to an arrogant self-regard to which humans are prone. We all would like to believe that our intuitive leaps always land on solid ground.

Reading Jones, Vaughan, Rachman, Weinberg, and the pronouncements of psychodynamic therapists throughout the century is a lesson in the true depth of hubris. They participated in a system of thinking designed to give therapists the most room for conceptual roaming while conferring on them scientific authority. Psychoanalysis and the derivative psychodynamic schools of talk therapy are structures for directing thought that appear to be strict but that, in reality, are the *least* constrictive to imaginative leaps made by the practitioner. It would be delightful to be able to believe that this sort of mental recipe results in a perfect interpretive soufflé. In reality, psychodynamic psychotherapy is a method for coming to any conclusion the therapist would like to form. It allows therapists to find patterns where none actually exist.

CHAPTER FIVE

Does Therapy Work?

Above all, what we as Americans prize are magic elixirs: simple solutions, closed and totalizing systems of explanation, grand schemes at once easy to understand, applicable to everything and everyone, and which thereby reduce the heart-stopping complexity of the world to a set of nostrums or dicta that we can recite like mantras, when things go bad, to quiet the soul.

—Peter Marin,
"An American Yearning"

Although some psychodynamic therapists persist in attempting to treat major mental disorders with psychotherapy, they are a dying breed. As we will see, a medical approach has become the key to the treatment of most forms of mental illness. While behavioral and cognitive therapists have carved out helpful ancillary roles in the treatment of some major mental illnesses, talk therapists in the psychodynamic tradition have largely retreated to the claim that they can address more common problems such as unhappiness or demoralization often associated with tragic life events such as divorce, trauma, and grief.

Does therapy work to alleviate the demoralization of the non-mentally-ill? Certainly if one were to go looking for stories of therapy's success, one would not have to travel far. Many people who enter therapy end up as believers in the effectiveness of the treatment they received. "I was feeling down and confused, I went to therapy, and now I feel better," they sincerely attest.

They had the good fortune to avoid the field's most aberrant treatments—that is, they didn't walk out of therapy believing that they had been abducted by space aliens, or that their sadness was the result of the unfairness of a patriarchal or capitalist culture, or that they had uncovered supposedly repressed memories of being abused as an infant by their parents. Rather, after some months of therapy they felt markedly better and were happy about the time spent with their therapists, whom they respect and admire. What could be wrong with that?

Such stories, common as they are, cannot be taken as proof of therapy's legitimacy. To begin with, such stories are anecdotal. In any meaningful reckoning of therapy's effectiveness, such accounts must be weighed against the number of times the same treatment was ineffective or left the patient feeling worse. Because going to therapy is usually a voluntary act, the process tends to exclude those who quickly become skeptical of the therapists' conclusions or methods. For this reason, the fact that most of the stories one hears are positive is not surprising.

The testimony of a single satisfied patient does not even prove the efficacy of that particular case, for a single patient cannot know how he or she might have felt after a few months of *not* going to therapy. The sadness or other symptom might have simply been a passing phenomenon caused by biological factors, or it might have been precipitated by the strain of a short-term problem in the patient's life. The perception that psychotherapy is the agent that changes the patient does not necessarily make it so. In addition, the individual patient can't know whether some other form of treatment or life pursuit might have made him or her feel better, faster, for a smaller investment of time, effort, or money. This is no small question considering the massive amount of societal resources we allot, individually and collectively, to psychotherapy.

Many questions cannot be settled simply on the basis of patient or therapist testimonials. To make an informed, sound judgment about the role of psychotherapy in modern life, it's critical to know, for instance, the power of the placebo effect in therapy—that is, the extent to which patients will feel better for the singular reason that they have taken the step of accepting help that they believe to be effective.

Separating the effectiveness of the individual healers from the effectiveness of their treatment is also critical in understanding whether therapy is a teachable technique or whether it relies on the fact that some people, regardless of their training or theoretical position, are simply more empathetic than others and therefore better able to give a patient solace and understanding through a crisis. Remarkably, the field of psychotherapy has just recently gotten around to considering these critical questions.

Until recently, treatment methods were mostly debated and adopted like philosophies or religious doctrine. While they were created and modified with great effort, they offered little empirical evidence that they could effect change, much less cures, for any sort of disorder. Not surprisingly, many schools, particularly psychoanalysis and its psychodynamic offshoots, have only grudgingly submitted themselves to rigorous testing. With both the practitioner's self-esteem and income on the line, these schools were willing to ride on the devotion that therapy could consistently create in their suffering or needy patients.

Without any empirical proof that certain therapies were effective at all or more effective than others, treatments would flourish, relative to their rivals, through various popularity contests. Some therapists appealed to patients' desires while others created treatments that fed off the cultural fears and enthusiasms of the moment. Other therapies came to prominence by winning the more challenging, but often equally speculative, debate contests within formal and informal professional circles. Psychoanalysis, as we have shown, came to prominence largely through a successful campaign of intellectual strong-arming in the nation's psychiatric schools and institutions. Through several decades of prominence, psychoanalysis offered no reasonably scientific proof of its ability to help patients. Winners of these informal but heated contests claimed the status accorded to university chairs and journal editors.

Psychodynamic schools of therapy (in the tradition of psychoanalysis) have largely divorced themselves from the question of proving their effectiveness in the treatment of patients. Relying for proof on the loosest measure—reports of the practitioners themselves—anecdotal success has been reported from every quarter. In the words of psychiatrist and researcher Jerome Frank, the field of psychotherapy could be characterized as "crowded with entrepreneurs, each of whom proclaims the unique virtues of his product while largely ignoring those of his rivals, and backs his claims with speculative pronouncements supported by a few case reports."

It was not until the 1950s, with the rise of competition from the earliest drug-based treatments, that the question of whether therapy worked was asked with any degree of seriousness or concern for empirical evidence. In 1952, in one of the first major studies on this question, Hans Eysenck found two-thirds of therapy patients improved significantly or recovered on their own within two years, whether or not they received psychotherapy. He reported, in short, that psychotherapy was utterly ineffective. With psychotherapy undergoing a dramatic postwar expansion at the time, Eysenck's study was not what the growing field wanted to hear.

Other studies by those more predisposed to psychotherapy soon appeared, showing that psychotherapy was indeed more effective than no treatment. After that, new studies were published reconfirming Eysenck's results. In the late seventies and eighties, along came the meta-analysis studies, which claimed, through the use of complicated statistical methods, to be able to combine the results of dozens or hundreds of other studies. Far from settling the argument, these meta-analyses only added to the controversy. Sometimes statisticians could take similar sets of studies and come to opposite conclusions. The problem was more basic than the complexity of meta-analysis statistics: The studies being meta-analyzed were often badly designed. "No matter how elegant the statistical procedures of meta-analysis, poor research is still poor research," wrote one scientist.

There were a variety of serious problems with many of the

studies and any number of other issues that made the question of measuring therapy effectiveness difficult in the extreme. Major mistakes included not using control groups by which to gauge changes that could be attributed to therapy. Given Eysenck's contention that the normal passage of time often finds people overcoming distressful periods on their own, it seemed obvious that some sort of control be established to understand the effect of time passing versus the impact of the therapy offered.*

Of those studies that had control groups, even fewer had control groups of patients who were given believable placebo treatments. Offering a control group a fake medication or some sort of nontherapy procedure (like a relaxation exercise) would equalize the positive effects both of the patients' having sought treatment and their expectation of being helped. The act of reaching out for help and having someone reach back is enough to inspire hope, which, in some cases, is the antidote to mild demoralization. The power of this effect was shown in studies that found a 75 percent improvement rate in patients who were given a long intake interview and then put on a waiting list to receive treatment. Apparently, these subjects perceived the intake interview as therapeutic, although it was nothing more than them answering questions and detailing their problems while an authority figure listened carefully.

Because no one agrees on what psychotherapy is, creating a talking placebo (where patients interact with someone but don't receive "psychotherapy") has been difficult. "Our understanding of the nature of the processes that induce change is imperfect (if not downright lacking)," wrote L. Prioleau and her colleagues of placebo treatments, which included talking to the patient. "Presumably the treatment is construed as a placebo in the belief that discussions that do not focus on specific problems are not therapeutically efficacious. But this belief may be no more than an act of faith. It may well be that the

---

*One example of a flawed study on psychotherapy is the *Consumer Reports* survey that came out in 1995. Because of the importance of this report in sparking consumer confidence in talk therapy, we've taken a closer look at its flaws in an appendix.

essential features of psychotherapy which account for its therapeutic effectiveness are well reproduced by this type of placebo treatment."

Despite this question, the studies with placebo groups still seem to be the best for judging therapy's effectiveness. When three researchers from Wesleyan University analyzed the data from thirty-two previous studies, which had compared psychotherapy to some sort of placebo treatment, the results were less than encouraging for therapy. Combining the results with meta-analysis techniques, they found that the benefits of therapy relative to those of placebo treatments were "vanishingly small." The analysis of these studies seems to indicate that if you control for the expectation of cure and the comfort of talking to a solicitous and respected helper, you have only a tiny effect due to the content of what is said and done in therapy. Said another way: What the therapist actually says to the patients in different modes of treatment appears not to matter to a significant degree.

The news for therapy gets worse. Other studies have indicated that the rates at which patients sometimes deteriorated in therapy was typically higher in those groups that were given treatment as opposed to those that were given placebos or no treatment at all. Still other research shows a lack of correlation between the experiences of therapists and the results they achieve. Therapists with little experience seem to perform as well as therapists who outranked them in seniority, years of experience, and training. Other researchers pushed these findings further, by comparing liberal arts college professors to therapists with an average of twenty-three years of experience. In counseling disturbed college students, the college professors did just as well as the seasoned therapists. In a review of forty-two studies comparing professional therapists with paraprofessional therapists (such as teachers given the job of counseling students), only one study showed that the trained therapists got better results. Twenty-nine studies showed no difference between the two groups, and the remaining twelve studies showed that the paraprofessionals actually outperformed the professional therapists.

"These are provocative findings for the psychotherapy community," wrote the authors of the study. "It is hard to imagine a study comparing trained and untrained surgeons, or trained and untrained electricians, for that matter. Dead patients in the first instance and dead trainees in the second could be the unfortunate outcome."

Three decades after his initial study blasting the effectiveness claims of therapy, H. J. Eysenck wrote that he could still find no compelling evidence that the practice of psychotherapy showed much value. Unfortunately, he notes, this lack of support had little effect on the profession, which has shown a propensity to ignore all findings that dispute the usefulness of its methods. He goes on:

> . . . it is difficult to see how, from the ethical point of view, we can reconcile this refusal to face facts with the social duties imposed on the applied scientist. Do we really have the right to impose a lengthy training on medical doctors and psychologists in order to enable them to practice a skill which has no practical relevance to the curing of neurotic disorders? Do we have the right to charge patients fees, or get the State to pay us for a treatment which is no better than a placebo? Do we have the right to continue to teach students general psychology theories, such as the Freudian, for which there does not exist any experimental evidence, and which have failed in their application to psychiatric treatment? . . . Freudian and other psychological theories have hitherto been under a preservation order which has made them immune to the killing effect of adverse facts, it is time this preservation order was rescinded.

The pervasive nature of this placebo effect may explain one of the most troubling aspects of these studies: that they often fail to find significant differences in effectiveness between different schools of treatment. Considering the radically different approaches of the hundreds of different schools of therapy, it defies common sense that all of them have equal (albeit a small) effect. Those who study the research on therapeutic effectiveness refer to the possibility that all therapy settings achieve roughly the same outcomes despite dramatic differences in theory and technique as the "dodo bird hypothesis." This label comes from the Lewis Carroll line in *Through the Looking Glass* when the dodo bird announces after a race: "Everyone has won and all must have prizes."

This upbeat spin, however, might just as well be put in opposite terms. If psychotherapy has shown only the ability to make marginal changes of questionable staying power, and if trained therapists show no more success than the minimally trained or even untrained counselors, and if there is no increase in the effectiveness of the treatment the longer the treatment is given, then it might just as well be said that all schools of therapy have lost and none deserves a prize.

Remarkably, proponents of therapy often point to the placebo effect of treatment with pride, sometimes even admitting that it is the true power of therapy. This argument seems as if it would be as welcome as poison by those who have studied, debated, and defended endless intricacies of one or another school of therapy. Imagine a doctor taking pride in the fact that the drug she spent her career developing has only a marginal placebo effect on the patient. Perhaps wisely, however, therapists seem unwilling to turn away any evidence that what they do has value.

It has long been noted that all therapies share a number of traits that make them all equally, albeit marginally, able to change or influence patients' attitudes about themselves, some self-defeating behaviors, and certain life circumstances. Jerome D. Frank and Julia B. Frank's seminal and respected book *Persuasion and Healing, A Comparative Study of Psychotherapy* is the most compelling and thorough defense of talk therapy along these lines. They argue that all schools of talk therapy battle demoralization by engendering in the patient a sense of hope and enhancing the sense of mastery the patient has over his or her life. The therapist does this by offering a compelling mythology to explain the patient's symptoms and employing impressive rituals or procedures (such as hypnosis, relaxation, or emotional flooding) by which the therapist demonstrates his or her power and increases the expectation of cure or change.

The problem therapists most commonly face, they argue, is that of demoralization brought on by a failure of what they call the patient's "assumptive world." "Each person evaluates internal and external stimuli in the light of assumptions about what is dangerous, safe, important, unimportant, good, bad, and so on," they write. "These assumptions become organized into sets of highly structured, complex, interacting values, expectations, and images of self and others that are closely related to emotional states and feelings. Such psychological structures and processes shape, and in turn are shaped by, a person's perceptions and behaviors . . . the totality of each person's assumptions may be conveniently termed his or her assumptive world."*

One's assumptive scheme (we have referred to the same concept, generally, as one's "life narrative") allows one to explain past events, as well as predict one's own behavior and the actions of others. Some of these assumptions are so deeply layered into our consciousness that their original source might be quite obscure. In order to live relatively normal mental lives, Frank and Frank write, one's assumptive world has to more or less correspond to the real world. It is when one's assumptions do not predict behavior (especially one's own behavior) that we can become troubled. "Since a person relies on the assumptive world to make the universe predictable, any event or experience that is inconsistent with a person's expectations creates surprise or uncertainty." Such uncertainty can lead to demoralization and anxiety, which can bring a person to therapy.

In *Persuasion and Healing,* the authors assume that all forms of therapy fix inconsistencies in the patients' assumptive systems—that is, they bring the patient a greater sense of personal

---

*In this conception of what therapists treat, Frank and Frank are clearly excluding many major mental illnesses, symptoms of which are far more debilitating than failures of one's assumptive world. The authors admit as much: "[I]t has become clear after years of dedicated effort that psychotherapy cannot cure most psychoses."

agency by helping the patient recognize the source and consequences of mistaken assumptions and by helping the patient create a stronger and more vital assumptive system. By doing so, they give the patient a greater sense of mastery over his or her reactions, feelings, and choices.

The fact that the framework of assumptive systems varies wildly from one therapy school to another is, they argue, beside the point. Frank and Frank admit up front that the many and various theories of the different talk therapy schools are better thought of as "myths" than scientific findings. As they explain: "We have chosen the term 'myth' to characterize theories of psychotherapy because such theories resemble myths in at least two ways: (1) they are imagination-catching formulations of recurrent and important human experiences; and (2) they cannot be proven empirically. Successes are taken as evidence of their validity (often erroneously), while failures are explained away."

Therapy is effective not as a result of its specific theories or methods, they argue, but as a result of clients *coming to believe* in those theories and methods. In this sense it's less important that the therapists' theories of mental behavior are true than that they are believable. Any believed-in assumptive system relieves the anxiety experienced when one is failing. While the authors think of their book not as a criticism of talk therapy but as a reconceptualized defense of the practice, in between the lines of their own arguments is something of an exposé of talk therapy.

By arguing that it doesn't matter whether the theory is scientifically valid, Frank and Frank dismiss the very reason we believe modern patients are willing to believe and avail themselves of treatment. All the trappings of the therapist, including the certifications, diplomas, and stuffed bookshelves, serve to distinguish the talk therapist from his or her more colorful colleague, the faith healer. These accoutrements indicate to the patient that talk therapists are not offering simply another myth to explain human behavior, but that they possess actual knowledge culled from the study of human cognitive behavior and emotional functioning. Patients believe in therapists' theories at least in part because of their claim to social status in the scientific-technological culture in which we live. This status is a combination of a number of factors, the most important of which is our expectation that therapists have access to valid methods of treatment.

Therapists from all schools of therapy have helped to encourage this conclusion in the minds of prospective clients. It is for this exact reason that many patients are willing to take the first step and enter therapy. If, however, the theories therapists employ are only myths (selected not for their fit with reality but for their believability), the social status we grant therapists is a lie to the extent that it is based on those theories.

In Frank and Frank's kind assessment of the psychotherapy-as-healing myth, we are asked to ignore all the grand scientific-sounding pronouncements (from Freud to the present day) about how the unconscious functions as well as the specific promises of the various techniques employed. This argument also ignores the fact that therapists themselves often believe that their treatment relies not on some broad placebo effect but on the specific things they say to their patients. Patients also come to believe that attention to the therapists' communications, insights, and interpretations is the road to healing.

Some defenders of therapy ask us to sympathize with the therapists' unfortunate position of having such an ineffective method in the face of clients who are so willingly credulous. "Consider the psychotherapist," Robert Woolfolk writes in *The Cure of Souls: Science, Values, and Psychotherapy.* "Every day of his professional life he is asked questions to which he does not have the answer and is confronted with problems he does not understand and cannot ameliorate. His patients assume he knows more than he does and constantly give evidence of their imprudent expectations. . . . The problems brought to (the therapist) are too recalcitrant, and the art and technology they practice are too weak. . . . The gap between therapeutic knowledge and effectiveness on the one hand, and the needs and hopes of the patients, on the other, can demoralize the therapist." Of course, it is hard to feel too sorry for the demoralized therapist, considering the real victim of his ineffectiveness is the patient.

Tellingly, Woolfolk does not address the question of why the patient is so credulous. The answer is that therapists themselves often oversell their abilities, a conclusion that can be found between the lines of Woolfolk's own book. Like most of his colleagues, he does not advise that the patient be warned that the techniques of therapy are "too weak" for most problems. "To be concerned only with efficacy," he explains, ". . . will lead either to therapeutic cynicism or to the collapse of therapeutic authority and credibility." He is correct: A clear and general understanding of therapy's effectiveness would indeed lead to a general collapse of therapeutic authority. We would argue, however, that this fact is no reason to keep the patient in the dark about the usefulness of therapy.

These respected professionals ask us, in effect, to ignore the inability of therapy to meet patients' expectations by arguing that everything works out for the best in the end and that any compelling and "imagination catching" theories learned in therapy will relieve the anxiety of having a weak "assumptive scheme," or shaky life narrative. Frank and Frank blithely assure the reader that "In our present state of ignorance the most reasonable assumption is that all enduring forms of psychotherapy must do some good or they would disappear."

This sounds like little more than wishful thinking. We should not assume that there must be some validity to a therapy simply because it has shown staying power. With this conclusion, the authors of *Persuasion and Healing* ill-advisedly lump all psychological theories together. We would argue that while some assumptive worlds learned in therapy are benign, others are manifestly harmful. In addition, *how* someone comes to believe in one narrative versus another (especially if they were coerced or seduced with false promises) is not of incidental importance.

When talking about assumptive systems learned outside of therapy, the authors themselves point out that inaccurate and delusional assumptive worlds can have perverse staying power in a person's mind. They admit, for instance, that assumptive systems can be compelling in certain settings and yet be monstrously evil and wrongheaded when viewed from outside those settings. "The overriding power of consensual validation explains how a person can feel and appear mentally quite healthy yet be involved in a highly deviant, destructive, or irrational group, such as the Nazi party or a Satanic cult." They admit, in short, that an incorrect assumptive scheme (even an abhorrent or obviously destructive one) can draw committed converts. Frank and Frank simply fail to draw out this argument to potentially damaging (or simply misleading) assumptive worlds that the patient comes to believe in during therapy.

Frank and Frank's rescue mission is made in good faith, but they succeed mostly in highlighting the reasons why many forms of talk therapy are doomed. Indeed, much of the book reads like someone calming the passengers on the *Titanic* by asking them to reconceptualize the vessel as a submarine. Does anyone really believe that psychodynamic psychotherapy can survive as a persuasive "myth" if the very persuasiveness of that myth relies squarely on its illusory empirical and scientific pretensions?

We suspect that proponents of therapy, including Frank and Frank, often confuse the patients' new *sense* of mastery of their lives with mastery itself. Just as the belief that you are a good writer may be contradicted by the words on the page, having a sensation of mastery over your life may have little to do with having any actual control.

Indeed, that *sensation* of mastery may come from giving up control to a charismatic leader or a restrictive set of theories about the world. Frank and Frank make this case for us by comparing therapy to aspects of faith healing and miracle cures from cultures around the world. "Revival meetings and cults share most of the characteristics of secular psychotherapies that help produce and maintain beneficial changes in attitudes and behavior," they write. "Successful instances of both psychotherapy and spiritual healing reduce psychologically caused suffering, increase self-esteem, and foster a sense of mastery in persons who seek their ministrations."

To further the parallel, they quote anthropologist Claude Lévi-Strauss's description of a religiomagical cure:

> That the mythology of the shaman does not correspond to objective reality does not matter. The patient believes in it and belongs to a society that believes in it. The protecting spirits, the evil spirits, the supernatural monsters and magical monsters are elements of a coherent system which is the basis of the native's concept of the universe. The patient accepts them, or rather she has never doubted them. What she does not accept are the incomprehensible and arbitrary pains which represent an element foreign to her system but which the shaman, by invoking the myth, will replace in a whole in which everything has its proper place.

Lévi-Strauss, as the authors of *Persuasion and Healing* imply, might as well be describing certain types of talk therapy. Belief in the therapy is the central fact, while the validity of the theories remains of secondary importance at best. The role of the talk therapist is closely analogous to that played by the shamans who have populated every prescientific culture around the world. Shamans claim the role of organizing the culture's beliefs about human existence, behavior, and disease, and perform rituals that rely on the expectation of cure, but they do not deal directly with the disease process. Frank and Frank are exactly right in drawing these parallels, but their case is far more devastating to the practice of talk therapy—particularly psychodynamic therapy—than they indicate.

Those who feel the rush of positive feelings from bathing in the springs in Lourdes or finishing a pilgrimage to a shrine may experience the sensation of relief from their demoralization or even from the symptoms of an illness with an accompanying sense of mastery over the anxiety that can accompany difficult life periods. But if this sense of mastery comes from the demand characteristics of the situation, one might legitimately ask whether the price paid is too high. Specifically, those experiencing such religiously inspired "cures" must pay the price of abdicating their personal will to unseen spiritual entities. They must psychologically genuflect to the religious leaders who claim to understand and channel supernatural powers. In the process, they often become subservient to powerful forces of group dynamics at the further expense of personal agency.

Certainly, such experiences can increase the sensation of mastery over the complexities of life, but we would argue that this is more an illusion of control than control itself. Certainly there is no proof that the diseases that afflict the pilgrims to Lourdes are routinely cured by the experience—the symptoms are simply temporarily masked by the thrall of the experience. The shaman/priest's ability to channel spiritual forces are an illusion made believable by the power of group belief.

Frank and Frank concede that any improvement experienced by the faithful at a shrine "probably reflects heightened morale, enabling a person to function better in the face of an unchanged organic handicap," which makes their comparison of faith healing and therapy less encouraging. Like the faith healers who cannot hope to cure illnesses, therapists cannot pretend to be able to effectively cure gross organic diseases.

But what about overcoming demoralization? Since neither the pilgrimage to the shrine nor the experience of therapy in itself changes anything in the patient's life, any uplifting effect of believing in the myths inherent in these encounters is likely to be short-lived. Far from being encouraging, the parallel with various forms of faith healing can be read as an admission of defeat.

The comparison between such faith-based practices and psychodynamic therapy should be abundantly clear. The impressive feat of the psychodynamic therapist is to convince the patient that his or her problems stem from unseen forces—not in the realm of the supernatural but in the unconscious. The therapist claims he or she can discern and interpret these forces by examining the patient's dreams, free associations, physical tics, ailments, and so on. In short, patients must give up both the belief that they are fundamentally in control of their decisions (since part of their behavior is shaped by forces they can't see) as well as cede the ability to interpret the expression of those supposedly causal forces to the respected therapist. Because whatever sensation of mastery gained by the patient comes from yielding to an outside authority, that sensation comes at a significant cost and a great risk.

Therapists may use the influence gained in this trade-off to recommend positive changes in a patient's life. They may, after a time in therapy, even cede back to the patient some ability to interpret his or her own unconscious influences. Of course, they may do neither of these things. Our argument is not simply that the belief in the dynamic unconscious is mistaken, but that any sense of mastery gained from such beliefs is often at the expense of personal agency. The history of therapy bears this out, as it is filled with stories of patients who become ever more dependent on the therapist throughout treatment. (If the recovered memory epidemic has taught us anything, it is that this dependency can grow ever more severe during treatment.) Of course, this is not surprising: The greater the patient's belief in the power of these unseen forces and the therapist's ability to discern and explain them, the greater the patient's need for the therapist's ministrations.

Frank and Frank implicitly argue that the relief from anxiety that accompanies deeply believing in such assumptive worlds makes all therapies similarly valid. We disagree. There is at least one obvious conclusion that can be drawn from the similarity in effectiveness across treatments, and that is, if you have similar outcomes between two therapies, one of which is dramatically more costly and time intensive, you have at least two good reasons for choosing or recommending the other.

In addition, it seems obvious that the real-world validity of these assumptive systems *does* matter in several important ways. One could ask, for instance, whether the assumptive theories have any use outside the group of like-minded adherents. In addition, if any number of assumptive systems can relieve the anxiety of not having one, might we assume that the ones that rely *least* on unseen forces (unconscious or otherwise), group belief building, and adherence to some charismatic shaman or healer might be better than those that do?

Recently, certain segments of our culture have been engaged in something of a love affair with "non-Western" religiomagical approaches to healing. (One can see this infatuation in Frank and Frank's description of benevolent shamans.) Western culture, however, has its own history of witch doctoring that doesn't get such good press. This is the history of nostrum peddlers who, in the days before the regulation of medicine, traveled the country offering various forms of elixirs or procedures (often accompanied by an impressive machine or apparatus) to cure illness.

It is wrong to immediately assume that nostrum peddlers were nothing but confidence men. Although some peddlers of herb concoctions or electromagnetic cures for cancer certainly knew that what they offered was useless, others, no doubt, held a sincere, if unwarranted, belief that their cures would sometimes perform the wonders described in their passionate sales pitches.

Frank and Frank's positive comparison of therapy to religiomagical cures of other cultures rides in part on our reflexive respect for multicultural practices. However, the comparison of therapists to our culture's own nostrum sellers might be equally revealing. As Frank and Frank point out, two of the common features of all talk therapies and the religiomagical practices of shamans are "hope or positive expectation" and "emotional arousal." This is certainly true of the nostrum seller. Indeed, those with mild medical ills such as lethargy, mild headaches, muscle aches, and other mild dysphoria may be so won over by the nostrum seller's sales pitch that they may claim to be cured, at least temporarily.

Not surprisingly, Frank and Frank do not look to the nostrum seller for a comparison of therapy's placebo effect. This is likely because there is a much wider realization of the dangers of the nostrum sellers' false cures. Most important among these dangers is that those with serious but treatable conditions might chose to believe the compelling rhetoric of the pitchman over their doctors' advice. Believing in a psychodynamic therapist may in the exact same manner cost the patient an actual cure. As we will illustrate in a later chapter, many cures for mental diseases exist, but they exist outside the knowledge and experience of most talk therapists.

CHAPTER SIX

Therapy's Retreat

CLIENT: Two or three years? Hmmm. This really is quite
a different matter than I had anticipated, and I'm not
sure . . .
THERAPIST: Yes, it is a major undertaking, Mr. Bellows. It
needs to be thought of as one of the major events of
one's life, for what we attempt to do here is to reexamine
the whole course and meaning of why you're alive.

—JAMES F. T. BUGENTAL,
The Art of the Psychotherapist

At the end of the millennium, therapy is facing a crisis of legitimacy. The field is reverberating with self-criticism. Nevertheless, there is an underlying unwillingness to understand the meaning of the sum of this criticism as well as a collective inclination to hide the import of these problems from the general public.

The fact that many of the leading figures in the profession have largely conceded that therapy has only a marginal effect on its patients has not stopped some from bravely trying to stake out a common defense of the discipline. But their search (as described in the last chapter) for specific notions or techniques that might be defended by a majority in the field has proven exceedingly difficult. Those who claim to know of a therapeutic bottom line often argue themselves right out of the possibility that the practice of therapy rests on any body of knowledge or technical expertise.

In his book *Cultivating Intuition: An Introduction to Psy-*

chotherapy, British psychoanalyst Peter Lomas has attempted to discern the heart of the practice. Perhaps too honestly, he begins with what psychotherapy is not. No, he admits, therapy cannot claim to be a science, nor can it pretend to have access to any proprietary tools or techniques. "The basic principles of our profession are embedded in ignorance," Lomas writes. "There is little agreement on the desirable qualities of the finished product and little agreement on the means of bringing it about." There is not even enough in particular to the practice of psychotherapy to "single it out from other activities of living," or to elevate it to what might be considered a "specialized procedure." What Lomas is left with is remarkable for its vagueness. "Therapy at its best," he writes, "is the outcome of two people meeting regularly over a long period of time during which one of them, respecting the ordinary conventions of conversation and behavior, has tried to help the other feel better and to lead a better life."

Lomas's defense of therapy *at its best* perfectly illustrates just how far therapists have had to fall back in order to find some element of the practice they might commonly defend. Not being able to mount a shared defense of any theory of mental functioning, or mental illness, or any specific procedures or techniques (besides meeting regularly over a long period of time) has left therapists without much ground on which to regroup. Lomas's description of the heart of psychotherapy can hardly be seen as specific to the enterprise, for it might also describe many friendships and parent/child or student/teacher relationships. Therapy has no more special claim to such a definition of human interaction than a particular school of literature deserves praise for using verbs and subjects.*

---

*This retreat into vagueness has also been enlisted in the modern defenses of Freud. Current therapists who might not attempt to defend any of his individual notions or cases will still gladly ally themselves with his eminence. Lomas resorts to just such uncompelling praise. "Freud was foremost," he writes, "in getting two people into the same room to talk about the anguish of one of them without the intervention of religious dogma." Lomas insists that it was "Freud who taught us to confront the basic state of being of our patients," while at the same time admitting that Freud's conclusions were most often "dehumanizing" and "atomistic."

Lomas is not alone in putting up such a wafer-thin defense of talk therapy. Instead of making special claims for the tools and theories of their practice, modern-day practitioners and promoters of psychodynamic therapy increasingly market the experience with ever-vaguer promises. "The primary goal of psychodynamic psychotherapy is insight," write Michael Nichols and Thomas Paolino in their book *Basic Techniques of Psychodynamic Psychotherapy*, adding, "When the therapist intervenes, the ultimate purpose would always be to foster understanding. . . . [The therapist] tunnels through the darkness of ignorance . . . bringing meaning and purpose where none existed." "Insight," another prominent therapist agrees in a professional book on therapeutic technique, "has been extensively singled out not only to refer to a phenomenon specially applicable to the psychodynamic therapies . . . but also as the patient's ultimate aspiration."

James Bugental advocates in *The Art of Psychotherapy* "life-changing psychotherapy," which he defines as "the effort of patient and therapist to help the former examine the manner in which he has answered life's existential questions and to attempt to revise some of those answers."

Therapists pursue the illusive goal of "insight" by employing equally ill-defined techniques and approaches. Bugental's therapy "calls for continual attention to the patient's inner experiencing, and it recognizes that the prime instrument needed for that attention is the therapist's own subjectivity." For Lomas, the quality best employed by therapists is "wisdom," which, he notes, is defined as "the capacity for judging rightly in matters relating to life and conduct." For this task the therapist must also possess degrees of "confidence . . . integrity, incisiveness, courage, strength, compassion, humility, warmth, tact, patience," and, importantly, that most ephemeral of all personal qualities: "intuition." Bugental agrees that the key in deep therapy is the therapist's "intuitive sensing" of what is behind the patient's conscious awareness.

"Some people," George Weinberg explains in his book *The Heart of Psychotherapy*, "see habitually into the grain of human exchanges. They feel it when a bank teller looks at them with ruthless impersonality while he hands them the change. They seem to experience every high and low. Life is an adventure for them and every moment counts. When someone like this becomes a therapist, the sessions are like big dates in which everything said or done is important."

In sum, these writers present talk therapists as essentially superior humans whose superhuman personal qualities can create an experience for patients that draws the psychological poison from their systems through the use of the therapists' intuition. It is not surprising, from therapists' self-descriptions, that they often receive the devotion that shamans and other faith healers expect from their believers.

Those who pursue such broad defenses of therapy rarely follow their arguments to their logical end—which is that therapy, conceived in such ill-defined terms, cannot be defended beyond the empathetic powers of *individual* therapists and their self-proclaimed abilities as guides through the rough country that less fortunate human beings tread. To defend therapy as the subjective imparting of life-wisdom or intuition is to give up its defense as a technical expertise with a particular application to mental illness or theory of mental functioning. Although they seldom concede the point, defenders of talk therapy rarely attempt to argue that the special qualities they single out (intuition, wisdom, compassion) can be effectively taught in graduate school or during clinical internships.

However, despite their common acknowledgment that therapists lack any semblance of agreement over what therapy is or how it should be practiced, many defenders of therapy often continue to emphasize therapists' training and knowledge as if claiming they give them special status. Lomas, for instance, points out that a therapist has undergone "arduous training" and has familiarized himself or herself with the "ideas of those who have pioneered this particular kind of task." This seems to run counter to his admission that therapy cannot be uniformly defended in any of its particulars and that it would be "immodest and rash for a therapist to proclaim, or believe, that she possessed more wisdom than her patient."

It seems that these defenders of therapy are seeking, on the one hand, a status for therapists similar to the standing of those who have received specialized "arduous training" in areas such as medicine and the law. On the other hand, they are hesitant to defend any *specific* claim to knowledge, technique, or outcome. Instead, they display practitioners' therapeutic savoir faire and rely on the patient's often-glowing assessment of therapy as proof of the therapist's intuitive abilities. It doesn't take much reading between the lines of much current therapy literature to hear a certain pleading argument. "We are thoughtful, caring people," this argument goes. "Our patients tell us we are kind and intuitive and that they value their time with us. Shouldn't this be enough?"

The defense of therapy in such prayerful terms has a variety of other consequences. Chief among them is that if psychotherapy claims nothing in particular in terms of method or outcome, it is more difficult to charge it with any particular failure. As long as the goals of the therapist are as amorphous as "insight" and "wisdom," nearly all therapists can claim a measure of success—if they can bring their clients to believe that they have discovered something deep in their nature. After all, the claim to have achieved such "insight" requires only the therapist's and the patient's agreement.

This retreat into such vague guarantees protects psychodynamic therapy from another obvious criticism—that it lacks any promise of consistency in how the patient comes to view his or her life. If the same patient were to go to two different therapists (even of the same school of theory), could they reasonably expect to receive the same advice about how they view their lives? To our knowledge, no one who understands the current state of the therapy profession would venture a "yes" to this question. The above defenders of therapy certainly don't try to argue that different therapists could be expected to arrive at similar life narratives given the same patient. Intuition, which is often cited as the therapist's key tool, is by its nature a personal and subjective quality and cannot be expected to have similar results from one therapist to the next.

This is particularly true of the techniques of psychoanalysis and other psychodynamic therapies. No one, for example, attempts to make the case that a dream analyzed by two different therapists would invariably yield the same interpretation or insight. How could they be consistent when they are so candid about the associative nature of thinking (on the part of the *therapist* as well as the patient) that surrounds this activity? Lomas, for example, does not make the case that the dream interpretation relies on any particular knowledge of therapeutic theory; rather, it relies on the therapist's "intellectual flexibility."*

In Lomas's description, we hear the clear echoes of Freud's belief in psychic determinism—that is, his belief that the therapist's free associations during therapy were deeply and specifically illuminating of his or her patients' thoughts. Although few modern therapists publicly make the case that their associative thoughts surrounding the patient's communications are as specifically telling as Freud believed his associations were, therapists still employ the same method and still insist that their intuitions are inherently meaningful.

Nichols and Paolino's book on the basic techniques of psychotherapy describes the forming of an interpretation as a "creative art," which "requires a similar free-floating use of the imagination that, in patients, we call free association." To do this the therapist adopts a "playful, experimental attitude that generates the freedom of thought necessary to penetrate the unconscious mind." Given the same patient, therefore, it is impossible to imagine that such a "free-floating" imaginative process might yield the same set of interpretations from two different therapists.

*Similar descriptions of the psychodynamic therapist's mode of thinking can be found throughout the history of the discipline. As Ferenczi describes it, interpretations arise through a complicated mental recipe. "[The analyst] has to let the patient's free associations play upon him; simultaneously he lets his own fantasy get to work with the association material; from time to time he compares the new connections that arise with earlier results of the analysis . . . his mind swings continuously between empathy, self-observation, and making judgments."

If therapists had expected that their techniques might yield consistent outcomes, they could certainly have devised tests to prove the therapist's ability to come to the correct conclusion from a set of patient's communications. No psychodynamic therapist we have heard of, for example, provides a record of a client's dreams or free associations for other therapists to double-check. There is no movement for such a process because therapists know that confirmation is impossible. Dream analysis and free association and the other techniques of psychodynamic therapy are not defended on the grounds that they will take patients somewhere predictable and specific, but only that they will take them somewhere that will, in the end, appear meaningful.

Psychiatrist Toksoz Karasu's essay on the general principles of psychotherapy argues that insights can be curative *regardless of whether they hold any truth at all.** Lomas, in *Cultivating Intuition,* agrees that there is a growing realization that "it doesn't matter whether an interpretation is true or not," and that "as long as we enable the patient to go away with a more coherent picture of his life, we have done our job." While he is not altogether content with this conclusion and hopes "our interpretations stay as close to reality as is possible," he gives us no reason to expect that this "reality" might be the same from therapist to therapist given his description of the techniques of therapy.

The admission that the truth of a therapeutic insight is of little concern to therapists is often mentioned so quickly that the reader can fail to understand its full import. In their defense of therapy as a path to insight, talk therapists cannot get around the obvious problem that most patients expect the ultimate insights gained in therapy not only to be compelling but *true.* This is almost always a false expectation, for if the insights being discovered were discrete to a given patient and if the methods of therapy were a reliable method of finding those

---

*He quotes A. M. Ludwig, another well-known therapist, saying, "There is no necessary relationship between the truth or falseness of insight and therapeutic results."

insights, we should expect that different therapists could come to the same conclusions. Few psychodynamic therapists venture the argument for consistency in outcome because, by their own descriptions, similar outcomes are impossible. Every utterance in therapy can be taken in dozens of different directions (or ignored altogether), and there is no reasonable way to expect agreement between therapy encounters.

Despite these admissions by those at the top of the profession, it is not surprising that patients haven't given up on the idea that, in therapy, they are discovering the truth about their lives. This is for the simple reason that many therapists continue to claim that getting to the absolute truth of the patient's mental workings and motivations is a principal goal of therapy. Pop-psychology books such as Judith Herman's *Trauma and Recovery*, for instance, state repeatedly that what gets revealed in therapy should be the absolute truth of the patient's inner life. "From the outset, the therapist should place great emphasis on the importance of truth-telling," Herman writes. "The therapist should make clear that the truth is a goal constantly to be striven for."

The street-level therapists, who often acquire information from the same pop-psychology books patients read, seem to have ignored the effectiveness studies and the agreement at the top of the profession that therapists are selecting narratives and employing compelling myths as opposed to finding truths singular to their patients. That the most clearheaded in the field have given up these myths does not keep these street-level therapists from continuing to sell their theories to their patients with the assurance that they will lead to the truth.

"When a therapist encounters new, highly touted theories and methods . . ." writes Woolfolk, "the allure is palpable. . . . Feelings of inadequacy are replaced with those of confidence and power. Sometimes new therapeutic remedies are employed as panaceas. New ideas and theories can become dogma and bigotry." The history of talk therapy is one of wave after wave of such enthusiasms.

There is no indication that therapists routinely inform patients that conclusions drawn out of therapy are arbitrary to huge degrees. Some sophisticated patients may understand this, but it is also clear that a large segment of patients don't. Most patients assume that when therapists offer to reveal the truth of their inner lives, they are talking about something specific to their individual experience. If patients understood how many therapists rely on their intuition and "intellectual flexibility" to come to their conclusions, we suspect that many would be much less inclined to show up and pay for treatment.

. . .

The intellectual retreat of therapy from its claim to reveal the unassailable truths hidden inside patients' minds and unconscious has been followed recently by a scattering of the troops. Therapists have established cozy relationships with a variety of social movements and cultural trends. Indeed, over the recent history of the discipline, talk therapists have demonstrated that a theory of psychotherapy can grow up around any philosophy, the treatment principles differing to the extent that the philosophies differ.

A recent *Utne Reader* article "Ten Innovative Therapists Who Do More Than Just Talk" illustrated the ever-wider ground being claimed by therapists. It features William Doherty, for example, who believes that therapists should promote moral responsibility, and once that's accomplished, should "guide [patients] to take responsibility for their communities." Rhea Almeida, for her part, hopes to make everybody into a therapist. She recruits people she knows from her community to help run sessions that are part "consciousness-raising" and part therapy.

Don Campbell is featured in the article for promoting the healing use of music in therapy. He attests that music has often brought people out of comas and helped others uncover memories of abuse. "Your body is music," Campbell says. "You can learn to listen to it and heal yourself." Jaime Inclan, according to the magazine, treats "the deeply rooted, ongoing family trauma of migration." Kenneth Hardy fights "spiritual homelessness" by teaching us to be accepting and sensitive to the racial and cultural differences around us. Therapy is key to this process because it offers us "opportunities for greater connectedness and the healing of relationships strained, fractured, and fragmented by prejudice, injustice, and misunderstanding."

Barbara Goodrich-Dunn is featured for promoting "body-mind" therapy by helping organize the United States Association for Body Psychotherapy. She hopes to bring together such diverse disciplines as dance therapy, bioenergetics (which analyzes the body to assess psychological character), and core energetics (which combines "touch talk and spirituality" in therapy). Connecting the body to the mind is the best way, she says, to "find the inner wholeness we all are seeking, the ultimate goal of all therapy." And the magazine profiles Mark Epstein, who encourages therapists to bring meditation and Buddhist thinking into the therapy setting. "Buddhism teaches that spirituality means uncovering the depths and intensity of our own belief in the central importance of our self," he says. "It talks about how we can recover our ability to love—and isn't this what everyone comes to therapy for?"

Perhaps the most popular recent outgrowth of this search for new ground is the talk therapists' interest in the psychological care of their patients' spiritual life. In some regions of the United States, major mental health clinics openly tie their treatments to fundamentalist Christianity, while in California many schools of therapy have developed around mystical New Age beliefs. Any number of recent books take on spiritual or quasi-spiritual subjects, from angels and prayer to the transformative power of love and the human spirit.

As the empiricists pursuing a medical model continue to show a satisfying and steady progress in the curing and/or management of mental illness, there are some signs from the psychodynamic therapists of an increasing sense that their status as the primary interpreters of human behavior is in grave danger. This can be seen between the lines of pop-psychology texts. After reading a few of these books in a row, one begins to hear the tone of a nervous suitor trying to flatter and romance us, while saying nothing that might put us off. "Each of us is uniquely important in the cosmos," writes psychologist Andrew Canale in *Beyond Depression*. "We are God's celebration of the goodness of being. . . . Each of us is a mysterious picture of mysterious love." This is not to say that these books were written cynically to lure us into therapy (or convince us to buy the author's next book). Their sincerity is obvious—sometimes even comically so. They trip over themselves in their rush to offer us solace in sentences like these: "If the Voice of Aloneness and Another Alone both incarnate, if their strategies and goals seem radically different, if they both embody, wouldn't we expect them to be involved with our body-beings? How else could it be?" Statements like this communicate nothing outside of the authors' heartfelt desire to help.

In particular, some talk therapists have begun to invoke the word *soul*, often claiming to be its caretaker. Psychotherapist Thomas Moore has taken the lead in this growth area with his immensely popular books, including *Soul Mates* and *Care of the Soul*, the latter of which lingered on the *New York Times* best-seller list for more than forty-six weeks. "The great malady of the twentieth century, implicated in all of our troubles and affecting us individually and socially," Moore writes in his opening sentence of *Care of the Soul*, "is 'loss of soul.'" What this means is hard to say, for he admits to having trouble telling us what the soul might be. "It is impossible to define precisely what the soul is," he writes at one point, reminding us that "definition is an intellectual enterprise anyway." Despite this, Moore goes on for nearly three hundred pages, giving advice in respect to the soul, addressing everything from "coming to terms with depression" to "wedding spirituality to the soul."

In the wake of this success, other mental health professionals rushed to market with books that emphasize that attention to the soul is the best path to mental well-being. Psychiatrist Jean Shinoda Bolen, author of *Goddesses in Everywoman*, *Gods in Everyman*, and the *Tao of Psychology*, writes that the "loss of soul creates a void, an emptiness, that people fill with addictive behavior," and recommends that people "become aware of how deprived your life is of sources of joy, sources of beauty, and sources of creativity, which are all soul sources." As a mystic for whom the "inner and outer worlds are equally real," Bolen reminds us that the "decision to reconnect with your soul is similar to any choice to change things for the better, whether it's to stop smoking or to lose 20 pounds." Psychologist Joan Borysenko, author of *Minding the Body,* whose vision is to "reunite medicine, psychology, and spirituality in the service of personal and planetary healing," writes that nourishing the soul "means to become kinder, more compassionate, wiser and more loving. . . . When we nourish the soul we nourish God, increasing the abundance of the life that we can see . . . and the levels of life we don't see at all." Borysenko, for her part, does have a definition for the soul: It is nothing less than "the basic substance of the universe."

To some degree, at least, the new role of therapists as guardians of the spirit can be seen as the psychological equivalent of the "God in the gaps" argument employed by creationists—that is, as science further explains the workings of the universe, God's role is steadily pushed back into the gaps of current knowledge. If science can explain the evolution of a wing but not an eye, the eye can still be proclaimed God's handiwork. Similarly, talk therapy has been pushed more and more onto ground that science does not claim. It seems likely that some psychodynamic therapists have become champions of the soul not because this is where their theoretical endeavors have naturally led them but because they are increasingly being boxed out of other areas by biomedical advances. In these new areas they can find happy respite from the constant hounding by those who demand that they show the legitimacy of their theories. When the subject is love, the soul, or the human spirit, no one is likely to take you to task for what you conclude. Anyone's opinion on these subjects is more or less as valid as anyone else's, and all are equally immune to scientific challenge.

Of course, the psychodynamic therapists who have ventured into these areas would not agree that they have been shunted there by the steady progress of science. Regardless of how they became defenders of the human spirit and soul, from this position, talk therapists have gone back on the offensive, attacking the medical model of mental health healing for cruelly ignoring the deeper needs of their patients. Psychiatrist Peter R. Breggin, author of *Toxic Psychiatry* and *Talking Back to Prozac,* for example, attacks the medical model for taking "love" out of the treatment of patients. Love is the key ingredient to healing the mind, he says, yet "there's no mention of love as a healing principle in the commonly used textbooks of psychiatry." Only when a therapist expresses love (which is defined as "a joyful awareness characterized by treasuring, caring, mutuality, a desire for closeness, and empathy") can he or she create "a healing environment."

In a similar manner, Moore, in his soul books, consistently belittles secular and rational explorations of human troubles and their shortsighted emphasis on the patient's symptoms. His work is not about "curing, fixing, changing, adjusting or making healthy, and it isn't about some idea of perfection or even improvement." What Moore does with patients, he tells us, has nothing to do with the aspects of psychology that come out of "secular science." Instead, he practices "a sacred art," which helps people realize their "mystery-filled, star-born nature."

It's toward this sacred art that he hopes psychology will turn. There is considerable interest, he writes, in bridging the psychological and the spiritual. "Our very idea of what we are doing in our psychology has to be radically reimagined. Psychology and spirituality need to be seen as one. In my view, this new paradigm suggests the end of psychology as we have known it altogether because it is essentially modern, secular, and ego-centered. . . . Psychology is incomplete if it doesn't include spirituality and art in a fully integrative way." Bolen and many others agree. The best therapy is when therapist and patient meet "at soul level," where the therapist can listen with "an ear for prose poetry" and "evoke love."

Bugental also agrees that psychotherapy (along with Western culture) has for too long overemphasized the empirical approach to understanding human behavior. We must move, he argues, toward the subjective appreciation of experience. "The realm of the true subjective has been neglected by Western culture and science for at least three centuries," he writes. Fortunately, however, "this chauvinist prejudice is receding to such backwaters as academic positivism, political conservatism, or religious fundamentalism."

Casting themselves as defenders and protectors of the human spirit, many psychodynamic therapists are understandably upset about the new restrictions being placed on them by health insurance companies. The actuaries and accountants, who are now asking the profession to prove that their treatments are efficient and effective at curing patients' complaints, are portrayed as troglodytes—unenlightened and empathy-lacking cave dwellers who have none of their understanding of the complexity and depth of the human mind. The restrictions of managed care are anathema to many therapists. They tell indignant stories of being told by insurance companies that the number of sessions should be limited according to the severity or nature of the client's problem. Six sessions for the treatment of a patient is, of course, downright ridiculous if you believe the job of the therapist is to revive the human spirit or protect the soul. That managed care providers are far along in restricting payments to therapists is portrayed as something akin to the onset of a new dark ages.

Whether or not these books are helping enliven the human spirit is a subjective call. However, if mental health professionals are going to begin offering themselves up as champions of the soul, love, and the human spirit, then one should ask how good they are in this new role. Although we do not claim to have the answers, some questions are in order: Do these books do a better job than literature, for instance, in giving us a mirror in which to examine our own humanity? Do they do better than music and other forms of art in sharpening our perceptions and deepening our emotional complexity? And what about religion itself? Without offering ritual or community, can these spiritual and quasi-spiritual texts offer much of a replacement for traditional organized religion?

Unfortunately, these books are often such viscous stews of platitudes that it is very difficult to discern the thinking behind their recipes. Despite their popularity, these books seem designed primarily to give therapists maximum room for conceptual roaming. The logic is often circular, and their language vague and littered with coined terms. Breggin, who promotes "love" as the answer to all ills, asks us to avoid "thingness" and to push past "doingness" to achieve "beingness." What can we make of Moore's suggestion that caring for our soul means we should buy good linens, a special rug, and a nice teapot or that we might consider hiring therapists for buildings to care for the structure's "suffering"? And what can be said of psychologist John Gray, author of *Men Are from Mars, Women Are from Venus,* who reminds us to take our love vitamins—vitamin S for self-love, vitamin P for parental love, etc.? And what about Bugental, who advises in *The Art of the Psychotherapist* that for therapy to be nurturing of the "spirit and soul," the therapist and patient must search "without a map" for "the wild god, the god of mystery, the god in back of god"?

To judge these books for their logical merit seems mean-spirited and, moreover, beside the point. These writings are, for the most part, flamboyant offerings of grand and sincere beliefs. Besides, one might ask, do the authors even make a claim to rationality when presenting arguments about the need for more love in the world, the search for the wild god, or greater caring for the soul?

The answer is that many of them often *do* make a claim to scientific status, at least implicitly. Those who prefer belief over reason do not reject science, at least insofar as it can be used as a rhetorical tool, and there are few myths in our day that don't lay some claim to scientific legitimacy. Such efforts, as anthropologist Christopher P. Toumey writes, give believers in myth the "stories they want to hear with the moral meanings they require, and it sets them upon a stage of scientific sanctification decorated with test tubes . . . monographs, geological expeditions, . . . and secular credentials." In our time, myths must appear studied.

Purveyors of myth engage in a kind of parasitic feeding off of science. Therapists often selectively choose from findings while blithely disregarding any disconfirming results (often arguing that the findings of effectiveness studies, for example, are too narrowly focused to be applied to their holistic view of the patient). When cornered by the fact that their work lacks scientific backing, they may concede. We doubt, however, that they often make such an admission to the patient. Sadly, neither the therapists nor their various professional organizations seem willing to disabuse naive patients of their belief that therapy is a precise science. Therapists, after all, have only a few tools to use in their effort to solve the clients' problems—chief among them is leveraging the clients' belief in the therapists' abilities. This belief comes in large part from the therapists' claim to special scientific knowledge of the etiology of feelings and behavior. There is no advantage to the therapist in giving the patient a reason to wonder if he or she has bet on the wrong cure.

Therapists happily accept—and often demand—the special status the lay population awards those who have deep and scientifically based knowledge. At the same time, psychodynamic therapists disdain the operational limitations any respectable set of scientists impose on themselves, including, most importantly, safeguards against overgeneralization from hunches and anecdotal observation.

Therapists try to maintain the best of two worlds: enjoying the status of scientists while practicing the free-roaming thinking of philosophers or priests. When their methods are challenged scientifically, modern talk therapists do a rhetorical sidestep, claiming that the challenger has missed the point. They are not narrow-minded scientists, they argue, and they should not be judged by scientific standards. They are, after all, protectors of the human spirit and soul.

CHAPTER SEVEN

Why Patients Believe

To what extent, we might ask, should the therapist woo her patients? Would they have the confidence to put themselves in her hands if they did not, at least at the beginning, have an exaggerated notion of her powers? The history of healing reveals a long-established conviction that it is necessary to seduce the patient into false beliefs. . . . It would be foolish to make a show of all [the therapist's] failings and incompetencies.

—PETER LOMAS,
Cultivating Intuition:
An Introduction to Psychotherapy

Psychodynamic psychotherapists usually duck the thorny issue of the patient's suggestibility by painting a comic picture of how a therapist might try to influence a patient's beliefs. They consider suggestion a situation in which therapists simply insist on their interpretations. No good therapist would do this, and besides, they argue, the patient would rebel. While the history of psychodynamic therapy clearly shows that many therapists did employ just such dogmatic insistence, it is true that this is the least often used (and least effective) type of influence. Even when such tactics induce the patient to verbally agree with the therapist's conclusion, they are not very effective in producing internalized acceptance.

Freud provides the clearest cautionary tale in the use of repeated insistence as a form of suggestion. The record of his early therapeutic methods, critiqued in our earlier book and by others, shows clearly that Freud bullied and harassed his patients into the belief that they had experienced early childhood molestation.* As he reports, he encouraged therapists to "boldly demand confirmation of our suspicions from the patient. We must not be led astray by initial denials. If we keep firmly to what we have inferred, we shall in the end conquer every resistance by emphasizing the unshakable nature of our convictions."

Freud learned early in his career the cost of such strong-arming: His practice was notorious for the defections of patients who broke off treatment when they faced his bold demands for confirmation of his theories. Dogmatic insistence is the crudest and *least effective* form of suggestion.

Because such insistence is indeed likely to raise red flags in all but the most vulnerable patients, it is in a way the least troubling form of suggestion. It is, however, the specter that therapists conjure when they argue that they never employ suggestive methods. If therapists were truly interested in addressing the problem of suggestion, they could begin by looking up the word in the dictionary. The *Random House Dictionary* defines it in part as: "The process of inducing thought or action, *without* resorting to techniques of persuasion or giving rise to reflection, in such a way as to produce an uncritical response." This definition implies a much more interesting challenge to talk therapy, for it identifies the key aspects of suggestion as those that happen in ways that are not likely to be noticed or provoke critical thinking by the patient. This is the sort of suggestive process that Freud learned and advocated later in his career. He advised that therapists should avoid making interpretations until they have built the structure on which the interpretations will hang—that is, they should slowly build evidence toward a conclusion *before* that conclusion is openly suggested to the client.

When we act without obvious and direct compulsion, con-

---

*He later claimed that the stories of molestation that he had demanded from his patients were actually their childhood fantasies. It was on this shaky ground that he founded psychoanalysis.

strained only by the social conventions of a situation, we typically maintain the illusion that we are acting with total freedom
and that the choices we make reflect only our internal values and
desires. The more subtle the pressures brought to bear, the more
likely we are to assume that we are in control of our own behavior. Because the process of slowly building evidence is not overtly
coercive but rather depends on the patients' willingness to carry
out their role, the conditions are optimal for patients to accept
and internalize the life stories they and the practitioners create.

Modern-day therapists, as Freud eventually recommended, do
not spring interpretations on patients but rather nudge the therapy conversation toward conclusions without openly telling
patients where they are going. "Only when the 'truth' takes on
an air of inevitability does an interpretation do its work," writes
psychodynamic psychotherapist Harold Boris. "Only insofar
as the patient and therapist have an experience in common to
advert to can either feel convinced."

By revealing the interpretation only after the evidentiary
framework has been completed, the therapist is much more
likely to convince the patient of the correctness of the therapist's
theory. That this strategy is less crude and obvious than outright
insistence does not make it any less a form of manipulation. In
fact, this approach is more likely to make the patient a loyal
believer while leaving him unaware of the process of influence
that brought him into line with the therapist's assumptions.

Freud clearly perceived that the argument that his psychoanalysis was awash with techniques of suggestion had the potential to
undermine the entire psychodynamic enterprise. He knew that
the most devastating critique of his practice was that patients
were not uncovering genuine fantasies or memories from their
childhoods but rather only adopting and reflecting back at him
his own perverse theories. He admitted as much, saying, "Our
opponents believe . . . that we have 'talked' the patients into
everything relating to the importance of sexual experiences . . .
this is the objection that is most often raised against psychoanalysis. . . . If it were justified, psychoanalysis would be nothing

more than a particularly well-disguised and particularly effective form of suggestive treatment and we should have to attach little weight to all that it tells us about what influences our lives, the dynamics of the mind or the unconscious."

Freud, of course, flatly dismissed this possibility, even when he was using the most ham-fisted methods of coercion on his bewildered patients. Although his phrasing often implies careful consideration of the problem, his denials were dogmatic. "The danger of our leading a patient astray by suggestion, by persuading him to accept things which we ourselves believe but which he ought not to, has certainly been enormously exaggerated. An analyst would have had to behave very incorrectly before such a misfortune could overtake him; above all, he would have to blame himself for not allowing his patients to have their say. I can assert without boasting that such an abuse of 'suggestion' has never occurred in my practice."

Freud is simply lying about his use of suggestion. His own admissions, as well as the other evidence of his brutal manipulation of his patients, leave no other possible conclusion. However, he was quite right about the impact a full understanding of suggestion would have on psychoanalysis and subsequent psychodynamic psychotherapies. It does lead us to conclude that the techniques are "nothing more than a particularly well-disguised and particularly effective form of suggestive treatment."

In addition to his belief in psychic determinism (examined in chapter two), Freud believed he had another silver bullet that could defeat this criticism of his practice. He simply declared that patients would never accept the therapist's assumptions unless those assumptions contained some amount of truth. "Conflicts will only be successfully resolved and his resistances overcome if the anticipatory ideas [the patient is] given tally with what is real in him. Whatever in the doctor's conjectures is inaccurate drops out in the course of the analysis; it has to be withdrawn and replaced by something more correct."*

*For Freud, this was a particularly spurious argument because of his propensity to chalk up any denial on the patient's part as "resistance," which he scored as *proof* of that inference—that is, resistance was not simply something to be gotten around but evidence that

Modern-day denials of the problem of suggestion have not progressed much farther than this exact tactic. Despite a wealth of evidence that people can be led to believe all manner of ridiculous things during therapy, therapists continue to insist that only *valid* interpretations will stick in the patient's mind. Listen, for instance, to Paul Wachtel defend therapy in his 1993 book, *Therapeutic Communication*: "[T]he therapist's comments . . . can easily be rejected if they are read as alien. And they are likely to be experienced as alien if they do not in fact resonate with some aspects of the patient's own aspirations, values, or vision." Or listen to Judith Herman, writing with a coauthor in her 1993 paper in the *Harvard Mental Health Letter*: "Therapists often make suggestions, but patients will respond only when those suggestions resonate with their own feelings and experiences."

There are a number of flaws in this "tally" argument. First of all, the demoralized people who seek out therapy are the least likely population to challenge the therapists' interpretations. Most people who seek therapy are at the least confused and at worst mentally ill, and they have sought the help of a talk therapist because they believe that these practitioners have some answers to their dilemmas. For this reason they seem unlikely to be in the position to "easily reject" the therapists' speculations or guidance toward certain conclusions. This is particularly true if the patient is in the thrall of the therapist because he perceives her as brimming with the psychodynamic wisdom of our age. The idea that a patient in such a vulnerable position will always be able to speak up and tell the esteemed therapist when the inferences are off course is wishful thinking. Patients, as we have argued, often believe they are seeing the equivalent

---

he was on the correct path. As Kenneth S. Bowers and Peter Farvolden wrote in the *Psychological Bulletin*: "It often seems that the more strongly his patients resisted, the more evidence it was that his theory and interpretation of the patients' difficulties were correct, and the more he pressed his patients to accept them. In other words, both resistance and acquiescence to them were accepted as validating his emerging theories. The upshot is that it was impossible for patients to say anything that could possibly disconfirm Freud's theory about why they were distressed . . . this of course puts psychoanalysis out of the reach of science."

of a medical doctor, whose knowledge is so extensive that dismissing his or her conclusions out of hand would be foolhardy.

In addition, the fact that the therapist largely selects the details to be focused on during therapy (from the millions of feelings, memories, and behaviors that make up a patient's history) dramatically increases the likelihood that the explanation for the behavior will appear to "tally" in the patient's mind.

The tally argument has other flaws as well. It relies on the notion that the patient knows *when* a therapist has made an interpretation. In actual practice, there rarely is such a moment. As we have seen, therapy is a process by which the therapist slowly moves the patient toward conclusions that the therapist's theoretical background has led him or her to suspect. The eventual cause-and-effect interpretation can be present long before it is ever spoken. The questions the therapist asks, the topics chosen for discussion, the choice of which information is repeated and which is ignored can all embody, and subtly steer the patient toward, the eventual content of the therapist's interpretation. This process is driven by the therapist and the patient who are searching for the thread connecting the therapist's questions and comments.

During this process the clear boundary between whose opinion is whose can be utterly lost. As Wachtel describes: "What is the therapist's viewpoint and what is the patient's is for the moment partially obscured." He goes on to point out how the therapist uses this blurring to his or her advantage in placing a notion in the patient's head. This technique can be used "to insert a new idea into the patient's inner dialogue, to encourage the patient to adopt a perspective from the therapist, to identify with a different point of view that, it is hoped, will be liberating." This is a good description of the subtler form of suggestion.

Kenneth Bowers, in a well-known paper, similarly emphasized "the importance of therapeutic maneuvers that [are] sufficient to establish some kind of therapeutic control over the patient's behavior, while being sufficiently subtle to *escape being viewed by the patient as influence attempts*" (italics added).

These descriptions—by therapists themselves—obviously run counter to the assertion that the patient can easily reject a therapist's influence. If the therapist successfully weaves his or her interpretation into the discussion such that the patient doesn't even realize where the idea came from, the patient is hardly likely to identify it as "alien," and put a stop to the process.

But there is more import to this blurring effect than these therapists admit. Within the therapeutic dialogue, the therapist is in no way immune to this dynamic, but can be just as unaware as the patient is to where an idea originated. The therapist is looking for theoretical themes at the same time that the patient is trying to figure out what sorts of thoughts, feelings, and memories are important to the therapy process. Therefore, evidence that seems to point to one of the therapist's conclusions is likely to appear to the therapist as if it sprang out of the dialogue. The therapist is predicting and, in all likelihood, the patient is expecting such themes as well. Once one possible theory comes into play, it can quickly build momentum. The brain is considerably better at stacking evidence to confirm patterns than it is at recognizing and giving appropriate weight to information that falls outside of a pattern. Because therapists get to pick and choose what is treated as important, it is unlikely that they would run across a patient with whom they couldn't employ their favorite psychodynamic theory.

It is likely that narrative threads have some momentum simply due to the fact that they have found their way into the therapy discussion. How these narratives evolve in therapy from a possible theory about a behavior to a believed-in theory is a slow and subtle bridging of the gaps between the therapist's beliefs about behavior and information from the client's experience. So organic is this process, it is entirely possible that the therapist and patient can create a fictional narrative or set of beliefs about a client's life without either of them having the understanding that they did so intentionally. The result of this process, however, can be that the story or beliefs created would simply appear to both the therapist and the patient, in hindsight, to be inevitable—nothing less than the distilled truth.

When one considers the therapist's input and interpretations not as punctuations to the patient's communications but as the stimulus that directs the patient's attention toward a hypothesis, dismissing the idea that suggestion is the central element of therapy becomes more difficult. Whether the therapist or the patient introduces an idea is, in the end, much less important than how the process of therapy continually stokes and builds the sense of certainty. "Throughout the therapeutic process . . . the therapist reexplores and refines his diagnosis by carefully observing the patient's interactions," writes Karasu. This is true; however, the therapist is also constantly influencing what he or she is observing. Unless the patient refuses the therapist's hypothesis when it is only hinted at (in which case he or she is likely to be labeled "in denial"), the idea that the patient's problems stem from a given source is likely to gain some momentum.

The interpretations that patients come to believe in therapy are usually cause-and-effect theories linking events in their past with the difficulties that brought them to therapy. Social scientists know that the most likely reason people will be wrong in their cause-and-effect reasoning is because they incorrectly apply a prior belief to a new situation. This is particularly true if, as Lynn Arnoult and Craig Anderson wrote in a paper on this phenomenon, a preheld causal belief is "strongly held, ego involving . . . or when a justifiable rationale for selectively valuing and devaluing new information is available." Therapists and their credulous patients are particularly vulnerable to this bias. As Arnoult and Anderson note, therapeutic theoretical approaches are just such "statements of cause-effect relations." Because of this, there is a grave "danger . . . that causal explanations consistent with therapists' own orientation will be so readily accepted that other possibilities are given insufficient consideration."

Once this bias has come into play in selecting a possible cause-and-effect narrative, other biases skew the process and cement the mistake. First, finding an applicable causal theory usually cuts short the process of considering other explanations. In experiments on this effect, subjects quickly picked up on and adopted the first causal theory hinted at by the setting of the experiment or by the testers. Alternative explanations were quickly abandoned and new alternative explanations no longer sought. Our desire to hold on to a causal theory leads us to selectively choose the information that seems to confirm it while dismissing or downplaying the information that would contradict it.

This effect is especially powerful when those cause-and-effect theories are of a social impression or a self-assessment. In a statement that should be printed on the front cover of next year's American Psychological Association convention program, Arnoult and Anderson write that "in particular, [research] showed that beliefs about one's own or others' social perceptiveness can survive even the total discrediting of the evidential base that gave rise to those beliefs."

It would be hard to imagine a process more prone to natural human biases than psychodynamic psychotherapy. The therapist and often the patient come into the treatment setting ready to apply a list of causal theories. This is aggravated by the fact that many therapists appear to focus on increasingly narrow sets of causal theories over the course of their careers. Because, as we've argued, they often believe they find the evidence for the causal theory they suspect in a given patient, it makes sense that they are more and more likely to jump to this same conclusion with subsequent patients.

"If such errors were easily corrected by exposure to specific case data," Arnoult and Anderson write of therapy, "then we would have somewhat less reason for concern. However, a large body of work from a variety of areas of psychology demonstrates that such expectation-based errors are extremely difficult to correct . . . the initial guess may get fixed and other information totally ignored."

Despite arguments to the contrary, patients are not in a position to play ombudsman in this process. They can't be expected to tell the expert therapist when therapy is off-course for the obvious reason that they themselves are engaged in the work of building evidence for the possible causal theory in question. Unless the patient has walked out on the therapist (in which case the process stops), he or she likely shares some belief that the therapy is on the right track. The patient is boxed out of dissenting at both ends of the process. In the beginning, the patient may not even realize that a therapist's theory has been introduced. By the end of the process, the patient is just as invested in the explanation as the therapist, for he or she has helped to find and order the evidence that seems to confirm the therapy's conclusion.

Psychodynamically oriented case reports illustrate how the therapist's interpretations of the client's behavior relies entirely on the theoretical assumptions the therapist brings into the session. The client's communications are sifted for evidence of these previously held theories. This process nearly always requires a narrowing of the patient's life narrative so that details that don't fit the story are ignored or not revisited. It is through this same process that the patient becomes convinced of the validity of the therapist's theory.

A brief example of a therapist's interpretation might illustrate the point. Several years into therapy, a thirty-six-year-old female patient of Harold Boris related numerous memories of her life. She told Boris how she examined herself naked in a mirror at age six. At the same age, she remembered her parents taking a trip to Europe, leaving her in the care of a nurse, while she was sick with the measles and bothered by constipation. She then told Boris of some preadolescent sexual play she engaged in with a young male friend and her sister, which she enjoyed at the time but felt bad about later. She also related some adolescent sexual experiences that she enjoyed except when her breasts were touched. She told Boris as well that she currently had sex with men but could have an orgasm only through masturbation. Boris explains that these memories were related over months in no particular order.*

---

*Boris notes that the scattered way in which the patient revealed these critical pieces of her past was a clear "hostile attack" on his deductive powers.

He begins his interpretation by considering the constipation his patient experienced when her parents left her with the nurse. "Whether she was defying the nurse, or holding on to her parents, or both, of course, matters, as does the question of earlier struggles with ownership and loss," he writes. "But of no less moment is the series of symbolic transformations: Breast=feces=penis=stay=come."

From this bizarre equation he goes on to shape his interpretation: "This material . . . tells a story of yearning, defect, fury, and a love in danger of being obliterated by envy. The material may be thought to say: Once I discovered I did not have a penis, I soothed my anguish first by believing the condition was temporary, then by forgetting the fact. Finally I had almost to rediscover it. Now all I want is to return to the days when there were no differences, and to feel alive and all of a piece and one of the guys."

As proof that his interpretation was on the right track, he notes: "An interpretation along those lines might (in fact did) produce a flock of additional memories, further elaboration of the patient's current experience." The patient, Boris notes, was left with "a sense of the absolute rightness of the construction of the child's experience to the grown-up patient."

Clearly there is a long list of psychodynamic assumptions layered into this interpretation, including:

- The belief that childhood and adolescent sexual experiences are more important than most other experiences in determining adult mental well-being.
- That not having a penis might be of deep psychological importance to a young girl.
- That all things scatological and sexual interrelate in deeply meaningful ways.

The therapist, it would seem, held the assumptions prior to the beginning of therapy with this patient. Without psychodynamic logic to justify his interpretation, the ties between his evidence and his conclusion are not compelling. We are left to wonder about the thousands of other details, memories, and feelings that surely also came up during the dozens of hours of therapy. What of them?

The inferential logic is so clearly backward, running as it does from theory to evidence, that Boris's patient must also have come to believe in these psychodynamic assumptions in order for her to become convinced of the "absolute rightness" of his interpretation. This convincing may have happened during therapy, with Boris layering his theoretical assumptions into the background of their conversation in such a way that they never came under direct scrutiny. It is also quite possible that the patient came into therapy fully expecting that treatment would lead to such conclusions. Without this shared agreement, we would suggest, the connections drawn by the therapist would be manifestly ridiculous.

In the end, as Boris implies, it is the patient's belief that the evidence from her life fits the theory that is taken as proof of the latter's validity. This sort of conclusion pervades the case reports in the psychodynamic literature. While some improvement in the patient's symptoms is usually reported at the very end of the story, that change is often the denouement to the tale. The case study does not turn at the dramatic moment when the symptom abates (as it might in a story of a medical cure) but at the point when the patient expresses belief in the therapist's insight into the cause of her problems.

CHAPTER EIGHT

Why Therapists Believe

I've observed a curious phenomenon in the careers of many therapists while they are undertaking to build a private practice. There comes a time when their following seems secure. . . . It seems at that very instant that patients sense the change. The therapist looks less needy, he's arrived. Suddenly the referrals start coming in from everywhere.

—GEORGE WEINBERG,
The Heart of Psychotherapy

A good deal has been written about how psychotherapy can influence the patient. There is another equally important dynamic in the therapy encounter that gets less attention: the manner in which the patient's eventual belief in the insights of therapy inevitably feeds back into the therapist's confidence, self-conception, and eagerness to promote his or her theories and techniques. To understand why generation after generation of therapists becomes so devoted and proud of its theories, one must first understand how the therapist's confidence is enhanced by the patient's eventual conversion during therapy. It is, after all, the therapist's belief in the power of therapy—as much as the patient's—that motivates individual practitioners and drives the field onward.

Although the power relation between the seemingly authoritative therapist and the untutored patient is profoundly uneven, in one sense the influence consequences are an even trade-off. When therapists offer an intuitive speculation to

171

compliant patients, they are likely to find not only genial acceptance but the patients reporting feelings, thoughts, and dream material consistent with the gist of the therapists' intuition. The therapists come to believe that their inspired guess was right on target, thus confirming their suspicion of their own insightfulness. The upward spiral created when a patient expresses confidence in a therapist's intuition opens a door for the practitioner to become more daring, sweeping, and profound in his or her pronouncements about the patient's psychological history.

The confidence the therapist develops is the lifeblood of talk therapy. As the quote at the beginning of this chapter indicates, the therapist who is confident will be the therapist who succeeds. A subtle and continual back-and-forth between the patient and the therapist lies behind this outcome. A patient expresses confidence in the therapist, who is inspired to act more confidently, which further raises the patient's respect for the therapist and hope for a good outcome.

Therapists' ability to achieve even a marginal placebo effect clearly requires that they be confident enough in their own abilities to raise clients' beliefs that the therapy is a valid treatment. This belief, as we have argued previously, can have the effect of engendering hope in the patient and, at least temporarily, relieving mild demoralization. As we have argued, there are multiple factors (therapists' social status, the demand characteristics of the therapy encounter, the demoralized state of patients at the beginning of treatment) that increase the likelihood that patients will come to believe and respect their therapists.

Self-proclaimed healers of all sorts can decrease a subject's sense of demoralization and anxiety even in the face of diseases they cannot hope to cure. Writing about psychic healers, psychology professor Nicholas Humphrey notes that "many kinds of illness, of the body as well as the mind, can be influenced by the patient's hopes and expectation and thus by the suggestions given him by an authority figure whom he trusts." The chronic stiffness or general pain of arthritis, for instance, can temporarily be overwhelmed by the adrenaline and excitement of believing one has received a miracle cure. While this is not a long-term remedy, the momentary effect can be dramatic. The level of the subject's belief in the cure, which is directly related to the confidence of the healer, is the critical factor in the process.

Humphrey argues that the faith healer is as influenced by this process as the subject. "The consequence is that a kind of virtuous circle can be established," continues Humphrey. "Success in bringing about a cure feeds back to the healer, boosting both his image in the eyes of the world and his image of himself. And thereafter nothing succeeds like more success. The process must of course be launched in some way. . . . But all that this requires is that there should already be some small reason—however unsubstantiated—why people should consider the healer a special person."

These "virtuous circles," however, can quickly spin out of control when healers pretend to be able to accomplish more than the marginal good they can affect. It is a common error to believe that the connections we perceive are deeper and more meaningful than they are. Such an assumption allows us to simplify a world that is far too complex to be easily understood or understood in all its particulars. Psychics, for example, should not be dismissed as con artists until one understands the all-too-common logical illusion they are perpetrating on themselves. Many psychics, perhaps most, wish to believe in their extrasensory powers because (like those who believe *in* psychics) they make the common mistake of remembering the times when their predictions were correct and overlooking the number of times they were wrong.

This is understandable, for the moments when psychics are accurate can be, for both the psychic and the observer, quite awe-inspiring. While the witness, at such moments, asks himself, "How could he have known if he didn't have paranormal powers?" the psychic may be asking a similar question, "How could I have known if I *wasn't* psychic?" The self-proclaimed seer (especially one who wants to believe in his or her own extrasensory abilities) has no guaranteed immunity to the infectious wonderment of such coincidences.

The memory of such moments may inspire the confidence in the psychic to suffer through the next set of incorrect guesses until the next breathtakingly accurate insight. The more confidence psychics have in their powers, the more guesses they will venture and the more times they will be accurate. This does not mean that such psychics are more *likely* to be accurate than anyone else, only that they are making more guesses. Even when psychics employ suspect methods to increase the chances of hits (such as expressing overly general insights or incorporating into their psychic visions information they have otherwise obtained about their subjects), it is still likely that many psychics believe they possess supernatural power. The devotion and respectful awe they receive when they are correct is simply too flattering to dismiss—and in accepting this praise, belief in their own supernatural abilities can be often internalized.

Like psychics, therapists' belief in their intuition and powers of insight feeds directly off the patients' belief. Patients' end-of-therapy testimony that therapists have seen through to the very center of their behavior and mental life is a heady thing to hear. It is not surprising that therapists do not critically examine all the factors that lead patients to such a flattering conclusion, but rather takes the patients' testimony as prima facia evidence of the therapy's success and the power of their own healing abilities.

The confidence-building process that goes on between therapists and patients is more troubling than the back-and-forth reinforcement that goes on between psychics and their subjects. While psychics rely on luck, intuition, and a little trickery to impress their clients with accurate visions, therapists can create or build the very evidence that will appear to confirm their insights. While psychics rather lamely employ strategies such as making their predictions overly general, therapists' methods are much more time consuming and complex. As we have argued, the therapist's method of exploring the patient's unconscious doubles as a way of manufacturing confirmation of the therapist's conclusions. The same process by which psychodynamic therapists perceive the workings of patients' thoughts and behaviors is also the process by which patients (who are already somewhat credulous because of their very participation) become convinced of the accuracy of the therapists' insights. Because therapists can manufacture the moments when they appear correct, they can increase the likelihood that their clients will believe their insightful powers. This, in turn, fuels the therapist's confidence to continue the process.

This back-and-forth confidence building is immensely helped by the fact that patients deeply hope that therapists will be able to see into their thoughts and motivations. The demoralization that accompanies most patients as they enter therapy often comes with a feeling of isolation, of being trapped and confused by their own thoughts and life circumstances. This desire of the patient to believe in the therapist's abilities is similar to the hopes of those seeking counsel with psychics. Any evidence of the healer's powers is quickly greeted with enthusiasm. Jeffrey Masson, in his book *Final Analysis,* describes this behavior from both sides of the couch. During his training therapy he writes of his analyst, "I desperately *needed* for him to be the man he claimed he was, the man I wanted him to be. . . . I had to believe that Schiffer was wise and kind and good and selfless, because only if he was would I benefit from the analysis. . . . It was in my own interest to maintain the delusion." Later, Masson experienced the other end of this interaction as a therapist: "An analysis, even a psychotherapy, could not succeed, I knew, if the situation was democratic and egalitarian. My patients were looking to *me* for answers. They would not welcome a shrug of ignorance and a question in return. And there was a constant push for me to be wise."

The process by which therapists come to believe in their wisdom is a simple combination of common human weaknesses. The patient's desire to be helped by a powerful healer dovetails with the healer's desire to be helpful and to be the person the patient wants to see. This process can be benign or marginally effective, temporarily relieving minor demoralization (although this often comes at a greater cost of time and resources than might be reasonably justifiable). A greater problem arises, however, when the confidence-building process spins out of control.

The modest placebo effect achieved by psychic healers, for instance, is dwarfed by the number of times they have reached beyond their abilities and, for example, given their customers false hopes of dramatic cures to serious illnesses. It is not surprising that psychics overreach the limits of their modest powers to give temporary hope, for there is nothing in the theoretical framework of fortune telling or faith healing that might incline healers to limit their practice to banal predictions or the momentary relief of minor ailments. If psychics truly believe in their power to channel healing energy or direct miracles from God, why wouldn't they believe that they had the power to stop the course of cancer or heal a spinal injury as well as "curing" headaches and joint pain? If something truly magical is going on, there is no reason to believe that such magic would have limited applications. The "virtuous circle," by which Humphrey describes the healer's increase in confidence, all but guarantees that psychics as well will eventually overstep the marginal good they can accomplish and falsely promise cures for diseases they have no hope of bringing about.

The extent to which healers of any sort understand their personal limits to help patients is exactly the extent to which they accurately understand the limits of their techniques. While there is a growing knowledge of the limits of talk therapy at the top of the profession, the psychodynamic schools are, as usual, the hold-outs. Although they have largely stopped promising to cure schizophrenics, they continue to assert more vague promises: to re-create patients' lives; to reveal their inner children; to expose the workings of their psyches; to reveal the horrible truths hidden in their childhoods; to release their imprisoned "souls"; etc. Like psychics, psychodynamic therapists have no agreement on *what they can't do,* and therefore therapists' steadily increasing confidence in their own powers make it likely that they will eventually overestimate the change they can bring about.

The self-confirming process of therapy has a cumulative effect on the therapist both within the work with each individual patient and within the therapist's career. How far from reality can this cycle of confidence building take the therapist's self-assessment? Very recent history tells us that the sky is the limit. In the late 1980s, for example, dozens of prominent psychiatrists, psychologists, and therapists announced that they had discovered, through therapy encounters with patients, a worldwide network of satanic cults that had existed for centuries and had killed thousands with impunity. The ridiculousness of these stories* is only the beginning of what is amazing about them. More telling, for our purposes here, is the dramatic role these therapists claimed for themselves in the heroic battle against these evil organizations. University of Utah psychologist Corey Hammond, in a lecture to other practitioners, claimed to know that this network of satanic cults was intent on global domination. These therapists, by exposing this network of cults, quite literally saw themselves as saving the world.

How did they come to such inflated self-assessments? Interviews with therapy patients suggest that they were responding to the confidence expressed in them by their patients during therapy. These therapists did not brazenly claim the role of hero-of-the-world in one swoop; rather, their self-conception slowly grew out of the confidence their patients expressed in them. Because of the constant reinforcement of their patients' devotion, these therapists became so confident in their conclusions that they proudly brought their startling findings before the general public. They no doubt hoped that everyone would come to see them, as their patients had, as heroic doctors exposing evil. The general public and the press, however, eventually became skeptical. In terms of the cycle of confidence

---

*Every bad guy on the planet was implicated in this fantasy. Psychiatrists such as Bennett Braun publicly implicated the Ku Klux Klan and "Nazis" as key organizations behind the international satanic conspiracy. Psychiatrist Colin Ross pointed a finger at the CIA. Corey Hammond, another prominent promoter of the scare, said that the Mafia and the producers of Hollywood horror films were also involved. For a detailed explanation of these claims, see the authors' previous book, *Making Monsters: False Memories, Psychotherapy, and Sexual Hysteria.*

building that the therapist gets subjected to, it is hard to imagine a more outrageous cautionary tale than the story of these misguided Satan hunters.*

Such a dramatic story of therapeutic overconfidence is not merely an aberration in an otherwise healthy discipline. It is, rather, an indicator of the lengths to which the seductive process of practicing psychotherapy can mislead the therapist. Other psychodynamic therapists who believe they are revealing the true explanation of their patients' behavior through the exposing of their unconscious forces are also influenced by their patients' deference and trust in their powers. Therapists believe they can see into their patients' unconscious, in short, at least partially because their patients believe they can do this. From the therapists' point of view, the evidence of their abilities coming from the testimony of patient after patient can leave little doubt in their minds that their procedures are valid and that they are the brave and insightful healers their patients expect them to be.

Because psychodynamic therapists neither accept theoretical limits to the power of their technique nor require objective proof of their effects, it is extremely unlikely that they will ever step back and examine the mistakes that might have misled the process. And, indeed, there is precious little record in the literature of therapists apologizing for previous mistakes after a theory or technique has proven ineffective or fallen out of vogue. Neither the profession nor those who have promoted psychodynamic cures for everything from schizophrenia to asthma, for example, have gone out of their way to publicly admit they were wrong.

This unwillingness to admit mistakes is not surprising, for even scientists with pet theories tend to stick with them even in light of compelling disconfirming evidence. But even though

---

*Recent years, in fact, have provided another equally outrageous example. Harvard psychiatrist John Mack's belief that, through his patients, he has tapped into the friendly communications from extraterrestrial creatures is certainly as grand a fantasy as his colleagues' satanic cult theories. Here again, we find a prominent mental health professional publicly attesting that he has discovered information critical to saving the planet.

individual scientists cannot be expected to turn on a theoretical dime and admit their long-held mistaken assumptions, it can be expected of scientific disciplines at large to be critical of new and old theories alike and to quickly expose at least the grosser mistakes.

Psychodynamic therapists, however, rarely hold each other to account for the simple reason that they all are relying on equally prayerful assumptions and using equally ineffective techniques. Even when their mistakes are brought to light, therapists are reluctant to relinquish their pet theories. Witness again the scores of therapists who pursued their satanic cult theories, often at the expense of their patients' well-being. In the half dozen years since their theories have been exposed to the public, court cases have been brought against dozens of them by disillusioned former patients who had been led to believe they had uncovered repressed memories of satanic cult abuse. Many of these cases have exposed the grossest therapeutic malpractice and have resulted in multimillion-dollar damage awards for the plaintiffs. Even with such public and outrageous proof of misconduct, none of these therapists has come forward with a public admission that he or she had used a technique that caused patients to form beliefs that confirmed the therapists' mistaken assumptions. They have never admitted to the damage done to their patients. Rather, these therapists continue to attest that they are the brave healers their patients once believed them to be. Such a grand self-assessment, once achieved, is difficult to surrender.

In *Why People Believe Weird Things: Pseudoscience, Superstition, and Other Confusions of Our Time,* Michael Shermer conveniently lists twenty-five fallacies of thinking, nearly all of which are directly applicable to the mistakes of the psychodynamic approach to therapy. Therapists interested in evaluating the possibility that they have deceived themselves may want to ask the following questions based on Shermer's list.

Have they, for example, made the classic scientific mistake of failing to understand how their theories influence their observations—that is, how, during therapy, they change the patient's beliefs? Have they examined how their techniques might create the expected results? Further, have they fallen prey to the central mistakes of pseudoscientific thinking, which are mistaking anecdote for data, jargon for scientific language, and rumor for reality? Have they rationalized their theories' failures or employed post hoc reasoning to draw theories of causation? Have they covered holes in their theories through the use of emotional language, false analogies, or grand metaphors? Have they employed ad hominem attacks on critics to counter those critics' arguments? Have they overrelied on the unsupported proclamations of authority figures in the field? And have they ignored or not sought evidence that disproves their theories?

Psychodynamic therapists are particularly prone to the mistakes listed above. The pursuit of knowledge through the scientific weighing of evidence against theory does not come naturally. Critical thinking is an arduous learned behavior that is difficult to maintain. The mistakes listed above almost inevitably pervade areas of thinking where scientific reasoning is not prized and constantly attempted, for these mistakes are not aberrations but the natural outcome of the human inclination to believe that our thoughts always reveal truth.

• • •

To avoid the criticism that the back-and-forth belief building is a central problem in the therapy encounter, psychodynamic psychotherapists will usually invoke the notion of transference. Freud proposed that the client's reactions to the therapist (both good and bad) had little to do with the therapist or the therapy but were reflections of the patient's reaction to his or her parents and other caregivers or authority figures in the patient's life. "The patient sees in his analyst the return—the reincarnation—of some important figure out of his childhood or past, and consequently transfers on to him feelings and reactions," Freud writes. "It soon becomes evident that this fact of transference is a factor of undreamed of importance."

Freud, not surprisingly, had little problem with positive transference. "So long as it is positive it serves us admirably," he writes. That the patient desires to win the analyst's "applause and his love" becomes "the true motive-force for the patient's collaboration." Feelings of anger, disappointment, or disillusionment with the therapist are another matter. "The danger of these states of transference evidently consists in the possibility of the patient misunderstanding their nature and taking them for fresh real experiences instead of reflections of the past," explains Freud. Patients, then, must be convinced of the idea of "negative transference" in order to understand that they are really not upset with the therapist but with someone in their past—usually their parents. For Freud and many of his followers, transference was a sign of the patient's pathology for the parental relationship (which therapy was supposedly mirroring).

The logic of allowing positive transference to grow while immediately pointing out the supposed pathological source of negative transference is one of Freud's low points in the use of his self-serving logic. It is, however, the same advice that can be seen repeated throughout the history of psychodynamic literature. "Negative transference can be expected to occur in most insight therapies, sometimes for long periods," J. Kotin writes in a book written for therapists. "In accordance with the rule of interpreting transference only when it becomes a resistance . . . positive transference should not be interpreted early in the course of therapy."* Positive transference is expected to fade away by the end of therapy (although there is plenty of reason to wonder whether this routinely happens), while the patient must be quickly convinced that the negative reactions to the therapist or to therapy are because he is upset with someone else.

No doubt a patient's reactions to a doctor or therapist will, in some ways, mirror relationships learned earlier in life. But by overemphasizing the primacy of such resemblances, therapists severely underestimate—often to the extent of dismissing altogether—the ways in which therapists solicit their patients'

---

*Freud, Kotin, and others warn therapists to be careful of positive transference that becomes extreme, but it is seldom indicated how such extreme transference would distinguish itself.

devotion and how they throw up roadblocks to any critical thinking by the patient. That the patients who come to therapy and stay in therapy think particularly highly of their therapists is hardly surprising, for they are buying the package exactly how it is being sold. That the therapist/patient relationship may mirror the other important relationships in the patient's life should take a conceptual backseat to the more obvious fact that the therapist cultivates the dependence that positive transference is supposed to explain away.

To make the case that there is something deeply significant to the patient's transference, Freud and other therapists often express mock-amazement at the deep emotional neediness that patients often express during treatment. "It was perhaps the greatest of the analyst's surprises to find that the emotional relation which the patient adopts towards him is of a quite peculiar nature. . . . For this emotional relation is, to put it plainly, in the nature of falling in love. . . . This love is of a positively compulsive kind. . . . In the analytic situation it makes its appearance with complete regularity without there being any rational explanation for it."

But the only real surprise here, as Richard Webster points out in *Why Freud Was Wrong,* is how Freud could overlook the many obvious and entirely rational reasons for such a reaction. The patient, who is likely already in an insecure state at the beginning of therapy, is put into situations where he or she is expected to speak his or her darkest and most private inner thoughts. This dynamic alone would raise the patient's expectation of emotional intimacy. "Freud seems not to recognize," writes Webster, "that by commanding his patients to reveal aspects of their lives and of their feeling which they would normally keep secret, he was placing them in a position of extreme emotional vulnerability. In normal human relationships such revelations tend to be reserved only for those who are emotionally close and intimately trusted."

Freud's contemporary, analyst Sandor Ferenczi, was aware of this obvious criticism. "Naturally the patient interprets the [imagined] deep understanding of the analyst . . . as a sign of deep personal interest, even tenderness," Ferenczi argued. "Since most patients have been emotionally shipwrecked [they] ... will cling to any straw." Considering what is expected of the patient in this setting, is it at all surprising that patients expect deep emotional concern, even love, back from their therapist or that they are eventually disappointed and annoyed when it is not forthcoming? At another point Ferenczi wrote simply: "We claim that the transference comes from the patient, unaware of the fact that the greater part of what one calls the transference is artificially provoked by this very behavior."

The explaining away of a patient's anger at the therapist as "negative transference" is an even more unseemly turn of logic, for it is an all too obvious way of dismissing criticism. As with positive transference, the argument that the critical patient is always angry at someone *other than the therapist* ignores the much more plausible reasons why patients often become disillusioned during treatment. Most likely, the patient at some point intuits that, as we have argued throughout, the therapist's ministrations cannot live up to his or her billing. If the source of such negative feeling is indeed the patient's dawning sense that he or she might have been fooled, the theory of "negative transference" can be seen as a rather brilliant, if Machiavellian, rhetorical gambit. That is, if the therapist convinces the patient of the theory of transference, the therapist can nullify the patient's criticism, claim the confirmation of Freudian theory, and at the same time rebuild his or her status in the eyes of the patient by claiming to *have predicted just such a reaction.*

Sometimes therapists will acknowledge that patients may be angry at the therapist because the treatment is falling short of their expectations. "Almost always, patients hope for more than therapy realistically has to offer," Kotin admits. "Thus, some disappointment is inevitable. . . . Some authors feel that disappointment is almost universal in the initial phase of therapy." Why does the patient have unrealistic expectations of therapy? Could it be because—as they often recommend—the therapist has allowed positive transference to grow unchecked?

So even when the patient's frustration is pointedly with the disappointing results of therapy, therapists can employ the theory of "negative transference" and turn the focus back on the patient. Kotin, writing in 1995, provides an example of what a therapist might say when the patient expresses such frustration:

> So I have really disappointed you. And you are very angry at me—angry enough even to consider stopping therapy. However, rather than doing that, it is important to see if we can work this out. One of the reasons you came into treatment was that you were having trouble working things out in your relationships. This is like a laboratory, and it may be very important for us to see this through. (Pause) What was the worst part of this for you?

As if transference wasn't enough conceptual armor to protect psychodynamic therapists from criticism, therapists also have the concept of countertransference by which they can explain away their own mistakes and shortcomings as deeply meaningful insights into their unconscious reactions to the patient. Carl Menninger lists some of the signs that the therapist may be under the spell of countertransference:

- Carelessness in regard to arrangements—forgetting the patient's appointment, being late for it . . .
- Persistent drowsiness (of the analysts) during the analytic hour . . .
- Repeatedly experiencing erotic or affectionate feelings toward the patient . . .
- Becoming disturbed by the patient's persistent reproaches and accusations . . .

The therapist is in no way responsible for these mistakes, for, as Menninger points out, "countertransference is by definition an unconscious phenomenon." Instead of reproaching himself, the therapist should "try to think through the analytic situation again and identify those features or acts or words of the patient which triggered off this reaction."

Kotin provides an even more amusing illustration of the use

of countertransference: "When a therapist thought about her vacation during her session with patient A, she was partly . . . wishing [she] could find some way to help her patient enjoy life more. When she thought about her upcoming lunch while with patient B, she was responding to the deep, primitive, oral needs of her regressed patient. . . . When the therapist remembered she needed to stop at the cleaners, she was responding to patient E's venomous hostility toward everyone in her life. The patient's lack of empathy for others' experiences made the therapist feel dirty, and she looked forward to changing into a freshly cleaned outfit."

There is virtually no misdeed or mistake a therapist can make that cannot be explained through the interplay of transference and countertransference. Freud, after participating in the surgical mutilation of one of his patients,* exonerated his surgeon-friend Wilhelm Fliess from obvious malpractice by invoking the notion that the patient's profuse bleeding was really only an expression of her affection for Freud. The repeated and nearly fatal hemorrhaging of the patient after a botched, unnecessary, and disfiguring surgery was blamed on the patient's attempt to win Freud's attention. She was, as Freud wrote to Fliess, "bleeding for love" of him. Later in psychoanalytic history, another analyst explained sexual encounters with patients by blaming their "overt transference." "About 10% [of patients] find it necessary to act-out extremely" with their therapists, writes Dr. J. L. McCartney, in 1966, "such as mutual undressing, genital manipulation or coitus."

It is hard to imagine a theory that more studiously ignores the obvious than that of transference. With the theory, patient's adoration, expectations, anger, and disappointment can all be explained away in a manner that, if convincing, will further

---

*In this now well-known case, Freud and his friend Wilhelm Fliess operated to remove a segment of bone from the nose of Freud's patient Emma Eckstein, believing that this procedure would cure her of her neurosis. Fliess managed to leave a half meter of surgical gauze in her nasal cavity, which caused a series of hemorrhages and infections, nearly ending Eckstein's life.

impress the patient with the insightfulness of the therapist and the importance of therapy. Given the frequency with which the concept of transference is trotted out, it becomes clear that this theory is more for the benefit of the therapist than the patient. It must certainly be reassuring for the therapist to believe that both a patient's high hopes and his or her disappointment has little to do with the therapist but rather are hints of important aspects of the patient's psyche.

That the patient's disappointment or disbelief in the therapist's theories can be dismissed as negative transference is one of the final ways in which the therapist is released from any possible accountability. The therapist can invoke this theory of transference at will, dismissing all manner of objection from the patient. Therapy, as Karl Menninger points out, "is an occupation in which practitioners work alone with nobody observing them and without any controls. . . . In this way the analyst works without checks other than those imposed by their sense of responsibility." There is, of course, one other person who witnesses the procedure; that is the patient, who is not a passive recipient of the procedure like the unconscious surgery patient, as Menninger implies. With the theory of transference, however, therapists effectively inoculate themselves against patients' criticism and so negate any chance that patients might steer therapists away from their favorite theory or whatever interpretation they are intent on making. The therapist can always claim to be on the right track regardless of the patient's loudest objection.

One final example is necessary in order to show the true lengths to which the concept of transference can be used as a shield to deflect criticism. Noting the overall decline of psychoanalysis in the seventies and eighties, Nathan Hale, a sympathetic historian of the field, invoked a kind of negative cultural transference. He speculated that because parents were divorcing at a greater rate, psychoanalytic patients were coming into therapy less capable of positive transference because they had less good feelings about their parents. "Perhaps with products of the fragmented family, psychoanalysis had been less successful," he wrote, "partly because of the large amount of hostility and underlying distrust patients bring to therapy, as if there had been no satisfactory models of love and closeness." Transference in this way can become an excuse for parents' failures large and small.

The confidence building that therapists often experience during their careers becomes more troubling to a global assessment of the profession when one remembers that the theories employed in psychotherapy are themselves discovered and honed in the practice of therapy. The belief building that affects the patient, the unsound confidence gained by the therapist due to the patient's admiration, and the psychodynamic theories that gain momentum in each generation of therapists are the result of an interconnected process that has no internal checks save for, as Menninger noted, the therapist's sense of responsibility. But this is *not* a safeguard on the process, for, as we have argued, some therapists are as vulnerable to the belief-building power of the therapy encounter as the patient. Therapists may come to believe in the validity of their theories at the same time patients learn to apply them to fashion a story of their lives.

That patients come to believe narratives that often mirror the vague anxieties present in the culture is the predictable outcome. The self-awareness fad of the seventies, child abuse in the mid-eighties, fears of cults and ritual abuse in the late eighties and early nineties—all of these were incorporated into the conclusions of psychodynamic psychotherapies. Even the fringe enthusiasms for past lives and space alien abduction found their way into the stories therapists and patients created together. Because the narrative-building process happens in such a piecemeal manner—slowly building evidence and momentum toward its conclusions—it is easy for the cultural concerns and interests that both the client and therapist share to seep into therapy without either party being fully aware of how they got there.

Advocates proclaim that the from-the-trenches origin of psychodynamic theory is its great strength. That the theorists of the field are therapists themselves, they argue, ensures that the theories never stray too far from the realities of the patient's life. This argument assumes that the patient's reality is solid enough to keep the therapist from pursuing theories of behavior that fundamentally don't tally with the patient. We have shown how patients are rather easily influenced by the subtle or brazen suggestions of the therapist. The history of psychodynamic therapy from Freud's day to today is filled with reports of patients quickly coming to believe in theories of the therapy in which they find themselves immersed. If this history has shown us nothing else, it has illustrated the power to convert patients to the notions of the therapist. The idea that the patient's eventual belief in the interpretations and theories of therapy is taken as a central point of confirmation of the validity of those theories should now give even the most credulous pause.

We have argued that psychodynamic therapy is flawed through the process by which the patient is molded by the therapist's suggestions and the therapist is influenced by the patient's eventual belief. Because there are no checks on the process that might help discriminate fact from fantasy, both are easily blown by the cultural winds of the moment. There is one final link in this interaction, and that is the manner in which therapists as a group influence our culture. That is to say, that for several generations therapists have not only built beliefs in their individual patients but also have had a hand in determining which fears, concerns, and interests we have focused on as a culture.

As Frank and Frank point out, the very fact that therapists give names to certain conditions and label them illnesses qualifies symptoms as pathologies and builds confidence in the rest of us that they can treat these conditions. "Variants of normal behavior and ordinary unhappiness become illnesses amenable to psychotherapy," they write, "when a theory exists to explain them as such." German psychiatrist Karl Jaspers put it this way: "Therapeutic schools unwittingly foster the phenomena which they cure."

The two most compelling examples of therapists affecting our culture's understanding of mental illness and therefore influencing the predispositions of all their potential patients are the promotion of post-traumatic stress disorder (PTSD) and dissociative identity disorder (which we will refer to by its more common name of multiple personality disorder, or MPD). In *The Harmony of Illusions,* anthropologist Allan Young makes a compelling case that PTSD is largely a culturally created disorder.

The power of this process by which the theories of mental illness generated in the mental health profession can influence society's understanding of mental illness should not be underestimated. Young argues that even though PTSD might not exist outside our cultural understanding of it, once the disorder has been accepted by society and by a patient population, it can have many consequences. Once it has been made real enough to "shape the self-knowledge of patients, clinicians, and researchers . . . the reality of PTSD is confirmed empirically by its place in people's lives, by their experiences and convictions and by the personal and collective investments that have been made in it."

PTSD found wide social acceptance because it mirrored the sociopolitical winds of recent decades. The idea of bringing trauma (such as the atrocities of war) into public awareness was mirrored in the idea that it was centrally important for patients to bring the worst moments of trauma into their awareness. The clues that seem to point to the idea of PTSD as a legitimate disorder are not discrete entities being dispassionately observed; rather, they are at least in part artifacts from an interconnected system that includes the beliefs of clinicians, patients, researchers, political activists, and society at large. The means by which all these groups communicate—from research, clinical papers, and conferences to the mass media—play back and forth on one another. All the pieces add, in their own way, to the aggregate process by which the patient comes to believe—and we as a society come to believe—that this disorder has an inherent legitimacy. This reverberation can create the harmony of illusion, which Young refers to in his title.

This growing acceptance of PTSD has led clinicians to look

for the disorder in an ever-widening population of patients, using ever-broader definitions of what might qualify as "trauma." According to the latest *Diagnostic and Statistical Manual*, PTSD can now be sparked by "trauma" that includes witnessing trauma, being threatened with trauma, or hearing an account of the trauma of a friend or family member. There is no time line on the expected response to such events, which means that symptoms experienced even decades after the event can be classified as symptoms of the trauma. Since most any disturbing event involving the knowledge of injury or death can be said to be traumatic, and nearly any problem can be said to be a symptom, any person can be diagnosed with PTSD.

The impact of media coverage can be clearly seen in the fast rise of multiple personality disorder. The American media, which has always fed off of the latest theories of therapists, was particularly interested in the fascinating symptoms of MPD, which included flamboyant displays of "alter personalities" supposedly brought forth by therapy. The fact that this disorder in its current form was virtually unheard of before 1970 did not stop newspaper and magazine reporters from credulously reporting the pervasiveness of the diagnosis. The book and subsequent 1977 movie *Sybil* had a dramatic impact on the general knowledge and acceptance of the disorder. Daytime talk shows were particularly important for spreading the news of this new disorder because these programs happened to match the demographics of potential MPD patients—women in their mid-twenties to forties. Nearly all the major daytime talk shows of the 1980s had broadcasts devoted to the topic. Often these programs showed MPD clients engaged in "switching" between their various personalities. The message of these shows was clear: MPD was not a rare disorder but rather common.

Reporters, book publishers, and talk-show producers have often made the same mistake that patients make when they show up for treatment: They have assumed that the diplomas, titles, and other trappings of the therapist mean that the therapist has access to reliable and accepted explanations for mental illness. Therapists, for their part, have every reason to encourage this belief and to appear in these public forums as confident experts.

Despite what we've learned in recent years, the profession continues to ignore the fact that each generation of therapists and patients shares a culture that influences their beliefs as to the causes and potential manifestations of mental illness. When the patient and therapist go on the hunt for, say, the "alter personalities" hidden in the patient's unconscious, they can be emboldened by the cultural consensus that such a disorder exists. Therapists, as Paul McHugh writes, "are not immune to the herd instinct . . . they may see in their patients what others tell them they should see. And because a harmony with the spirit of the times may be . . . crucial for therapeutic purposes . . . [they] may repeat a version of the same story on occasion after occasion."

As previously discussed, Freudian concepts such as repression, the dynamic unconscious, oedipal conflicts, and so forth have seeped into popular culture, becoming divorced from their specific Freudian origin and becoming a type of accepted common wisdom. The most general psychodynamic concept (that the powerful unconscious hides and controls the deepest currents of our mind) has proven itself malleable enough to mold itself to different schools of therapy. What specific types of forces the unconscious hides can change from generation to generation, while the notion that the dynamic unconscious harbors the key to the patient's behavior can retain its appeal and cultural momentum. Those who seek out psychodynamic treatment likely understand at least the rudimentary idea of the therapy and have already inferred from the culture in which they live the unconscious demons that they should expect to find.

Those who don't believe in the space alien abduction stories can quickly see that they are an outgrowth of a cultural interest in all things related to UFOs. If one could magically remove from our culture during the last twenty years all the UFO books, movies, television shows, and chatter on the Internet, one would no doubt discover that they had also eliminated all the stories of space alien abductions coming out of therapy settings.

Sometimes even the therapists who are in the midst of such trends can see these cultural forces at work. Psychoanalyst Charlotte Krause Prozan, in the midst of telling a story of how she interpreted the vague dreams and memories of her client as a narrative of sexual abuse, writes, "In 1973 and before, analysts were looking for penis envy. In 1990, we are looking for sexual abuse. . . . Patients and analysts are living in the same culture, and are being formed by similar trends. They may collude in what they believe is an accurate diagnosis of the patient's problems. But because they are both culture-bound, the truth may elude them both." Such remarkable self-awareness did not, unfortunately, keep Prozan from encouraging her patient to accept the abuse narrative.

While it may appear to therapists that patients are presenting evidence of certain unconscious forces *before* they are suggested by the therapist, this may mean only that the patient was exposed to the myth of the psychodynamic mind prior to therapy and was thus predisposed to the "discovery" of such forces. It is quite possible that the "sense of truth," which comes when a therapist gives an interpretation, arises from the way that interpretation dovetails with culturally shared beliefs, and does not arise from its match with the patient's internal life. There is no excuse for the therapist staying blind to the cultural influences at play in the therapy setting.

CHAPTER NINE

The Myth of Privileged Access to Our Own Thoughts

One of the key assumptions of therapy is that it can give patients a better understanding of why they take actions and harbor certain feelings and thoughts. With the help of the therapist we learn to explain ourselves to ourselves. Because patients most often seek out therapy because they feel troubled, this search for reasons often focuses on self-defeating actions, feelings, and thoughts. The therapist and the patient try to explain why we often seem to act against our own best interests, often to the point of appearing self-destructive.

One prominent psychiatrist has suggested that in talk therapy, the patient and therapist are engaged in something akin to writing a novel, in which the patient is the main character. Together they choose those facts—from the billion pieces of data that form the patient's actual life experience—that establish a narrative thread that is a good story. By "good story" we do not mean that it's happy, but rather that the cause-and-effect interactions that motivate the main character make sense given the theoretical assumptions that the therapist and the patient collaboratively impose on the patient's life. The goal is not to make the story appear enviable, but rather to create a narrative of cause and observable effect that feels inevitable.

Therapy, of course, isn't the only setting for this sort of story creation; in fact, it is an extension of what we all do naturally. We are all what might be described as lay scientists of our own behavior. We monitor our thoughts and usually assume that our feelings and behaviors are caused by reasons that are knowable.

Each day we explain to ourselves (and sometimes to those around us) the thinking behind a hundred different decisions and impressions. We can quickly say why we think we were put off by someone during a brief meeting or what thoughts led us to choose a particular restaurant. "I was thinking X," we say, "and then Y occurred to me, so I decided Z." We also tell stories about more carefully considered and evaluated life decisions, such as why we decided to move to another city or end a relationship. We share the assumption that the more we think about our behavior, the closer we will come to the true reasons we act the way we do.

Faith in therapy springboards off these common beliefs. Psychodynamically inspired therapists promise to add missing pieces to the patient's narrative—that is, information about basic and fundamental motivations that are central to the narrative but, for a variety of possible reasons, are outside the patient's awareness. These therapists promise to reveal the hidden pieces through an exploration of our unconscious minds. The literature of psychodynamically oriented therapy is rife with confident statements about this ability. The most important skill the psychoanalyst must possess is the ability to "translate the patient's thoughts, feelings, fantasies, impulses, and behavior into their antecedents," advises R. Greenson in his book *The Technique and Practice of Psychoanalysis.* "He must be able to sense what lies behind the various subjects his patient is talking about . . . [to] hear the hidden (unconscious) themes. . . . He must look at the fragmented pictures the patient paints and be able to translate them back into their original and unconscious form." The results of such insight, therapists maintain, manifestly prove their ability. "If the unconscious cause or causes can be discovered," writes C. Brenner in his book *An Elementary Textbook of Psychoanalysis,* "then all apparent discontinuities disappear and the concrete chain of sequence becomes clear."

The idea that therapists possess a technique that can reveal hidden forces is a compelling idea, for we sometimes sense an inability to explain the origins of our thoughts and feelings. At moments when everything in our lives appears to be going along swimmingly we can feel quite sad. Or conversely, we feel elation in times when we have plenty of reason to be depressed. Sometimes, looking back, we appear to have acted irrationally and in our own worst interest. The disconnect between the narrative of how we think we should feel and how we actually feel can provoke a good deal of confusion and anxiety. We know there is something else going on in our minds and that we don't have an adequate theory to explain our conduct.

To understand the value of narrative creation that goes on in therapy, we must begin by looking at our innate abilities to assess the sources of our own thoughts, emotions, and decisions. So we ask the question: Are we decent lay scientists of our own behavior? Social scientists have looked carefully at this question and have come up with some surprising conclusions. To put it simply, there is a growing body of evidence that we humans (even though we are the best problem-solvers evolution has produced) are not very good at identifying the reasons for even our moment-to-moment thoughts and actions and are singularly *incapable* of illuminating the mental processes by which our own brains make those decisions.

The substantial literature on the issue indicates that we mold our behavior in such a way that our actions appear invariably to be the result of conscious choices made among considered alternatives. We want to believe that we would not do something without adequate justification. In fact, subjects in hundreds of experiments have demonstrated remarkable willingness to deceive themselves in order to protect the belief that they always act in rational and responsible ways.

The "counter attitudinal advocacy experiments" are classics of the literature. In one experiment, high school students were asked their opinion on a number of social issues, including their feelings about mandatory integration through school busing. A couple of weeks later the same students were asked to participate in a small group discussion of the busing issue. The researchers placed students of like opinion in small discussion groups with one plant who was armed with persuasive arguments that countered the students' opinion. When the students rated their opinions after the discussions, they found their position had sharply changed. The antibusing students had sharply moderated their opinions while most of the probusing students actually converted to an antibusing stance.

Researchers then asked the students to recall what their opinions had been a few weeks earlier (the students were reminded that the experimenters had their original responses and could check the accuracy of their accounts). Remarkably, students who were originally against busing incorrectly remembered their opinion to be much more probusing than it actually had been. Most of the original probusing students incorrectly remembered that they had actually been against the policy.

As the researchers surmised, these students seemed to be blissfully unaware that their beliefs on this controversial issue had radically changed. Watching the students during the discussion begin to nod their heads at the confederate's arguments, the researchers wrote, "They seemed to come to agree with him without any awareness of their earlier attitude . . . [later] they gave every indication that the position they adopted after the discussion was the position they had basically always had. No subject reported that the discussion had made any difference in modifying his position."

In another classic experiment, social scientists asked subjects to undergo a series of strong electrical shocks after being told that the experiment would yield valuable medical knowledge. With the first round of painful jolts completed, the researchers asked the subjects to repeat the process. To some they gave ample justification for the second series of shocks, explaining how important the research was and that nothing could be learned without the second test. Other subjects were given relatively inadequate reasons, such as the researchers wanted to satisfy a passing curiosity. Even though the subsequent shocks administered to both groups were equal in strength, those given the insufficient justification reported that the shocks were less painful. Without any apparent awareness of what they were doing, the subjects who were given the inadequate excuse under-reported the discomfort of the shocks in order to protect a conception of themselves as people who made rational decisions.

The belief of the subjects that the shocks weren't that painful appears to go deeper than one might first guess. The subjects who were given the inadequate reason to undergo the second round of shocks actually showed less *physiological* reaction to the shocks as well as a greater ability to perform learning tasks while experiencing them than those who were given adequate justification. This would indicate that much more is going on here than the subjects simply lying to the researchers to avoid embarrassment. Even at the level of nonaware brain function (i.e., those that control heart rate, respiration, etc.), the test subjects reacted in such a way that it actually appeared that the shocks were less strong than in the other group.

These sorts of experiments have been done over and over in many different variations. What they tell us is that when we are asked about our actions after the fact or are given an expectation we mold our perceptions, memories, and stories of our conduct to fit the conception of how we believe we should act, given that we have previously learned what is a socially appropriate *story* for such action. When researchers manipulate our actions so that we perform outside of that belief, we change our perception of the experience so that our belief about how we behave is maintained.

The experiments on such post hoc story creation of our moment-to-moment behavior leads to an important question: If we indeed have access to our own internal thoughts and these thoughts explain our conduct, how do we manage to lie to ourselves? Social psychologist Richard Nisbett, Darryl Bem, and Norman Alexander have looked deeply at the first part of this question—that is, into the question of whether we have access to our own internal thought processes.

To find an answer, Nisbett designed experiments in which subjects were put into simple non-ego-threatening situations where they made decisions that the researchers knew they could influence in unconventional ways. The question at issue was whether the subjects had sufficient access to their own decision-making mental processes to correctly identify the source of the researcher's influence.

In one experiment a group of test subjects was asked to memorize pairs of associatively related words, like "moon" and "ocean," with the researcher's expectation that when later asked another question they would be more likely to pick a target word. In the case of the subjects who memorized the words *moon* and *ocean* as part of their word list, they were expected to answer Tide when days later asked to name a brand of detergent. This is indeed what they found: Subjects who memorized the list were twice as likely than members of a control group to pick the target word. Despite the fact that the word pairs they had memorized were still in their memory, however, almost none of the students could report that the word memorization had influenced their decision. When asked to explain the reason for choosing Tide, the subjects gave the same set of responses as those who had not been influenced, such as "Tide is the best-known detergent" or "My mother uses Tide," etc.

Nisbett and his associates did a variety of experiments on this theme, testing whether subjects could accurately report the source of influences on their behavior, evaluations, judgments, or choices. In each case Nisbett and his colleagues chose unusual stimuli—that is, they influenced the subjects' behavior in ways that do not fall into commonly accepted beliefs about the way the mind works. (It is not obvious, for instance, why memorizing a word list might, days later, influence one's choice of a name-brand detergent.) While subjects always reported a reason as to why they made a certain decision, judgment, or action, *they were virtually never accurate in identifying the ways the researchers were manipulating their behavior.*

Test subjects were utterly blind to the thought process that led them to certain decisions. Even when the experimenters pointed out to the subjects how their decisions were manipulated, subjects would most often stick to their story of how they came to their decision. The ability of people to report on their mental processes was "so poor," Nisbett and his colleagues report, "that any introspective access that may exist is not sufficient to produce generally correct or reliable reports." It appears that we often have as little conscious awareness of how we make a decision as we do of how our brains triangulate the perception of our two eyes to determine the distance of an oncoming car. While we might assume that because we live inside our bodies we should be better than someone observing us from the outside in terms of understanding our decision-making thought processes, this assumption is not borne out in Nisbett's tests.

The fact that much of our thought process goes on outside of our ability to describe its functioning may at first seem to give credence to the idea of a powerful unconscious entity deciding things for us. There is, however, good reason why this research does not argue for the unconscious mind psychodynamic therapists propose.

It is clear that most day-to-day behavior requires much out-of-awareness processing. Activities such as driving a car, which at first require our entire attention, become more and more automatic as time goes on. This does not mean that some powerful entity such as Freud's conception of the unconscious is driving the car for us, but rather that most complex activities are a mixture of conscious attention and behavior that is so well learned that it happens without our notice, attention, or conscious effort.

This sort of out-of-awareness mental processing happens with many mental tasks. The more complex the activity (say, for instance, making a judgment about someone's personality), the more likely it is to incorporate levels of learning of which we are unaware at the moment. But despite the deep complexity of our thoughts, humans seem particularly prone to proposing after-the-fact theories of why they behaved in certain ways or made certain judgments. It appears to be human nature to assume, when looking back at our actions, that they were the products of traceable thoughts and decisions. Usually, we can immediately offer a theory about why we did something, and once we propose such a theory, we tend to doggedly stick to it. We can get rather indignant when told we are wrong. Most people insist, quite simply, that they can look into their own thoughts.

Nisbett's research shows, however, that this out-of-aware-ness processing is largely inaccessible to scrutiny. He demon-strates that mental-cause-and-behavior-effect interactions are often not appreciated by the person doing the behaving. Because we can direct our conscious attention to problem solv-ing and weigh in our minds the pros and cons of an upcoming decision, we assume that we invariably regulate our behavior in this rational and considered way. However, the habits of thought that regulate our behavior are often so deeply learned that our post hoc explanations for why we act as we do are only sketchy and often inaccurate rationales.

Nisbett is not implying that we are always wrong about the source of our behavior. If a stranger walks up to us and punches us in the nose, we will be able to accurately report later exactly why we dislike the stranger. The cause is available to our conscious awareness, it is a plausible reason for our response, and there are few other factors in play. But even in this case, our understanding of why we dislike the stranger has less to do with our having accessed the pathways or patterns of our own thoughts than with the fact that we have a socially shared narrative that one dislikes strangers who punch them in the nose. An outside observer with no access to our mental processes would be just as likely to predict our dislike of the stranger and our reason for that response.

This conclusion—that outside observers are just as likely to' accurately choose our reasons for our actions—is exactly what Nisbett and his colleagues also found in all their experiments. Outside observers—that is, people who were given only brief descriptions of the experiments but were not test subjects themselves—were just as likely to be able to identify or, rather, *misidentify* what the subjects would believe to be the salient influences on their behavior. As they report, "The most remarkable result was that subject and observer reports . . .

were so strongly correlated for each of the judgments that it seems highly unlikely that subjects and observers could possibly have arrived at these reports by different means."

If knowledge of our own thought processes is not the means by which we determine the reasons for certain decisions and behaviors, what is? Nisbett proposes that the key to our beliefs about why we have behaved in a certain way relies on what we *have learned to believe is a plausible reason for that action.* "We propose," reports Nisbett, "that when people are asked to report how a particular response is influenced by a particular stimulus, they do so not by consulting a memory of the mediating process, but by applying or generating causal theories about the effects of that type of stimulus on that type of response. They simply make judgments, in other words, about how plausible it is that the stimulus would have influenced the response."

While some of these assumptions about the plausibility of cause-and-effect relations come from our own experience and observations, Nisbett proposes that many others are supplied by shared cultural (or subcultural) agreement about how certain stimuli and responses are supposed to interact. (That all the subjects in the word memorization experiment offered similar commonplace reasons for their choice of a detergent is one example of how we pick and believe socially conventional explanations of our actions.) We repeat these narratives to each other and thereby perpetuate the belief in them. It is not that these narratives are in all cases wrong; the point is rather that we appear to have little ability to go outside them, nor do we have any reliable ability to internally gauge when they are right or wrong. This would explain why subjects' explanations of their own behavior in Nisbett's experiments are almost always the same as observers' predictions of their explanations.*

*Anthropological knowledge about the variety of accounts of the self and conduct over human history and across cultures bears out the importance of learning in the way individuals select narratives. The observable variations across human groups in the ways in which people account for themselves cannot be explained either by some biological difference or by an instinct-driven unconscious. It can be accounted for only by the human ability to learn these explanations and by the history of the particular culture that directs the individual as to what learned explanation to believe.

Social psychologist Darryl Bem has sharpened this point and used it to oppose the cognitive dissonance explanation for the experiments such as the shock test described above. Cognitive dissonance theorists explain the above experiment by proposing a mental mechanism by which the mind resolves dissonance between how one behaves and one's beliefs about how one *should* behave. In the case of the subjects who submitted to the second round of shocks for no good reason, cognitive dissonance theorists point to the fact that these subjects subsequently underreport the severity of the shocks as proof that this mental process is hard at work lessening the dissonance.

Countering this theory, Bem has proposed that our explanations of our behavior are so similar to what outside observers would surmise that in all likelihood they are the same thing. To put it another way: When we explain our own behavior, we look at our own actions and pick plausible explanations in the *exact same manner as someone who was observing our actions might.* As opposed to having internal insight into our decisions (or having a mental mechanism that lessens dissonance), we observe our actions and make post hoc explanations. When experimenters are able to manipulate our behavior, we observe our actions and choose a plausible story or rational that assumes our actions were the result of our rational choices.

What makes one theory more plausible than another? The answer, Nisbett, Bem, and other researchers believe, comes from the culture or subculture in which the person exists. They theorize that cultures provide rules about why people behave the way they do in certain situations. In fact, they believe that the only times people can accurately report how they came to a decision are when culturally accepted explanations happen to match up with what the researchers know actually influenced the actions in question. We appear to have no sensation or special access to how our mind juggles the variables in a certain situation. We appear dependent on these culturally agreed-upon stories to explain our thinking and have no internal sensor for the times when we adopt the wrong explanation.

*   *   *

That our thoughts cannot trace their own course can be an odd notion at first, but it is one that has widening importance for the idea of psychotherapy. The basic work of psychodynamic therapy is to do exactly what the research shows we have little capacity to do: trace our thoughts and behaviors to their mental origins. If the patient and therapist have no ability to trace the course of thoughts, and if the patient has no internal sensitivity to when such cause-and-effect stories are wrong, what is really going on in therapy? Is there any reason to believe that the patient and therapist are any more accurate in identifying strings of causation than the subjects and observers in Nisbett's studies?

The final link in this chain is provided by the work of Norman Alexander and his colleagues. Their research builds on the idea that we adopt the notion that we are acting rationally (i.e., consciously choosing each of our actions), and that we are enormously sensitive to the texture of the social situations in which we find ourselves. Alexander's research explains why Nisbett's and Bem's observers predicted the attitudes reported by the subject in the experiments (even though the observers were told only about the problem confronting the subject). The experiments conducted by Alexander and his associates demonstrate that when people are not pursuing goal-oriented activity, they choose behaviors and report attitudes that are precisely those alternatives and sentiments that will yield the most approval from any third party who learns of their actions. In other words, when we are uncertain of our goals or hold no well-established position on the subject or situation at hand, we appear to choose the actions or opinions that will gain the maximum amount of favor from anyone who might learn of our actions.

What we are apparently working to accomplish is to present the identity that will be most strongly approved of by others. We have a finely tuned ability to discern—with as little conscious effort as it takes to calculate where a ball will land when we throw it—the norms and values that attach to a particular social situation. We appear remarkably able to calculate how we should act and how we are supposed to feel if we want our identity to appear appropriate in a given setting.

Our skill at analyzing ambiguous social situations and our sensitivity at how to present ourselves is such a fundamental part of being socialized that we often don't experience much effort in making the judgments about how to act or what to say when explaining the reason for our actions.

The lessons for therapy should be becoming clear. The onus is now on the therapy community to demonstrate that it has not composed a complex fugue on the theme of this research. That is, it must answer the question of whether its patients, who are put into the ambiguous social situation of therapy, are not reporting the attitudes and making the self-assessments that are most likely to win approval of the therapist.

Of course, the stimulus/response relationships that these social science experiments reveal are simplistic compared to the cause-and-effect narratives proposed in therapy. Psychodynamic therapists claim the ability to help clients connect current behaviors to long-past traumas in childhood, for instance, or to repressed fantasies decades in the patients' past. To compare what is attempted in therapy with these social science experiments is to compare addition to calculus. But if these researchers show that our addition is often wrong (and further, that we have no innate capacity to sense when it's accurate or inaccurate), what is the likelihood that the calculus done in therapy is correct? If we can't trace the influences of simple actions and decisions to their correct sources, can we be expected to do better making etiological connections between complex current life and events or fantasies from our childhood?

These experiments are also important in that they highlight the importance of culturally and subculturally shared narratives as explanations for behavior. Looked at over time, the vast number of psychodynamic schools of talk therapy appear as nothing more than a testing and breeding ground for these shared cultural narratives. Psychodynamic therapy offers a new and interesting world of possible narratives by which patients can come to *believe* they understand the origin of their thoughts and behaviors. These narratives become plausible in the patient's eyes through the process of influence embedded in therapy.

Considering that patients have little or no internal capacity to disconfirm such cause-and-effect stories, it is not surprising that each generation of psychodynamic psychotherapists has had patients who have adopted its narratives. To convince patients of the validity of the cause-and-effect narrative, therapists need not offer a true explanation, they need only immerse the patient into a new subculture and overwhelm the patients' previously held narratives. In some area—recovered memory therapy, for example—talk therapy seems nothing more than a narrative-creating machine, a place where the patient and therapist choose from a very small set of possible explanations for the client's problems and proceed to spend long hours building evidence for that conclusion.

With the deeper knowledge of how we observe our own behavior and pick socially accepted explanations for it, it becomes much clearer why schools of psychodynamic psychotherapy often mirror social trends of their times. The therapeutic process is deeply influenced by cultural notions of behavior because both the client and the therapist share assumptions (as well as a large amount of childhood socialization) on these exact issues. This problem becomes thornier because our current culturally shared theories of behavior are strongly influenced by the psychodynamic theories of therapy themselves. The bottom line is that to explain changes in a patient's behavior and beliefs while in treatment with a psychodynamic psychotherapist one need go no further than the analysis of the moment-to-moment influence process in which they are engaged. While this process can effect behavior and beliefs, it has nothing to do with altering the cause of mental illness. None of what happens in therapy is explained by the principles assumed to govern the psychodynamic unconscious—which does not appear to exist.

The experiments described above are just the tip of the iceberg in terms of the knowledge that has been gained about out-of-awareness human mental processing. Much has been learned, for instance, about sensory overload. We know that the amount of information in a visual display that exceeds our conscious processing capacity can nonetheless influence subsequent behavior. Our understanding of our thoughts can also be overwhelmed by preconscious sensory stimuli. Magicians rely on the fact that we will make quick and incorrect theories about what we believe we have experienced with our own eyes. Frequently, our senses may set our mind on a course for an incorrect conclusion before our highest level of consciousness has a chance to intervene.

All of this research point to a rather homely version of what some might call unconscious awareness. What these scientists describe is certainly not Freud's dynamic unconscious, which functioned as a mediating force between memories, fantasies, instinctual impulses, and our conscious minds. The out-of-awareness processing that the above experiments point to implies little unconscious intelligence.

Still, the manner in which our own thoughts are prone to misperceiving our mental motivation based on incorrect social narratives is something that should be deeply meaningful for therapists who claim to be helping their patients understand themselves. Has this knowledge been incorporated into the practice of therapy?

We agree that it might be good for patients (and every one else for that matter) to understand the import of out-of-awareness mental functions and our ability to deceive ourselves with incorrect beliefs about our behavior. We should all, as Kenneth Bowers of the University of Waterloo writes, "recognize the possibility for self-deception" and learn to take "the authority of one's own conscious experience with a grain of salt." But the central question remains: Do therapists have any authority to claim that they can replace such self-deception with a true (or even a truer) understanding of a patient's behavior?

Most patients do not, when they enter therapy, want to be further demoralized by a lesson in how arbitrary our personal theories of behavior can be or how such narratives are mostly a product of socialization and cultural learning. Certainly they expect therapists to have more in their bag of tricks than this rather disturbing news. It seems highly unlikely that therapists will ever stop offering the promise that they can help patients see through their incorrect assumptions and theories of behavior to their true ones. More likely, therapists will simply reinflate the ideas of out-of-awareness processing right back into the full-blown idea of the dynamic unconscious—and then claim to be able to interpret its true forces and meaning.

Bowers shows this exact tendency when he encourages therapists to have a greater appreciation for the "multiply determined" nature of consciousness. In one therapy case Bowers tells the story of a middle-aged woman suffering from agoraphobia. Her fears were so severe that she stayed in her upscale house for most of each week. Her relationship with her husband was sexless, which, we are told, caused considerable tension and frustration. We also learn that this woman felt guilty and shameful about being sexually active before her marriage. Although Bowers does not tell us what the woman said in therapy, we are told that at one point she made "veiled" sexual advances toward the therapist. Bowers concludes that a good clinician would likely consider that "this woman's presenting complaint of agoraphobia was at least in part a defense against a great deal of sexual frustration, and that at some level she fantasized psychotherapy as a potentially safe place to solve her problems." The patient, Bowers theorizes, was afraid to leave the house for fear she would become sexually active and lose her "self-esteem" and "affluent lifestyle" in the process. All of this, we are told, was likely hidden in the unconscious of the patient.

Here we have a fine example of the entirely unambiguous, *singularly* determined narratives to which therapists who believe they can see into the unconscious of the patient are prone. Although this narrative has a certain intuitive appeal, there are many reasons to wonder about this explanation. For instance, we are led to believe that the sexual interest in the therapist was unconscious because her advances were disguised. How disguised were they? Were they so disguised that the therapist, perhaps expecting "erotic transference," might have misread them? And if the therapist was correct that the woman had a sexual interest in him, is it at all surprising that her first entreaties might be "thinly veiled"? Such advances are the norm, after all—moderately well-socialized Americans very rarely simply ask to have sex.

And what is there to tie agoraphobia to the patient's supposed unconscious sexual longings? The literature on agoraphobia suggests that sexual frustration is a very unlikely cause for this severe disorder. All in all, the explanation is classically psychodynamic. It assumes the primacy of sexuality in the etiology of mental illness. It looks for transference (in this case erotic transference) for the prime clues as to the patient's problems. And it ignores the research into possible genetic and neurobiological sources for the patient's illness. What this narrative has to recommend itself is not a deep understanding of the complexity of consciousness but its simplistic narrative appeal—it is a good story. One can only wonder what this patient thought if the therapist decided to inform her that her agoraphobia was caused by her repressed sexual longings and that she unconsciously desired to seduce him.

To say that we have no internal mechanism to sense when our explanations for our behaviors are correct or incorrect is not to say that all explanations are equal. Some cause-and-effect narratives, as we have noted, can be more or less accurate than others. Some can be complete fantasies, such as when someone comes to believe that his insomnia is due to past-life trauma. The payoff for choosing the more accurate theories is that they are likely to have some predictive power. The explanation or narrative that a patient creates with a therapist cannot exist for long in a vacuum; it must meet the test of continually explaining our future behavior. If we come to understand that the correct explanation for our insomnia is the fact that we smoke tobacco or exercise just before bedtime, to choose a simple example, then that explanation will have predictive value: When we don't smoke or exercise before going to bed, we will sleep restfully. The predictive value of the theory bears the theory out.

If we are correct that the psychodynamic unconscious is an

invalid narrative (and thus has no predictive value), we must explain how it has existed for so long in the minds of so many people. Continuous social support is one reason invalid or myth-based behavioral theories remain in place. Constantly revisiting and reasserting incorrect narratives—even ridiculous ones—can give them remarkable staying power. People can go through their entire adult lives believing that, for instance, their wicked thoughts are due to demons or that their good decisions were made with the help of angels. Patients who stay in therapy (or those who continually avail themselves to these ideas through friends, books, or other media) can maintain their belief over long periods even if those theories lack predictive usefulness.

But there is another, more insidious way that psychodynamic theories gain momentum and staying power in the patient's mind. Psychodynamic therapists can utilize patients' inevitable *failure* to predict their behavior as proof of the theory that the patients are at the will of forces outside their awareness. As we have noted, people often go into therapy to bridge the disconcerting gap they feel between their feelings, thoughts, and behavior (on the one hand) and their mind's ability to explain, justify, and predict those factors (on the other).

If the psychodynamic explanation for their thoughts and behavior actually *decreases* patients' ability to accurately understand their thoughts and predict their behavior, then therapy can *increase* the very gap patients are trying to bridge. For patients who are grappling with their desire to believe the theories therapists are offering, the source of this tension may not be immediately clear. As patients become more a mystery to themselves, they may likely experience a greater sense that some unseen entity is at work. Psychodynamic therapists can then explain this sensation by pointing to the central tenet of the psychodynamic theory—that is, that patients are at the will of powerful unconscious forces.

In this way, the psychodynamic explanation actually utilizes the very fact that those who adopt it will largely be frustrated by attempts to explain their own behavior. The broader the gap between the believed-in theory of behavior and the predictability of future behavior, the more distressed the person is likely to become and the more likely he or she will be to cling to the ministrations of the therapist who promises that all will eventually become clear through therapy. In this way, psychodynamic explanations of behavior that rely on the idea of the unconscious can create the need for themselves.

CHAPTER TEN

Medicine Meets Myth

Until Prozac came along in its drugstore banality, every means of getting things straight between you and the cosmos had a romance about it: Zen meditation; heroin; "joining the French Foreign Legion, the Communist Party or a nunnery . . . and of course Freudian psychoanalysis."

—HENRY ALLEN,
Washington Post

During his training at Harvard in the early seventies, psychiatrist Harrison Pope witnessed the last grand days of the psychodynamic conception of mental illness. It was a time when psychoanalysts and their intellectual kin held sway over many of the nation's most prestigious psychiatric training programs. At Harvard, the biological approach to treating mental illness was in such disregard that students of psychiatry were not even required to complete a yearlong medical internship. Knowledge of medicine was considered so peripheral to the treatment of mental illness that it wasn't considered worth the extra year's investment of time. Instead, Pope's training focused on practicing long-term psychodynamic psychotherapy and presenting his notes from each session to a senior supervisor.

Pope remembers learning at the feet of renowned analysts who told stories of bravely curing all manner of mental illness armed only with their knowledge of psychodynamic theory and talk therapy. To say these men were respected and admired would be an understatement. Pope remembers their lectures as quasi-religious experiences. Some of these famous therapists even told stories of having cured cases of schizophrenia.

"I remember as a first-year resident both marveling at these stories and being a little skeptical," Pope says. "I marveled at the time that these men could have such extraordinary wisdom and insight that they would be able to cure a schizophrenic patient purely through words."

At the same time these elder statesmen of the mental health profession told of their victories, a beachhead was established for the biomedical approach to mental illness. In 1970, lithium was approved in the United States for the treatment of manic depressive illness. By the time Pope graduated from Harvard in 1974, the drug was being widely used to treat the disorder. The drug's effectiveness was beyond doubt, but its impact on the profession was broader than its effect on patients. Manic-depressive illness was perhaps the first disorder for which the psychodynamic theories completely collapsed.

Watching a manic-depressive patient go through a period of three or four days without sleeping, or experience the dramatic hyperactivity and euphoria, it was clear to many observers that the problem was biological in origin.* When lithium, a simple naturally occurring salt, was shown to completely eradicate the symptoms in most patients within ten days, it was the first loud ring of the death knell for psychodynamic theories. "The use of lithium for manic depressive illness was the first of many psychiatric disorders where the biological approach was able to take over and flush out the psychodynamic theorist," says Pope.

As other opportunities for the biomedical approach presented themselves, the claims of Pope's charismatic teachers were being put to the test. At McLean Hospital,† where Pope began his career, researchers conducted the largest most method-

---

*Even Pope, a student at the time, remembers suggesting to one of his supervisors that a manic-depressive patient appeared to be suffering a biological illness. The supervisor rebuked him and put a notation in his permanent file that the young trainee was "engaging in his biological interpretation in order to bind his own anxiety." This sort of diagnosing of the people who disagree with psychodynamic wisdom remains an often-used tactic in debate.

†McLean Hospital is Harvard's only teaching hospital devoted solely to psychiatry.

ologically sound study of the effectiveness of psychotherapy in treating schizophrenia. Schizophrenic patients were assigned to senior psychodynamic therapists for three hours of treatment a week while a control group of patients with the same disorder were given just a half hour of supportive talk once a week. When the results came in, they soundly contradicted the claims of the famous therapists. The patients in the control group performed just as well in every measure and quite better in a number of respects. There was no evidence that therapy (long-term or short-) could effectively cure schizophrenics. The brave stories Pope had heard during his training were beginning to look like wishful thinking or misdiagnosis.

Another influence in the debate over schizophrenia came from the introduction of magnetic resonance imaging (MRI), which made it easier to show the physical effect of schizophrenia on patients' brains. Doctors could safely create pictures that clearly showed the atrophy of the brain and the dilated cerebral ventricles. "The widespread use of such imaging machines made a big impression on the debate," recalls Pope. "If you could actually hold a picture of a schizophrenic's brain in your hand and see that part of the brain was no longer functioning, then it started to get very difficult to explain that the patient's disorder had been caused by his mother."

Such leaps in the debate were reminiscent of many medical advances over the course of the last hundred years. Theories about the cause of one illness or another raged until technology advanced to the point where a researcher could find a piece of evidence that would silence the debate almost overnight. Isolating the microorganism that causes tuberculosis, for example, quickly ended the debate over its cause.

Such discoveries have been and continue to be difficult but not impossible with mental illnesses. What makes them so problematic is that the brain has an altogether higher order of complexity than the body's other organs. With mental illness, root causes have been much more difficult to pinpoint. "The debate surrounding many mental illnesses continues to rage over whether the cause can be found in the environment or par-

enting or in biological factors or whether there is some hetero-
geneous mixture of factors," says Pope. "Often it has not yet
been possible to make definitive findings such as [of] a microorganism, but certainly the evolution we've seen has been a grad-
ual withering away of the psychodynamic theories and toward
an appreciation of biological factors."

Currently there is a growing consensus at the top of the mental health profession—at places like McLean Hospital, where
Pope is now chief of the Biological Psychiatry Laboratory—that
the major advances have and will continue to come from the
biomedical quarter. Unfortunately, just because there is agreement at the top of the profession does not mean that the rest of
the profession will quickly (or even inevitably) fall in line.
Because the mental health profession at large has no effective
mechanisms for quickly disseminating new research or coming
to a consensus about what procedures should be accepted
as new standards of care, the psychodynamic approach may
continue to mislead therapists and patients alike for years to
come.

"When the twentieth century is looked back at from a sufficient vantage point, I think that our successors will really be
shocked at what terrible damage was done to patients' lives and
the lives of their families by psychodynamic theories of illness
and behavior," says Pope. "These theories failed to understand
the possibility that patients were often suffering from a simple
biological illness. In addition, they often blamed the patient
and the family for the creation of the illness and in doing so
they added to people's misery. Psychodynamic theories have
done incalculable harm over the last decades."

The description of science proposed by those who argue for psychodynamic therapy is often a simpleminded one. Those who
claim to address the patient on a spiritual, existential, or subjective level often paint a picture of a biological or empirical
approach that dramatically understates its particular strengths.
Because the scientific approach to any disease (or, for that matter, any phenomenon) is often complicated and not quickly

explained, therapists have often succeeded in this rhetorical move. The popular debate, for this reason, has largely centered around the comparison of various commonly overprescribed drugs to talk therapy. Supporters of talk therapy continually point to drugs like Prozac or others that do little more than mask symptoms—such as Ritalin for hyperactivity and Valium for anxiety—as the alternative science offers to therapy. This ignores the fact that these medications are among the least exciting of the recent advances (not to mention one of the most misused approaches) in the treatment of mental disorders.

If these drugs were all the medical approach to mental illness had to offer, therapists would have a stronger case that they should be allowed to continue their haphazard romp through their patients' psyches. But Ritalin, Prozac, Valium, and their kin are not even close to the sum of recent medical advances. As the brain has become increasingly well understood, medical science has begun to understand a host of severe mental disorders.

The brain can be negatively affected by thousands of diseases or environmental stresses. These diseases and other factors can impact the brain in particular or the body and brain in a more global manner. Medical science has developed an impressive array of tests to determine exactly what is happening to a patient. Careful doctors can test blood and find out, for example, if the patient has higher-than-normal levels of lead, copper, or carbon monoxide. With sophisticated tests, they can learn whether someone is suffering the long-delayed effects of a typhus exposure, a brain tumor, or a heart problem that is limiting oxygen supply. Through other means they can detect thyroid problems, sleep disorders, Lyme disease, metabolic defects, and hundreds of possible infections, viruses, and lesions. All of these things can cause (and are often first noticed because of) changes in behavior and mental processing. Many of these problems can cause symptoms of depression; others can bring on hyperactivity or psychosis, and still others (like copper buildup) can spark bizarre and antisocial behavior.

Medical science has treatments for all the problems mentioned above and in many cases can effect complete cures.

While the amount of knowledge about the biological diseases that can lead to mental health problems is enormous, the percentage of times this knowledge is used when a patient comes to a psychologist or even a psychiatrist is distressingly small. A 1982 study found that 63 percent of the patients admitted to a psychiatric hospital and labeled with "untreatable dementia" actually had treatable disorders. Another study of 131 randomly selected patients at a prominent Manhattan psychiatric center found that 75 percent of the patients reevaluated were likely misdiagnosed when admitted. Even as late as 1990, a study of patients in state treatment programs found that only half of the patients with detectable physical diseases had been diagnosed as such. The harm of such lax methods is obvious, as the author of this study concluded: "A physical disease incorrectly diagnosed as a mental disease can lead to a lifetime on psychotropic drugs, loss of productivity, physical and social deterioration and shattered dreams."

Indeed, it can do worse than that. Many serious diseases can initially cause mild symptoms that therapists often naively believe they can cure through talk therapy. A client receiving talk therapy for a heart condition that is causing symptoms of depression can get sicker past the point where medicine can save him. One prominent psychiatrist is forthright in his contention that thousands of patients have needlessly died because they have been given useless talk therapy that can do nothing to cure an underlying disease.

Disorders of the brain cannot be cured by talking to a therapist. More important—and more disturbing—they are not likely to be *recognized* by a therapist or even most psychiatrists. Sadly, most schools of talk therapy are so loosed from the science that underlies the medical approach to mental illness that those trained in these methods have no clear understanding of what it means to make a diagnosis of a patient's problems. Therapists and most psychiatrists presented with any of the problems mentioned above will likely never know that they are treating a patient with a curable disease that is affecting the brain and therefore behavior.

The mental health profession is currently deeply confused about the difference between *describing* a patient's symptoms and diagnosing a patient's problems. Description and diagnosis are not the same. A description lacks the central component of a diagnosis, which is the discovery of the pathological *cause* of the disease. Noting that a patient is anxious or depressed, for example, is a far cry from diagnosing the patient, for there is no mention of what might have caused the depression or anxiety. Depression or anxiety is no more a diagnosis than "fever" and "aches and pains" is a diagnosis for a patient of a medical doctor.

Unfortunately, these sorts of general labels are often exactly what pass for a diagnosis among therapists. The problem is not simply that symptoms such as depression and anxiety are vague, but that they are meaningless in pointing toward a cause of the problem. Depression can have hundreds of causes, and it is only through an accurate determination of the source of the problem that a healer can have any real hope of selecting a meaningful treatment. As physician Robert Taylor, author of *Mind or Body*, has argued, such identifications "signify nothing with respect to specific causation," and furthermore, "descriptive labeling does not provide causative understanding." It's not difficult to see how the lack of a proper diagnosis can lead directly to the mistreatment of a patient. If the healer does not search for the cause of the patient's symptoms, there is little likelihood that he or she can treat those causes.

For a skillful medical doctor, the description of symptoms is just the start of the diagnostic process. Competent doctors will collect a thorough medical and personal history (including information about the patient's family history of illness) and complete a full physical examination of the patient. In addition, no medical diagnostic process would be complete without using the appropriate medical tests and neurological evaluations. "This medical detective work, known as the deductive differential diagnosis, is the cornerstone of medicine," psychiatrist Sydney Walker notes. "But modern psychiatry has attempted to shortcut the process . . . psychiatry has replaced the science of diagnosis with the pseudoscience of labeling."

This confusion can be seen most clearly in the bible of the mental health field: the *Diagnostic and Statistical Manual of Mental Disorders* (DSM IV). The DSM mostly concerns itself with the description of behaviors while largely ignoring the issue of what causes those behaviors. You can be given the label of borderline personality disorder, for example, if you manifest five out of a list of nine rather vague behaviors, such as inappropriate intense anger, chronic feelings of emptiness, a persistently unstable self-image, or a pattern of unstable and intense interpersonal relationships.* But there is no mention of what might cause such symptoms. Often avoiding the issue of cause, the DSM encourages psychiatrists and therapists alike to believe they have diagnosed the patient when they have only described the patient's symptoms.

"Reliability, and not validity, is the goal of the DSM," write psychiatrists Paul McHugh and Phillip Slavney. The DSM gives rules that make it likely that two different psychiatrists will give the same label to a given patient. This is little more than an extensive and complicated word game, for there is nothing in the DSM that would guide these two psychiatrists to come to the same conclusion about *the source* of this patient's problems. As McHugh points out, the questions the DSM does not address include: "How do these disorders come about? How are they to be avoided? What is necessary to correct them?" In short, the questions the DSM does not address are precisely the central questions a differential diagnosis seeks to answer.

In a "Cautionary Statement" at the beginning of the DSM, readers are warned that the criteria listed are offered only as "guidelines for making diagnoses, because it has been demonstrated that the use of such criteria enhances agreement among clinicians and investigators." They go on to warn that "the proper use of these criteria requires specialized training that provides both a body of knowledge and clinical skill." One

---

*Indeed, the patient might not even have to have these symptoms to be stuck with the label. In the introduction, the DSM authors write that "the exercise of clinical judgment may justify giving a certain diagnosis to an individual even though the clinical presentation falls just short of meeting the full criteria for the diagnosis."

wonders *what kind* of "specialized training" yielding *what sort* of "body of knowledge." Surely training and clinical work in phrenology, for example, should not count. But what should?

We are left guessing on this score precisely because the mental health field is not in agreement on the questions of what is the best training and theoretical orientation for practitioners. The DSM authors do not mention the clear upshot of this problem: While different clinicians might (thanks to the DSM) be able to label a patient's problems by the same name, they are unlikely to agree on how to treat the patient. Although published by the American Psychiatric Association, the DSM is marketed to the entire mental health field. Because the field is hopelessly splintered on the issue of where disorders come from and how to treat them, it is not surprising that the primary "diagnostic" manual is largely mute on the subjects of cause and cure.

The recent research on the causes of brain disorders requires a good deal more medical and scientific knowledge than the vast majority of therapists possess. Describing behavior, however, requires little specific medical knowledge. Anyone, from the medically trained psychiatrist to the master's degree–level social worker or the holder of a degree in educational and family counseling, can use the DSM.

Without any agreement on the etiologies of the problems listed in the DSM, it is not surprising that the inclusion or exclusion of any given disorder is little more than a popularity contest. The labels the DSM gives to sets of behavior are proposed, lobbied for, and defended based on consensus among the APA elite, with no necessary scientific or even orderly study underlying them. "To read about the evolution of the DSM is to know this: it is an entirely political document," writes Louise Armstrong in *And They Call It Help.*

The DSM, as a labeling word game, is not wholly without value. Indeed, compared to what came before, it is something of an advance in that it at least gives clinicians some way to know when they are talking about the same sets of symptoms. As Guze points out, it was only a generation ago that American psychiatrists were largely intent on arguing against the central importance of any diagnostic system—even one as shaky as that of the DSM. The DSM, despite its blindness to the issue of etiology, is at least an indication that the field is interested in some semblance of categorization of the disorders it claims to treat.

Unfortunately, the danger is still present that the non-medically trained practitioner might mistakenly believe the use of this labeling system is the equivalent of a differential medical diagnosis. For the medically trained doctor, the diagnosis is the critical step in selecting from a wide range of treatment options. Perhaps this is why differential diagnosis is so undervalued in therapy circles. For the committed of Johns Hopkins Medical School therapist, after all, there is only one treatment choice.

When the DSM process of categorization replaces differential diagnosis, the results can be disastrous for patients. Walker, in his book *A Dose of Sanity,* cites example after example of patients whose underlying disorder was ignored for years after psychiatrists incorrectly believed that they had completed a "diagnosis" with a DSM label.

Bobby, a shy eight-year-old, is one of those stories. Failing three of his classes and constantly in trouble at school for "acting out," Bobby had been diagnosed with classic attention deficit/hyperactivity disorder, because his behavior fit into the correct number of indicators* listed in the DSM. But these behaviors and the DSM label said nothing of the many possible causes for such behavior. Regardless, a psychiatrist put Bobby on Ritalin in hopes of masking his symptoms.

When he was eventually examined by Walker, the actual causes of Bobby's symptoms became clearer. Walker first noticed a number of compelling signs that the previous doctor had overlooked: Bobby was suffering from joint pain and fatigue; his neck veins stuck out prominently (indicating possible problems

---

*These descriptions of behaviors include fidgeting with hands and feet, squirming in seat, often running about in situations where it is inappropriate, having difficulty playing or engaging in leisure activities, having difficulty waiting his or her turn, and talking excessively.

with his heart); and his fingernails had ridges (pointing to the possibility of infection). Further tests revealed not one but several possible sources for Bobby's symptoms. An EEG showed that he was suffering from frequent mild seizures. Tests indicated that he had higher-than-normal lead levels while other tests showed that his joint pain was likely due to a previous strep infection. Further, abnormalities in blood tests pointed to possible heart ailments.

Bobby's diagnosis revealed a number of specific and, more important, *treatable* causes for the problems that plagued this child. The DSM diagnosis of hyperactivity and the prescription of Ritalin would do nothing for Bobby except perhaps hide his most obvious symptom of fidgeting in school. Indeed, the DSM diagnosis can be worse than nothing because it can give patients (or their caretakers) the false impression that they have received a clear understanding of an illness. This illusion decreases the likelihood that they will seek help from a doctor who understands diagnostic procedures and has the tools at hand to do an adequate job. In Bobby's case, ignoring his heart condition could have proven fatal.

Bobby's story is anecdotal support for Walker's general point: "The impressive medical terms in the DSM conceal a myriad of underlying medical problems, many of them curable—and many of them dangerous if left untreated." As Walker notes, many psychiatrists would miss the causes of Bobby's condition because they would stop at the categorization of his symptoms.

We should point out that Walker's criticism is pointedly directed at his fellow medically trained psychiatrists—those in the mental health field with the most claim to scientific status. That psychiatrists rely on DSM labeling and often fail to follow state-of-the-art diagnostic procedures is indeed troubling. Many psychiatrists, who are trained in medicine, have unfortunately opted to concentrate on psychodynamic theories that trace sources of problems to their patients' social/developmental histories and to their unconscious. As the studies on misdiagnosis indicate, the psychiatrists who have concentrated on talk therapy often overlooked the growing knowledge surrounding brain dysfunction and its relation to physical health. If they have focused primarily on psychodynamic theories, they have likely not stayed sufficiently abreast of the medical research. Some have become hardly distinguishable from the tens of thousands of psychologists and social workers who never had medical training.

Aside from the fact that they can lead to the misapplication of therapy, poor diagnostic procedures can also lead to the use of the wrong medications or medical intervention. In particular, the overprescription of Prozac is due to the inadequate understanding and misuse of diagnostic procedures within psychiatry. A psychiatrist who prescribes Prozac to every patient who has symptoms of depression is not doing his patients any favors unless he has ruled out the hundreds of underlying conditions that can lead to symptoms of depression. (Many serious but hidden illnesses can cause depressionlike symptoms.)

Since the accepted diagnostic procedures duck the issue of what is at the root of the problem, some psychiatrists and virtually all psychotherapists continue to guess about the cause of symptoms based on their various theoretical backgrounds.

A commonplace piece of advice for young doctors learning diagnostic technique is "When you hear hooves, think horses, not zebras." This is another way of describing the Occam's razor approach to reasoning—that is, to shave off less plausible theories in favor of more plausible ones. Unfortunately, the psychodynamic therapists often have not simply made the mistake of assuming zebras when hooves are heard, they have continued to theorize the existence of unicorns and satyrs.

The incorrect assumptions of mental health healers in regard to the expected symptoms and etiologies of mental illness can have effects beyond the mistreatment of patients. It is quite clear that behavior, including the symptoms of mental illness, can be gravely influenced by the beliefs of a culture and the expectations of those around us, particularly those who claim to understand the forces of our mental life. For proof, one need look no farther than the last pages of the DSM, where the authors list twenty-five "Culture-Bound Syndromes" from around the world. There is, for example, a syndrome particular to China and Taiwan called "shenkui," which can bring on dizziness, backache, fatigue, general weakness, and insomnia. Shenkui is supposedly caused by excessive semen loss and is often feared to be life-threatening. There is also a syndrome common to East Asia known as "koro," which is a sudden and intense anxiety that the penis will recede into the body and possibly cause death. Koro has been know to spread in local epidemics. In Arctic and sub-Arctic Eskimo communities, to choose one last example, there is a syndrome known as "pibloktoq," which is characterized by bizarre tantrums followed by convulsive seizures. It is clear from these examples that the expression of mental illness (and even the mimicking of symptoms by the non-mentally-ill) can be greatly influenced by cultural expectations and by the shared agreement on the source of the problem. This suggestibility makes it extremely important that therapists not indoctrinate their patients with speculative theories about the source and expected expression of symptoms or disorders.

The demeanor necessary for an accurate differential diagnosis is that of humility in the face of the unfolding evidence. Even a doctor with a hunch, or one on the trail of a suspected pathogen, should understand that a good diagnosis is discovered through an accumulation of evidence and not imposed on the basis of belief.

It is another debate tactic of psychodynamic therapists to suggest that the application of a differential diagnosis and the medical model to mental health fundamentally ignores the environmental factors that influence or precipitate mental illness. This is an unfair extension of the argument that only psychotherapists treat the "whole patient" while those who follow the medical model cruelly ignore patient histories and treat patients as if they were biomedical machines. But, of course, medicine does not ignore influences outside the patient's body or in their past, and neither should the medical approach to mental health.

In fact, the medical approach to illness does not assume one etiology over another until evidence begins to stack up. "The medical model," writes Guze, ". . . can accept social and psychological events as causes just as well as physical and chemical events. It can accept single causes or multiple causes. It can even be applied when etiology is unknown, as in many clinical investigations." Psychodynamic therapists seem to be projecting their own mistake—that of seeking a single sources of pathology in patients—upon medical practitioners. That the medical model takes into account evidence besides a patient's developmental history does not mean it is *limited* to that other evidence. In fact, as with any system of complex interactions, careful empirical work is the only hope of attaining any understanding of the relationship between social, environmental, and developmental forces on the functions of the brain and body.

There are currently myriad causes for brain dysfunction that are understood, and many for which there are treatments. The rapid development of this body of knowledge during the last fifty years has finally begun to provide a legitimate basis for the social status granted those who claim to be skilled at treating disorders of the brain.

There are reasons to believe that the advances will accelerate in the coming years. Improvements in biotechnology make it possible to synthesize thousands of compounds and to screen them in order to choose those with the highest possibility of having an effect. According to psychiatrist Pope, the time it takes to get a new compound to the human trial stage is one tenth the time it took fifteen years ago.

"Over the next ten years we will see the introduction of vastly superior psychiatric drugs to the point where the things we had in the 1970s will seem like Pleistocene relics compared to what will be on the shelves by 2005 or 2010," says Pope. "Once people start getting better, there will simply be no reason to spend years in talking therapy to try to analyze their problems."

While there is little doubt that the pace of progress along these lines will increase, there is also the possibility of dramatic breakthroughs that will revolutionize our understanding of mental illness. Pope and his colleague Jim Hudson have foreseen just such a shift in thinking. Writing about a whole spectrum of disorders including depression, panic disorder, anxiety, obsessive-compulsive disorder, and bulimia nervosa, Pope and Hudson predicted in 1990 that these seemingly dissimilar illnesses will turn out to share a pathological abnormality. Research since the publication of this paper has given weight to their stance. Drugs that have proven effective in treating depression have shown similar benefits across the spectrum of disorders that Pope and Hudson predict have a common root.

Even without considering future advances, there is presently enough knowledge to justify a shift in the way we think about mental health professionals. It is no longer enough to offer theories of mental functioning that are compelling or believable to the patient. It is time that the claim to jurisdiction over the province of mental health should be directly related to the ability to diagnose, manage (or cure), and predict the course of disorders of the brain.

Of course, there are diseases of the brain that medicine cannot cure. Autism, schizophrenia, and many types of brain tumors are currently beyond the reach of medical treatment. But even in these cases a proper diagnosis can be helpful. Knowing the classification and likely cause of such problems can, for instance, avoid anxiety heaped on patients who come to believe that their behavior results from their lack of control of their unconscious mind. Inappropriate blame is also likely to be avoided. Parents of an autistic or schizophrenic child who understand what medicine knows of the causes of the disease can stop blaming themselves for their child's state and learn a great deal about the best ways to care for a child with these severe disorders. At the very least, a well-founded understanding of the cause of a condition will avoid wasted time, effort, and money in pursuing procedures that offer no real likelihood of providing a cure.

Shifting our conception of a mental health healer would leave the psychodynamic therapist largely out of the loop.

However, mental health professionals with a more specific understanding of what can be effectively achieved in rehabilitative counseling would have a place as an ancillary treatment tool. These counselors, for instance, could manage the stress, anger, and anxiety often associated with mental illness. "Chronic anxiety . . ." writes Walker, "tends to make individuals breathe shallowly, which alters carbon dioxide levels; this change, in turn, alters the pH balance in the body, which can lead to sensations of panic. Anger alters levels of both neurotransmitters and hormones. Therapy, by relieving these normal but often counterproductive emotions, can also ameliorate their biochemical effects. . . . In this very limited sense, therapy can alter brain chemistry."

It is almost as important to define this sort of rehabilitative counseling by what it does not do. It does not attempt to rebuild the patient's personality, nor does it expect allegiance to a theoretical scheme of mental behavior or to any group or political or social cause. Treatment need not last for years and the therapist does not expect to create a global rationale for the patient's behavior or believe that such an explanation is essential for change. The patient's sense of self does not have to be torn down before it is rebuilt. Philosophical questions along the lines of "What is the meaning of my life?" are largely left outside the province of counseling. Such assistance is not expected to solve existential dilemmas, but rather to help in the removal of stumbling blocks in the individual's ability to function.

The major advances in the medical approach to mental illness have not come about because of Freud or psychodynamic therapies, but largely in spite of them. As we have explained, it was psychiatry—the very branch of mental health healing with the most scientific pretensions—that led the mental health field on its psychoanalytic misadventure in the mid-century. For this reason, it has not been from the field of psychiatry that the most promising medical advances have come. Sadly, psychiatry itself has been a latecomer in the scientific understanding of brain dysfunction.

Because psychiatrists lost themselves in the psychodynamic forest for the better part of this century, an entire generation was largely left out of the major medical advances. "Psychiatrists are becoming increasingly aware that their field hasn't kept up with modern science," writes Walker. "There is a growing discontent among psychiatrists regarding the poor quality of psychiatric 'diagnosis' and research over the past few decades, as well as a growing realization that advances made in other medical fields have made much of psychiatry obsolete. Psychiatrists are growing tired of watching neurologists, geneticists, immunologists, and microbiologists make dramatic progress in understanding the brain, while the 'brain doctors' themselves sit on the sidelines." The people who claimed status as healers of mental disorders have often been those most critically *lacking* in the ability to diagnose and treat them.

For this reason, it is hardly surprising that psychiatrists have overprescribed medications like Prozac and Ritalin. The enthusiasm for such medications does not resemble the careful practice of medicine, for the use of these medications often does not involve a careful diagnostic procedure, but rather looks very much like the excitement that surrounds the promotion of the latest talk therapy. Promoters of Prozac have made appearances on talk shows, been profiled and quoted in thousands of news magazines, and have written pop-psych books on the topic. Real medical advances—say, in the treatment of hyperthyroidism—do not get this sort of attention. Good treatments, like good diagnoses, are most often quite sophisticated and specific. They defy mutation into cure-alls.

Nevertheless, the American Psychological Association is currently busy lobbying to win prescription privileges for their clinical membership. Considering the lack of diagnostic skill on the part of the psychiatrists in the profession, the possibility that tens of thousands of psychologists may someday win the right to prescribe medication is a profoundly frightening notion. Is there any indication that these nonmedically trained therapists won't be a good sight worse at diagnosing patients than psychiatrists?

The ignorance of much of the mental health field to the advances in the area of brain dysfunction has often been defended with a spurious use of the mind-brain dichotomy. Psychodynamically oriented psychiatrists and therapists have often maintained that they are superior in helping patients understand their mind (which implies a big-picture understanding of quasi-metaphysical entities such as the unconscious and the psyche), while all but dismissing what is known of the brain's specific functions, disorders, and neurochemical makeup. By claiming that the mind is somehow distinct from the brain, they can argue that therapy is still the best treatment for matters of the mind. While this distinction can make for an endlessly interesting philosophical debate, it ignores the obvious fact that the brain is the organ from which human behavior emanates, and that without the brain there is no mind.

Psychodynamic psychotherapists spuriously argue that the medical approach to treating brain disorders will leave the patient bereft of a compelling life narrative by which they can organize their conception of themselves. Besides repeating our contention that life narratives (or "assumptive systems" in Jerome Frank's terminology) are socially supported myths, we would note that patients need not see their choice as an either/or dilemma. That a mental health professional might treat you without addressing your personal life narrative does not mean that you will be left without one. And if the disruption in your life narrative or sense of self comes about because of treatable brain dysfunction, there is no need for a therapist to reexamine or suggest changes in your life narrative in order for you to be treated.

• • •

Paul Starr, in his Pulitzer Prize–winning book, *The Social Transformation of American Medicine,* sums up the state of medicine at the turn of the century: "In the nineteenth century, the medical profession was generally weak, divided, insecure in its status and its income, unable to control entry into practice or to raise the standards of medical education." Snake-oil salesmen of all types roamed the country offering useless (and often harmful) medicines in impressively shaped bottles. The advertisements pushing these bogus medicines offer ample opportunity for us to laugh at these bunco men. The medicine China Stones, for instance, claimed to cure not only toothaches but also cancer and the bites of mad dogs. Lydia Pinkham's Vegetable Compound was touted as a cure for "all weaknesses of the generative organs of either sex," as well as "all diseases of the kidney." Tobacco-filled Cigars de Joy were advertised to give "immediate relief in the worst attack of asthma, hay fever, chronic bronchitis, influenza, cough and shortness of breath, and their daily use effects a complete cure." Dr. Johnson made these claims for his Mild Combination Treatment for Cancer: "No matter how serious your case may be—no matter how many operations you have had—no matter what treatments you have tried, do not give up hope. . . . I will furnish ample evidence of my integrity, honesty, financial and professional ability."

As with the mental health profession today, medicine a hundred years ago was charging ahead in all directions. Medicine's slow and imperfect transformation into a discipline driven by science was in no way inevitable. Contrary to popular belief, advances in the understanding of the workings of the human body did not have an immediate correlation with an increase in the professionalism or scientific standing of the average doctor. Change was not easy, for many had a financial incentive to maintain the status quo. Human misery has never been in short supply, and the fear of disease and death creates willing believers. Those with the confidence to lie convincingly often made fortunes exploiting these realities.

Indeed, the worst scams were perpetrated on the sick and desperate during the same age that Louis Pasteur and Robert Koch demonstrated that bacilli can cause disease and that inoculation could promote immunity. Legitimate scientific advances often spawned only more sophisticated claims from charlatans. William Radam, for example, gave credit to Pasteur and Koch in the marketing of his Microbe Killer, playing off the public's misunderstanding of the new breakthrough research. The Microbe

Killer, which consisted mostly of water with tiny traces of red wine and hydrochloric and sulfuric acids, was said to kill all the microbes in the body. Historian James Harvey Young, in his book *The Medical Messiahs,* reflected on the paradox of that time. The period in history when doctors could begin to explain many diseases "was the very age in which patent medicines reached their apogee."

It was only with great effort that the profession of medicine closed the gap that existed between science and the practitioner. To do so, professionals and journalists had to raise their voices and exert their influence. In the fight against pseudoscientific medicine, muckraking journalism became nearly as important as professional outrage. At the turn of the century, *Ladies' Home Journal* began running articles warning readers about the dangers of patent medicines. The most famous investigation came from *Collier's Weekly* in October of 1905. In a two-part series, the writer Samuel Hopkins Adams blasted the patent medicine industry. Naming 264 individuals and companies, Adams wrote a passionate jeremiad against these cynical drug sellers. "There is but one safeguard in the use of these remedies," he concludes, which is "to regard them as one would regard opium."

In 1906, a young educator named Abraham Flexner conducted an investigation of the nation's 131 medical schools. Flexner's findings proved devastating: America, he declared, had a few of the best medical schools in the world but many of the worst. Dozens of these schools lacked basic laboratory equipment and medical texts. Because of the poverty of the training at most institutions, he argued, society was overrun with poorly trained doctors and would be better off with fewer but better-trained physicians. Because many medical schools had drifted so far from the science of medicine, he concluded that "society reaps at this moment but a small fraction of the advantage which current knowledge has the power to confer."

Flexner's conclusion could not be more true of the mental health field at present. As medicine was a hundred years ago, the mental health field is now plagued by a large gap between its research and clinical applications. Largely unknown to the public, this split is fracturing the profession. While there are encouraging trends, the sheer number of clinical practitioners is so great that they effectively control the therapy industry. An alternative professional organization, the American Psychological Society, has been established as a place for scientifically oriented researchers and clinicians to flee the flood of romantic practitioners who are often contemptuous of science.

The revolution in medicine illustrates that change requires two types of force: momentum toward a new system, and an equally compelling argument as to why the status quo must be abandoned. As Lewis Thomas wrote in *The Medusa and the Snail*: "The real revolution in medicine did not begin with the introduction of science. That came years later. . . . Like a good many revolutions, this one began with the destruction of dogma. It was discovered that the greater part of medicine was nonsense."

We are in the midst of just such a revolution within the mental health field. Currently, there are mentally ill patients who are curable who are not being cured. This is not the patients' fault, for they have every reason to believe that they are putting themselves in the care of trained healers. Large segments of therapists have failed to understand or incorporate the massive advances in knowledge about the conditions they claim to treat. The specter of someone remaining sick while a cure exists outside the knowledge of their self-proclaimed healer should make anyone angry. That these very same healers who lack current knowledge about the treatment of mental illness often claim greater compassion in treating the "whole person," with their superior "intuition" and "wisdom," is an added insult.

Conclusion:
Therapy's Delusions

[Humans have] an almost limitless capacity for self-deception. The very nature of our brains—evolved to guess the most plausible interpretations of the limited evidence available—makes it almost inevitable that, without the discipline of scientific research, we shall often jump to wrong conclusions, especially about rather abstract matters.

—FRANCIS CRICK,
The Astonishing Hypothesis

In a *Harper's Magazine* essay, Peter Marin describes the four elements of the American passion for the latest existential enthusiasm: "(1) our desperate need to feel morally superior to others; (2) our need to believe that we alone have access to truths that can redeem or perfect the world; (3) our yearning to be the chosen of God—or, if we are secular, of history; (4) our tendencies to mistake our wishes for ideas and our ideas for truth by which we judge others, and find those others, of course, in need of change."

To the extent that psychotherapy feeds these appetites, it will always have defenders regardless of its ability to ameliorate the problems it claims to remedy. For many committed advocates, the questions we have raised in this book are beside the point. It doesn't really matter, after all, whether therapy works if there exists enough anecdotal testimony to increase or maintain the current number of patients. And to the extent that belonging to the group of enlightened people gives therapists and patients a sense of moral superiority, it is not likely to be undone by criticism from outside (and therefore unenlightened) skeptics. Who needs proof from outside sources when one has colleagues, friends, and acquaintances who agree on talk therapy's transformative powers?

When faith and social consensus become the standards of evaluation, social scientists usually stand back and accept the fact that people are often satisfied to have a share of faith, despite the inconsistencies or disconfirming evidence. If psychodynamic therapy is closer in kind to a trip to church than a visit to the doctor, the dire results of all the studies and critiques on the therapy are worth no more than their tonnage value at the paper recyclers. Faith need not be altered by negative empirical evidence; in fact, it often becomes stronger and more recalcitrant when faced with such challenges. It should be no more surprising to note that patients do not abandon therapy that has proven ineffective than it is to note that many still believe in creation myths that date the earth as a few billion years younger than scientists have estimated. This is not to say that social scientists can't do much when it comes to explaining the manufacturing of such beliefs, as we have attempted to do with psychodynamic therapy, but rather that they know that emotionally committed patients and therapists are not likely to be convinced through arguments based on mere fact.

The heart of therapy's power is that it feels meaningful to those who engage in it. Shouldn't that be sufficient? In one sense, the answer is yes. People should be free to pursue any beliefs they wish and, either collectively or individually, support the activities they value.

However, when the truth of a system of thinking can be understood only by those who already believe, the buyer should beware. What is being offered for sale in psychodynamic psychotherapy is not a cure to a problem but a system of myths about mental behavior and illness that requires a leap of faith to enter—that is, it requires the patient to ignore both common sense and empirical evidence. While psychodynamic therapists may promise that down the road, after a time of sincere adherence and devotion, the value of the system will become apparent, they cannot give compelling proof of this value to the uninitiated. Beliefs that require periods of indoctrination deserve careful inspection from the outside first. By their nature, belief systems that require building faith (either in a healer's power or the immutable truth of his or her doctrine) are not easily tried on for size, then returned.

So while our arguments may do little to convince those patients who believe they have experienced the healing power of psychodynamic therapy firsthand, they should make a difference to a prospective patient. We believe there is good reason to warn people, in the strongest possible language, away from explanatory theories and treatment methods that claim respect because they are scientific but in reality are built on myth. Similarly, if we as a society recognize that therapy depends on faith and not proof of its effectiveness, we may want to allocate our collectively gathered health care resources elsewhere.

Some therapists decry that their profession is being attacked unfairly from all sides. Managed care has limited the access of many practitioners to health insurance reimbursement. In addition, the profession is facing hundreds of lawsuits (with thousands more expected to come) against therapists who have practiced treatments such as recovered memory therapy and have diagnosed multiple personality disorder, which rank among the worst mistakes the profession has made in recent decades.

There is little doubt that managed care will fundamentally change the mental health care industry. In the past two decades, as the battle for scarce health care dollars heated up, psychotherapy was increasingly being asked not only to prove that patients ended up marginally better but that, at least for our most common mental health ailments, it could post a cure rate equal to that of medicine's. Psychodynamic therapy has not yet come close to being able to do that. As Carol Shaw Austad concluded in her book *Is Long-Term Psychotherapy Unethical?*,

"To date . . . we have not been able to achieve a level of certainty about the effectiveness of our treatment methods comparable to that which exists within the medical profession. . . . The type of outcome data that would enable us to use psychotherapy with the precision and certainty with which a physician operates to remove tonsils or gallstones simply does not exist." Under particular attack, as Austad's title hints, is the practice of long-term talk therapy, which, for all its mystique, has been able to post only the marginal effects of short-term treatment.

Therapists bemoan the fact that they are not treated by insurance companies with the same respect as medical doctors, often implying that critics and insurance companies are cruelly ignoring the ranks of the mentally ill. But it is not the fact that there are millions of mentally ill that is at question, it is the effectiveness of talk therapy as a treatment. With many disorders, it is no longer true that any treatment is better than any other. In terms of treating serious mental illness, it is time for the mental health professions to begin agreeing on the methods that are effective and to *limit their practice to those methods.* The testing of new treatments should now be done outside the general patient population before new procedures are adopted for use. It is unfortunate that actuaries of the managed care industry, not the mental health field's professional organizations, are the ones suggesting these changes.

In a 1994 article entitled "The Rape of Psychotherapy," former president of the American Psychological Association Roland Fox wrote: "I feel that psychotherapy and the profession of psychology are under attacks that are virtually unprecedented." While deploring the changes managed care has brought, Fox also points to what he calls the "media circus" surrounding the exposure of recent therapy misadventures, such as recovered memory practices. It is clear that Fox believes the amount of attention paid to these issues, and the result of that attention—which he says is a "black eye for psychotherapy"—is unfair and unwarranted. This attention, combined with the growing number of lawsuits, has "threaten[ed] to erode all public confidence in psychologists' services." Adding to the problem, according to Fox, therapists are suffering "secondary traumatization," because these trends will force them to "wonder if they somehow caused or encouraged" their patients to come up with false memories of abuse.

To lay the blame for the supposed harm done to the profession on the media or overzealous lawyers is, simply, outrageous. If the profession had any internal mechanisms with which to stem the spread of the acceptance of unsound speculations or unproven, dangerous techniques among its membership, it might have avoided at least some of the damage that has resulted in such bad publicity. It is not the media that has given the profession a "black eye" but the profession itself. Given that the profession so lacks standards, the media has an obligation to expose malpractice. And given that there are few internal mechanisms with which to hold therapists accountable, it is far from surprising that mistreated patients have looked to civil courts to air their grievances.

But what about the poor therapists who must now worry that they will be exposed to public criticism for employing potentially misguided theories and techniques? Those who have thoroughly acquainted themselves with the damage the reckless application of baseless theories of mental illness can visit on patients will, no doubt, shake their heads in wonderment at such an argument. It is, in fact, far past time that therapists begin worrying about the possibility that their well-meant ministrations might harm patients. To assume that such concern will cause the therapist "secondary traumatization" is a jaw-dropping example of the manner in which the profession tries to defend itself with its own jargon.

Psychodynamic therapists have attempted to hold their ground not by pointing to the studies that show their time-consuming and expensive approach to be differentially effective (there are no such studies), but by claiming that they are being bullied by forces with no compassion for the deeper questions that trouble us.

"Many practitioners and clients lament managed care's perversion of psychotherapy's most daring promise . . . to trans-form patients lives," wrote one protherapy essayist recently in *New Age Journal*. "Psychology, once a revolutionary approach to understanding reality and realizing one's inner potential, has under managed care been enlisted in the service of helping peo-ple adapt to the illusory security of the 'real world.'" The arti-cle disparages the work of HMOs for measuring success "simply in terms of what percentage of clients are functioning better at work and in their daily life." The article quotes one therapist as comparing managed care to McCarthyism, where "it is not communism that must be disavowed, but beliefs in a long-term treatment relationship, even though we know that a reliable, enduring relationship is no less necessary for the tor-mented individual of today than it was for such individuals in days gone by."

Articles like this one, entitled "Therapy Under Siege," expose the underlying biases and assumptions that continue to buttress the psychodynamic schools of therapy. It assumes that therapy has already adequately shown its ability to "transform patients' lives," "understand reality," and help clients realize their "inner potential." It avoids the obvious questions that should spring to mind: Transform patients' lives into what and on whose claim to authority? Whose assumptions of "inner potential" are we using? And most important: Whose view of "reality" does therapy attempt to lay bare? Is it something akin to Freud's "reality" of an inner mental life swirling with con-flicting unconscious desires and fantasies?

The way such advocates disparage the idea of "functioning better" in the "real world" also tips their intellectual hand. This sort of pious thinking is rife among psychodynamic ther-apists, for it mirrors their approach to patients, which assumes that if a problem is obvious, it must not be very important. Their promise is to reveal what is hidden from the patient, and so they assume that current problems are only indicators of deeper troubles in the patient's past or unconscious. Trouble on the job must be an indicator of something much more impor-tant; perhaps the patient is unknowingly reliving a bad parent-child relationship, or perhaps her unhappiness at work is an expression of her unconscious masochism. Learning ways of taking pleasure from that job (or building the strength to find a new one) would only be tricking the client into adapting to the "illusory security of the real world."

If mental health professionals focus on treating mental illness, who will be the guardians of the psyche and soul? Will we be forced to retreat into a mechanistic view of the brain and behavior? Will we be required to think of ourselves as biochemical machines? Who will take soundings of the deeper subjective mysteries of human experience? These are the questions psychodynamic therapists ask loudly in a last-ditch effort to save their teetering profession and declining practices.

The very premises of these questions are faulty. They imply, for instance, that humanity was incapable of addressing existential issues before Freud came along with his conception of the dynamic unconscious. Humanity has a rich history of literature, art, and philosophy that has always spoken to the mystical and subjective experience of humans. Second, such questions imply that psychodynamic therapies have actually done a respectable job in addressing these eternal human mysteries. As we have argued throughout this book, the promise that psychodynamic therapy will give patients a deep and complex understanding of themselves has simply been a cover for what are really *overly deterministic* views of human behavior and development. The psychodynamic literature is awash with case studies that report the key influences in a patient's existence in twenty pages or less. Although the influences pointed out by these therapists vary widely, these papers are similar in their certainty that they have discovered the central events of the patient's life and that these events without a doubt explain the patient's current perception and ability to function. These reports, in their very brevity, belie the notion that the psychodynamic approach to human behavior is very deep at all. It may claim superior attention to the whole person, but in practice it has most often shown only the narrowest determinism.

The argument that the biomedical model of mental health treatment will lead us all to be treated as biochemical machines is the most simpleminded of straw-man arguments. No one imagines that our current efforts to understand the human brain will lead to any such dismal conclusion. There is nothing about human experience to indicate that we are automatons, or simplistic rote learners, or mechanical responders to our environment. Whatever empirical understanding of the brain is revealed through science, it is unlikely to support a view of the human animal that's so different from what we can already observe.

What such research is likely to do, however, is draw a clearer delineation between normal mental functioning and disorders of the brain and begin to solve the great human mystery of mental abnormality. Mental illness is arguably the last large class of human affliction to be demystified. It was not so long ago that epileptics and others with brain disorders were viewed as being possessed with evil spirits or in some other way deserving of their fate. It was even more recently that the severely mentally ill were treated with lobotomies—a procedure that entailed little more than blindly sticking an ice pick in the patient's brain.

The progress in the biomedical understanding of mental illness that we have seen in the last half-century has been so heartening that for the first time in human history it is reasonable to expect that mental illness will someday soon lose its stigma. As the knowledge inevitably grows as to how to treat each specific malady, the quasi-philosophical debates surrounding the psychodynamic explanations will fall away from broad public discourse. When was the last time you had a passionate philosophical argument about the possible reasons everyone in your office was coming down with the flu?

Psychodynamic theories of mental illness and human development arose during a time when there were no provable or useful theories of brain function or dysfunction. They succeeded in winning followers partially because they filled the obvious vacuum in our ability to respond to the frightening presence of mental illness. As the biomedical model increases our knowledge of serious mental disorders, it will eventually destroy the myths we have held in the meantime.

The psychodynamic approach has failed not once but twice. First, it failed to illuminate specific causes of behavior and mental illness as Freud hoped it would. Second, it proved lackluster in its Freudian intention of giving humanity a language and a technique with which to illuminate its most complex experiences. Its history is one of false promises at both ends of this spectrum.

As Robert Coles writes, every generation is "on the hunt for a body of thought that promises to tell us almost everything about ourselves—our origins as individuals; our habits of thought; the nature of our affections; our interests; our likes and dislikes. For every demanding ideology there are, alas, all too many adherents, if not believers." Looking back at the superstitions and mistaken beliefs of previous generations is an easy way to feel superior. The flat earth, the divinity of kings, spirit possession, alchemy, phrenology, mesmerism—we can look back at all these beliefs and smugly wonder at the credulity of humans throughout recorded history. Charles Mackay, in his 1841 book, *Extraordinary Popular Delusions and the Madness of Crowds,* wrote: "Every age has its peculiar folly; some scheme, project, or phantasy into which it plunges, spurred on either by the love of gain, necessity of excitement, or the mere force of imitation. Failing in these, it has some madness, to which it is goaded by political or religious causes, or both combined."

The ease by which we can look back and dissect the widely held beliefs of the past can lead to its own type of delusion. Because we can so clearly see the social pressures that led to the adoption of past mistakes, we may believe that we are immune to those forces. If we are particularly self-assured, we can arrogantly believe we are the chosen generation in human history— the people who have finally come to a clear and meaningful understanding of the world around us. It is the nature, after all, of commonly shared delusions that they do not appear delusional during the time they are commonly held.

However, if we were to more closely examine any of the misguided notions from times past, we would see a legacy of very human mistakes—mistakes we are still prone to make. Humans are intensely curious, but the innate curiosity we possess (or, perhaps, are plagued with) is rarely expressed through dumbstruck awe. We show little ability to view a complicated set of evidence without quickly proposing some thesis about what we are examining. Our curiosity propels us to seek answers and, as history shows, we prefer incorrect answers to uncertainty. Our tendency to prematurely propose hypotheses about the world around us is the very expression of human curiosity.

The history of human thought prior to the rise of a scientific approach to knowledge is one of the hypotheses adopted because they have gained social consensus. Incorrect hypotheses have often gained such sway for reasons entirely independent of their validity. The tenacity with which humans hold these incorrect theories, once they have gained social momentum, can be extreme. Myths are often held and protected despite evidence against them and regardless of the lack of evidence in their favor. Those in the position to protect prominent myths have often responded to critics with everything from social censure to torture and execution.

Considering this, a more challenging mental game is to wonder what superstition are we currently laboring under that future generations will recognize as merely a social product of our times. Our answer, at this point, should surprise no one: The myth we are burdened with is the psychodynamic mind, as proposed by Freud and manipulated by psychodynamic therapists throughout the century. It is a myth worth challenging because it is not of the benign fireside variety that keeps away the fear of the darkness outside. This is a myth that has promised to cure the mentally ill. It is a myth that has claimed to advance our understanding of human mental functioning and behavior. It has done neither of these things and it is time for it to give way.

Still, the question remains that if the conception of the psychodynamic mind has made the foundation by which we have created the narrative that explains our lives, what will we do without it? To answer that question, it should first be noted that the biomedical approach to the brain offers a narrative itself. The brain-disorder explanation for something like depression seems at first an implausibly thin one, particularly for those who have spent time in therapy piecing together a psychodynamic explanation. Take, for example, a patient who comes to understand that she suffers from depression because of the deleterious effects of a sleep disorder caused by a combination of environmental factors and genetic propensities. While this is a shorter and less compelling story than a psychodynamic one (for it lacks the villains, intrigue, and exciting exploration of the hidden elements of the psyche that the psychodynamic therapy narrative offers), it is, nonetheless, a narrative that the patient can tell herself about her life.

Currently there is a cultural resistance to such brain-disorder explanation. Because we have been indoctrinated to accept the psychodynamic myth, we are often more comfortable believing that our variations in mood and idiosyncratic habits are solely or primarily reflections of experiences during our upbringing, even if those past events (as psychodynamic therapists often tell us) are hidden from our awareness. To learn that the basis of a symptom like depression may actually exist in one's current environment and brain chemistry can be perplexing to those who have fully accepted the premises of the psychodynamic view of the mind. The new information can be as disorienting as learning, after spending years searching the world for a buried treasure, that the treasure is back home in the attic.

In describing how well medication worked to cure his depression, novelist Walter Kirn wrote that he was at first greatly uncomfortable with the idea that his feelings were a function of chemistry. He writes that he had to resign himself to "a humbling new self-image: neurochemical robot." But this often-repeated negative reaction is, in all likelihood, an expression of the current awkward transition period between socially accepted narratives. A few generations from now, once the psychodynamic attempt to explain behavior and cognitive functioning has been fully exposed as an elaborate myth, the biomedical explanation is likely not to carry with it a sense of humbling moral defeat.

Of course, there will always be a gap between understanding the brain at its neurological level and our understanding of the mind through our shared descriptions of our feelings of consciousness. We have no intuitive ability to explain or describe, for instance, the function of synapses, or where memory exists in our brain, or the different functions of our right and left hemispheres. Careful scientific study, not introspection, has yielded what information we have on these subjects. The bulk of the brain's work happens outside our ability to describe its activities. The brain allows us to see out rather than in.

The scientific knowledge of the chemical makeup of the brain tells us little about the sensations, emotions, and thoughts it produces. Knowing where memory is stored, for example, tells us nothing about how memory affects how we think about ourselves. Paul McHugh describes the dilemma we are left with: "Synthetic explanations from the molecule up and reductionist analyses from the thought down do not meet, but leave a gap so wide that the most obvious feature of mental life—its subjective sense of purposefulness and meaning—remains disconnected from the objectively demonstrated dependence of that life on neurological integrity. It is from this fundamental problem that confusion arises over whether mental events are in themselves real things and how they are best explained."

The biomedical explanation will likely always appear thin compared to the dramatic stories patients learn to believe in therapy. However, and here is a key point, *the need to have a mythology to explain our circumstances is greatest when those circumstances are an unchangeable mystery*. To put it another way: We most desperately need an explanation for a condition like depression when we repeatedly experience it without any ability to escape its deadening symptoms. If the brain-disorder approach is correct and has yielded effective treatment techniques, then the story we tell ourselves about why we became depressed becomes much less important. When we gain actual control of the world, the myths we tell ourselves about how we are controlled by mysterious outside forces (or unseen internal ones) are no longer required.

That our beliefs about ourselves will likely always be rooted in language and story does not mean that science cannot inform this pursuit. Science has many specific things to teach us about ourselves and our behavior, but it also holds this clear aggregate lesson: The universe is an extremely complicated place; explaining even a small piece of the reality that surrounds us often requires Herculean effort. Human behavior, in particular, is a puzzle of vast and stunning complexity. Although our brains are evolved to manifest human behavior, they are paradoxically not well suited to explain that behavior. This does not make such explanations impossible, only tremendously difficult. While it is true that science can add to our individual understandings of ourselves in specific ways, it is certainly far past the time for us to incorporate its larger lesson—that of a humility in the face of our own complexity—into any story we tell ourselves about our lives.

It seems possible, moreover, that we might learn not to fear the complexity of the universe or the fact that it was clearly not designed for easy human comprehension, but rather that we will find solace and beauty in its intricacies and randomness. With a bit of humility and a modicum of skepticism, we may also learn to identify and avoid the endless parade of healers, shamans, and gurus who, while claiming to expand our view of existence, actually narrow our ability to appreciate its true depth.

To compare the scientific and psychodynamic conceptions of the mind for their level of humanity in the face of the complexity of the human mind is not difficult. The landscape science has glimpsed is far more wondrously elaborate than Freud, or any of history's myth makers, imagined. Science, as Francis Crick writes, "has not diminished our sense of awe but increased it immeasurably. . . . One must be dull of spirit indeed to read about it and not feel how marvelous it is. To say that our behavior is based on a vast, interacting assembly of neurons should not diminish our view of ourselves but enlarge it tremendously."

There is no reason, medical or moral, why people need to view their lives through the simple narratives cultures adopt. In the end, prescientific narratives have been less useful in explaining the vagaries of existence than they have been for signifying membership in a social group—a demonstration of support for its norms and values. The very idea that an all-explaining life narrative is necessary for human happiness may just be another story we have invented.

Appendix

One study deserves particular attention, not only because of the widespread coverage it received but because of how well it illustrates one major flaw in such studies. Published in 1995, the *Consumer Reports* article "Does Therapy Help?" was greeted with open arms by an industry beset by controversy, division, and increasing consumer skepticism. The magazine reported that the results of a survey of its readership indicated that therapy was remarkably successful. After so many years of marginal or negative results, the APA and other organizations embraced the *Consumer Reports* article with open arms. It's worth taking a close look at the results because the study was so influential in the national debate about psychotherapy, and it contains a number of flaws that make its conclusions questionable at best.

The article was based on a survey of 7,000 people who reported seeking help for mental health issues. While 3,000 sought help from friends, clergy, or relatives, others sought help through family doctors; 2,900 went to psychologists, psychiatrists, or some other form of mental health provider. It was these 2,900 that the survey focused on.

In particular, of the 426 people who remembered feeling very poor when they began therapy, 87 percent reported feeling "very good" or "good" by the time they were surveyed. Of the 786 people who were feeling fairly poor at the outset, 92 percent were feeling "very good" or "good" when surveyed.

According to Martin Seligman, who was consulted on the study and held the post of president of the American Psychological Association's division of clinical psychology, the survey sent a "message of hope" to people dealing with emotional problems.

The first problem is that the survey had no semblance of a control group—that is, people who reported having mental health problems but did not seek treatment. To know the extent to which therapy helped, it is critical to know not only what happened to those who sought treatment but also to those who didn't. Even Seligman accedes to this drawback in one sentence of his otherwise glowing *American Psychologist* report about the *Consumer Reports* survey. "Because there are no control groups," he writes, "the *CR* study cannot tell us directly whether talking to sympathetic friends or merely letting time pass would have produced just as much improvement as treatment by a mental health professional." Which is to say that the survey, which is intended to show us how helpful psychotherapy can be, actually tells us nothing of the sort.

The problems with the *Consumer Reports* study do not end there. The study bases all its weight on the respondents' ability to accurately remember and report their mental health from years past. The study's authors and promoters have grievously underestimated the way the memory of our emotional lives can be skewed in retrospective narratives. A full century of studies on the abilities of medical patients to accurately report symptoms shows that they are highly unreliable.

Seligman defends the survey's use of retrospective reports but not by citing studies showing how consistently people can accurately report feelings from years past. Rather, Seligman makes the case that *Consumer Reports* has used such retrospective surveys in the past and therefore they must have passed the test of time. "If retrospection was a fatal flaw, *CR* would have given up the reader's survey method long ago, since reliability of used cars and satisfaction with airlines . . . depends on retrospection."

Here we have a fine example of wishful thinking on the part of therapy's defenders. Assessing one's emotional and mental functioning over a long period of time is, of course, an entirely different undertaking than remembering whether one has had trouble with his car over that period. In the *Journal of Nervous and Mental Disease*, Lloyd Rogler and colleagues summed up this research on the ability of patients to recall symptoms simply: "Questions prefaced by the phrase, 'have you ever . . .' are assuredly not likely to produce what the retrospective requirement intended." The various factors that might unintentionally skew the response include the "type of symptom episode being recalled and the current mood of the respondent at the time of recall." All the studies we have seen on the accuracy of such self-assessment have pointed to the opposite of Seligman's cheerful assurance.

Notes

Introduction

11 "But there are always men . . . to some other group": Kuhn 1996, p. 19.

15 "zealots and charlatans" . . . "represented by psychiatry and psychotherapy": McHugh 1995, p. 201.

20 Technology such as . . . on the X chromosome: McHugh 1987, p. 916–17.

23 Thomas Kuhn's seminal analysis . . . the idea of a paradigm: Kuhn 1996, pp. 1–9.

25 Astrology and astronomy . . . the same thing: Ibid., p. 19n.

Chapter One: A Profession in Crisis

29 "Out in the rough-and-tumble . . . currency of guilt and blame": Crews 1995, p. 223.

30 "The field of modern psychology . . . and the real life": *Chicago Tribune* 1997, sec. 2, p. 1.

32 "As a profession clinical psychology . . . more important than prescription": Cox 1997.

36 "interpret literature . . . prescribe for the millennium": McHugh 1992, p. 497.

41 "people harboring disease . . . envious, passive, and amoral": Crews 1995, p. 71.

41 "all sciences have to pass through an ordeal by quackery": As quoted in Shorter 1997, p. 313.

44 For these reasons they maintain . . . rigor than medicine: Guze 1992, p. 35.

47 "Psychoanalysis gave us a vernacular . . . not given us such a vocabulary": Allen 1997, p. D1.

48 "longing to be able . . . single key": Freud 1953, p. 25.

Chapter Two: Freud's Forest of Resemblances

51 "Now listen to this . . . manage to contain my delight": Masson 1985, p. 146.

51 "I no longer understand . . . kind of madness": Ibid., p. 152.

51 The exhibit was going to be . . .: Crews, in press, p. 3. Many of the details used to describe the controversy surrounding the Freud exhibit in the following pages were taken from the introduction of *Unauthorized Freud,* which was in press as we were writing. The authors were grateful to have an advance view of the book. Pages cited are of the work in manuscript form.

52 A prominent independent . . . ". . . modern intellectual history": Ibid., p. 3.

53 "censors" . . . "Ayatollah's fatwa against Salman Rushdie": Ibid., pp. 4–5.

54 "prejudice that still . . . primitive psychology of faculties and humors": Ibid., p. 7.

55 "The movement's anti-empirical features . . . confirmation' of it as well": Crews 1995, p. 61.

56 *Freier Einfall:* Macmillian 1997, pp. 109–16.

56 Freud dogmatically insisted . . . *preceding* idea: Ibid., pp. 568–70.

57 "[T]he etiological pretensions . . . hysterical symptoms": Ibid., p. 209.

58 "subtle but *strong* interconnections": Ibid., p. 208.

58 "Conclusions about a causal link . . . presence of confounding variables": Rind 1997, pp. 237–55.

58 " 'Free' associations aren't free at all . . . being influenced by that bias": Crews 1995, p. 151.

59 "[T]he tendency not to reply . . . break out of the circle": Macmillan 1997, pp. 569, 610–12.

60 As Crews and others . . . had been "castrated": Crews 1995, p. 46.

61 "[Freud] assumes that since he . . . is not normally associated": Webster 1995, pp. 165–66.

61 "imaginative equation between babies and feces . . . replace one another freely": Ibid., p. 18.

62 "enduring discoveries . . . psychoanalytic formulation": Ibid., pp. 104–5.

63 "two-step . . . no further harm": Ibid., p. 134.

63 "the encompassing explanatory reach . . . test of time": Ibid., p. 106.

63 "Freud's ambiguity . . . survivals of Calvinism": Hale 1995b, p.6.

64 "Unfortunately I and many others . . . built their own churches": Stone 1995, p. 1.

65 "thicket of similar overlapping . . . same conceptual context": Heinz Kohut as quoted in Ibid., p. 2.

65 "Freud did not even feel the need . . . inspired speculation": Ibid., p. 5.

65 "It is astonishing to see . . . collected works of Sigmund Freud": Ibid., p. 6.

66 "My reading about the Frink affair . . . over our idealized leaders": Ibid., pp. 9–10.

67 "Our critics might be right . . . individual more daunting": Ibid., p. 12.

67 "not in disrespect . . . possibilities of sexual gratification": Ibid., p. 6.

67 "artist/subjectivist . . . proofs of their contentions": Ibid., p. 8.

68 "This is a post modern . . . hermeneutic uncertainty": Ibid., pp. 12–13.

69 "The analyst is loved, admired . . . catalyst of change": Ibid., p. 10.

69 "I still believe . . . one's self": Ibid., p. 13.

NOTES

Chapter Three: Rise and Fall
of the Psychodynamic Mind

71 "We stand at the threshold . . . than the atomic bomb": Levitas 1965, p. xi.

71 "before Freud there had been . . . ignored sexuality and childhood ": Hale 1995b, p. xi.

73 "The émigré analysts . . . highly respected pathfinder": Shorter 1997, p. 172.

74 America, it was noted . . . leading psychiatric trend: Shorter 1997, p. 170.

74 The postwar years . . . "something of a gold rush": Hale 1995, p. 211.

74 Fewer than 100,000 patients had completed . . . by these professionals: Ibid., p. 289.

74 In October of 1945 . . . able to walk, unaided: Ibid., pp. 279–80.

75 "eager to convert others . . . a wide audience": Ibid., p. 291.

75 "popularization further inflated . . . became abundantly clear": Ibid., p. 282.

75 "any doubts about . . . uses of the new therapy": Ibid., p. 280.

76 "in the highest . . . are to a metallurgist": Jones 1955, pp. 431–32.

76 "According to Sigmund Freud . . . hardly aware of them": Freud 1951.

76 "By discarding the old methods . . . the person concerned": Ibid.

77 "Psychoanalysis was the caisson . . . into private practice": Shorter 1997, p. 161.

78 "most people . . . illness at some time": Menninger 1963, p. 33.

79 "committed to the . . . in the United States": Hale 1995b, p. 214.

80 "A boy loves his mother . . . to his old man": Ibid., p. 285.

80 "These clashes of opinion . . . delight of their opponents": Ibid., p. 218.

80 "We are laughed . . . not enhanced thereby": Ibid., p. 219.

81 "I remember certain statements . . . we cannot help them": Masson 1988, p. 88.

82 "excessive, unresolved dependence": Hale 1995b, p. 259.

83 In particular . . . of destruction and guilt: Ibid., 261.

84 PATIENT: "You are a son of a bitch . . . wish to lay under it": Ibid., pp. 265–67.

84 Avoiding prosecution . . . license in 1983: Masson 1988, p. 126.

85 Hale recounts . . . "at the time opposed": Hale 1995b, p. 330.

85 More common were comments . . . ". . . with pioneering enthusiasm": Masson 1988, p. 128.

85 "He must make up . . . treatment of schizophrenia": Ibid., pp. 127–28.

89 The National Institute of Mental Health . . . ". . . not really convincing facts": Hale 1995b, p. 331.

90 "most stupendous . . . twentieth century": Medawar 1975, p. 17.

93 "psychoanalysis was conspicuous by its absence": Hale 1995b, p. 331.

94 "no consistent evidence exists . . . predisposed to this condition": Molden and Gottesman 1997, pp. 554–55

94 "switched to something else . . . could have imagined": Sifford 1987.

95 Opened in 1910 . . . hiding the patient's symptoms: Boodman 1989.

96 Osheroff's treatment . . . for more than a half a year: Klerman 1990.

98 In 1982, Osheroff brought a lawsuit . . . depression: Stone 1984.

98 "indicate that a large . . . minority rule": Sifford 1987.

99 "make a number of . . . shy and nervous": Ibid.

Chapter Four: Three Cases from a Legacy of Intellectual Hubris

101 "Psychodynamic psychotherapy . . . is a complex art": Nichols and Paolino 1986, p. xvii.

101 In 1912, Ernest Jones . . . The couple soon drowned: Jones 1912, p. 16–17.

102 "Her efforts to escape . . . side of the assailant": Ibid., p. 18.

102 "It is known . . . informed circles": Ibid., pp. 10, 19.

103 "We may thus imagine . . . of her deepest desire": Ibid., p. 21.

104 ". . . when the act of defecation . . . condition of dying together": Ibid., p. 15.

104 "the sense of security . . . intolerance of illusion": Roazen 1975, pp. 334, 342.

108 "probably products of . . . theoretical problem lay": Elisabeth Young-Bruehl in Stafford-Clark 1965, pp. xiv–xv.

108 "Our forefathers . . . other so-called 'deviants' ": Weinberg 1984, pp. x–xi.

110 "From this incident . . . practice was going badly": Ibid., pp. 4–5.

111 "One day, he was busily . . . he never forgave it": Rachman 1991, pp. 221–22.

112 "During his first year . . . resignation pervaded his existence": Ibid., p. 220.

112 "giant mole" . . . "of his body and mind": Ibid., pp. 220–29.

113 "[The consultant] concluded that the mother's . . . . effect on the therapist": Ibid., pp. 234–35.

113 "she practiced almost total . . . adult personality problems": Ibid., p. 235.

113 "satisfied that the proper diagnosis . . . who was thwarted": Ibid.

114 Charlotte Prozan . . . rodents in just this manner: Prozan 1993, p. 261.

115 "The scene was set . . . free to create": Rachman 1991, pp. 235–36.

116 "demonstrated a warm, sensitive feeling": Ibid., p. 238.

116 "I am a microsurgeon . . . not speaking metaphorically": Vaughan 1997, pp. 3–4.

117 "I dreamed I was at your office . . . felt scared and sad": Ibid., p. 1.

118 " 'It's as if . . .' . . . Katie begins to cry": Ibid., p. 7.

119 "I believe the cerebral cortex . . . relationships in daily life": Ibid., p. 17.

120 "our neural networks seem . . . patient's neural networks": Ibid., p. 5.

121 "I bought stock . . . when I woke up": Ibid., p. 179.

121 "The fact that Johnson & Johnson . . . with her own life": Ibid., pp. 181–87.

Chapter Five: Does Therapy Work?

125 "Above all, what we as Americans . . . to quiet the soul": Marin 1996, p. 40.

128 "crowded with entrepreneurs . . . by a few case reports": Frank 1974, p. 325.

128 "No matter how elegant . . . is still poor research": P. Kline 1983, p. 20.

129 "Our understanding of the nature . . . this type of placebo treatment": Prioleau et al. 1983, p. 277.

130 "vanishingly small": Ibid., p. 279.

130 Other studies have indicated . . . no treatment at all: Lambert et al. 1986.

NOTES

131 "These are provocative findings . . . could be the unfortunate outcome": Rutter 1994, p. 13.

131 ". . . it is difficult to see how . . . this preservation order was rescinded": Eysenck 1983, p. 290.

133 "Each person evaluates . . . his or her assumptive world": Frank and Frank 1991, pp. 24–25.

133 "Since a person relies . . . creates surprise or uncertainty": Ibid., p. 141.

134 "We have chosen the term 'myth' . . . while failures are explained away": Ibid., p. 42.

135 "Consider the psychotherapist . . . can demoralize the therapist": Woolfolk 1998, p. 132.

136 "To be concerned only . . . authority and credibility": Ibid., p. 135.

136 "In our present state . . . they would disappear": Frank and Frank 1991, p. 19.

138 "That the mythology of the shaman . . . has its proper place": Ibid., p. 99.

139 "probably reflects heightened . . . unchanged organic handicap" Ibid., p. 105.

Chapter Six: Therapy's Retreat

143 CLIENT: "Two or three years? . . . why you're alive": Bugental 1987, p. 210.

144 "Therapy at its best . . . and to lead a better life": Lomas 1993, pp. 4–5.

144 "Freud was foremost . . . state of being of our patients": Lomas 1993, p. 7.

145 "The primary goal of psychodynamic psychotherapy . . . where none existed": Nichols and Paolino 1986, pp. 13–14.

145 "life-changing psychotherapy . . . some of those answers": Bugental 1987, p. 6.

145 "calls for continual attention . . . own subjectivity": Bugental 1987, p. 3.

145 For Lomas, the quality best . . . ". . . relating to life and conduct": Lomas 1993, pp. 16–17.

145 "intuitive sensing": Bugental 1987, p. 11.

145 "Some people . . . said or done is important": Weinberg 1984, p. 4.

146 "ideas of those who have pioneered . . . than her patient": Lomas 1993, p. 17.

148 "playful, experimental attitude that generates . . . unconscious mind": Nichols and Paolino 1986, p. 17.

148 "[The analyst] has to let . . . self-observation, and making judgments": Menninger 1958, p. 140.

149 "it doesn't matter . . . we have done our job": Lomas 1993, p. 64.

149 He quotes A. M. Ludwig . . . ". . . insight and therapeutic results": Karasu and Bellak 1980, p. 11.

150 "From the outset . . . constantly to be striven for": Herman 1992, p. 148.

150 The street-level therapists . . . pop-psychology books patients read: Woolfolk 1998, p. 93.

150 "When a therapist encounters . . . can become dogma and bigotry": Woolfolk 1998, p. 132.

151 A recent *Utne Reader* article . . . ". . . and isn't this what everyone comes to therapy for?": Markowitz 1997, pp. 57–64.

NOTES

153 "Each of us is . . . How else could it be?": Canale 1992, p. 87.
153 "The great malady . . . is 'loss of soul' ": Moore 1992, p. xi.
153 "loss of soul . . . which are all soul sources": Carlson and Shield 1995, p. 197.
154 "reunite medicine, psychology . . . the basic substance of the universe": Ibid., pp. 46–47.
155 Love is the key ingredient . . . create "a healing environment": Breggin 1992, p. 135.
155 "mystery-filled, star-born nature": Moore 1992, p. 20.
155 "Our very idea . . . fully integrative way": Ibid., pp. xv–xvii.
157 "stories they want to hear . . . and secular credentials": Toumey 1997, p. 96.

CHAPTER SEVEN: WHY PATIENTS BELIEVE

159 "To what extent . . . failings and incompetencies": Lomas 1993, pp. 174–76.
160 "boldly demand confirmation . . . nature of our conviction": Bowers and Farvolden 1996, p. 363.
161 "Only when the 'truth' . . . can either feel convinced": Boris 1986, p. 295.
161 "Our opponents believe . . . mind or the unconscious": Bowers and Farvolden 1996, p. 365.
162 "The danger of our leading . . . occurred in my practice": Ibid.
163 "[T]he therapist's comments . . . aspirations, values, or vision": Wachtel 1993.
163 "Therapists often make . . . own feelings and experiences": Herman 1993.
163 "It often seems . . . out of the reach of science": Bowers and Farvolden 1996, p. 365.
164 "What is the therapist's viewpoint . . . will be liberating": Wachtel 1993.
164 "the importance of therapeutic . . . *as influence attempts*": Bowers 1987, p. 97.
166 "Throughout the therapeutic process . . . patient's interactions": Karasu and Bellak 1980, p. 35.
166 "statements of cause-effect . . . are given insufficient consideration": Arnoult and Anderson, p. 219.
169 "Whether she was defying . . . feces=penis=stay=come": Boris 1986, p. 297.

CHAPTER EIGHT: WHY THERAPISTS BELIEVE

171 "I've observed . . . from everywhere": Weinberg 1984, p. 39.
172 "many kinds of illness . . . figure whom he trusts": Humphrey 1996, p. 111.
173 "The consequence is that . . . healer a special person": Ibid.
175 "I desperately *needed* . . . to maintain the delusion": Masson 1990, p. 78.
175 "An analysis, even a psychotherapy . . . to be wise": Ibid., p. 146.
180 "The patient sees . . . undreamed of importance": Freud 1949, p. 66.
181 "Negative transference can . . . in the course of therapy": Kotin 1995, p. 180.

256

182 "It was perhaps the greatest . . . rational explanation for it": Freud 1953, p. 225.

182 "Freud seems not to recognize . . . close and intimately trusted": Webster 1995, p. 347.

182 "Naturally the patient . . . will cling to any straw": Masson 1988, p. 82.

183 "We claim that the transference . . . this very behavior": Ibid., pp. 148–49.

184 "So I have really disappointed you . . . What was the worst part of this for you?": Kotin 1995, pp. 183–84.

184 "Carelessness in regard to arrangements . . . reproaches and accusations": Menninger 1958, p. 88.

184 "countertransference is by definition . . . triggered off his reaction": Ibid., pp. 89–90.

185 "When a therapist thought . . . freshly cleaned outfit": Kotin 1995, p. 195.

185 "About 10% . . . genital manipulation or coitus": Masson 1988, p. 178.

186 "Perhaps with products . . . models of love and closeness": Hale 1995a, p. 389.

188 "Variants of normal behavior . . . the phenomena which they cure": Frank and Frank 1991, p. 9.

189 "shape the self-knowledge . . . have been made in it": Young 1995, p. 5.

191 "are not immune . . . on occasion after occasion": McHugh 1995.

192 "In 1973 and before . . . may elude them both": Prozan 1992, p. 207.

Chapter Nine: The Myth of Privileged Access to Our Own Thoughts

193 We are all what might be described . . .: Nisbett and Ross 1980.

194 "He must be able to sense . . . original and unconscious form": Greenson 1967, p. 365.

194 "If the unconscious cause . . . sequence becomes clear": Brenner 1955, p. 14.

196 "They seemed to come to agree . . . in modifying his position": Nisbett and Wilson 1977, p. 236.

198 When asked to explain . . . "My mother uses Tide," etc.: Ibid.

199 The ability of people . . . ". . . to produce generally correct or reliable reports": Ibid., p. 233.

200 "The most remarkable result . . . by different means": Ibid., p. 205.

201 "We propose . . . influenced the response": Ibid., p. 248.

202 Countering this theory . . . the same thing: Bem 1967.

207 "this woman's presenting . . . to solve her problems": Bowers 1987, p. 103.

Chapter Ten: Medicine Meets Myth

211 "Until Prozac came along . . . 'and of course Freudian psychoanalysis'": Allen 1997.

212 "I remember as a first-year resident . . . purely through words": Pope's comments in this chapter were recorded in a personal interview with the authors.

216 A 1982 study found . . . had treatable disorders: Hoffman 1982.

216 Another study . . . misdiagnosed when admitted: Herring 1985, p. 3.
216 "A physical disease . . . shattered dreams": Koran 1990.
217 As physician Robert Taylor . . . ". . . does not provide causative understanding": Taylor 1982, p. 251.
217 "This medical detective work . . . with the pseudoscience of labeling": Walker 1996, p. 5.
218 "Reliability, and not validity . . . What is necessary to correct them?" McHugh and Slavney 1983, p. 32.
218 In a "Cautionary Statement" . . . ". . . body of knowledge and clinical skill": *Diagnostic and Statistical Manual* 1994, p. xxvii.
219 "To read about the evolution . . . an entirely political document": Armstrong, 1993.
220 Bobby, a shy eight-year-old . . . categorization of his symptoms: Walker 1996, pp. 30–37.
224 "The medical model . . . many clinical investigations": Guze 1992, p. 38.
226 "Chronic anxiety . . . therapy can alter brain chemistry": Walker 1996, pp. 124–25.
227 "Psychiatrists are becoming . . . sit on the sidelines": Ibid., p. 26.
228 "In the nineteenth century . . . financial and professional ability": Starr 1982, p. 80.
230 The period in history when doctors . . . ". . . patent medicines reached their apogee": Young 1967, p. 25.

CONCLUSION: THERAPY'S DELUSIONS

233 "[Humans have] an almost limitless . . . rather abstract matters": Crick 1994, p. 262.
233 "(1) our desperate need . . . in need of change": Marin 1996.
236 "To date . . . simply does not exist": Austad 1996, p. 26.
236 "I feel that psychotherapy . . . confidence in psychologists' services": Fox 1995, pp. 147–55.
237 "Many practitioners and clients . . . in days gone by": Dennis 1994, pp. 90–97.
241 "on the hunt for a body . . . if not believers": Coles 1995, pp. 117–18.
241 "Every age has its peculiar folly . . . or both combined": Mackay 1996.
244 "Synthetic explanations from the molecule . . . how they are best explained": McHugh and Slavney 1983, p. 3.
245 "has not diminished . . . enlarge it tremendously": Crick 1994, p. 206.

APPENDIX

249 "Questions prefaced by the phrase . . . respondent at the time of recall": Rogler 1992, p. 222.

Bibliography

105th Annual Convention. 1997. Program. Chicago: American Psychological Association.

Abelson, R. P. 1968. Psychological Implication. In *Theories of Cognitive Consistency: A Sourcebook,* edited by Robert P. Abelson, 112–39. Chicago: Rand McNally and Company.

Abraham, C., and S. E. Hampson. 1996. A Social Cognition Approach to Health Psychology: Philosophical and Methodological Issues. *Psychology and Health* 11: 223–41.

Adelman, H. S. 1995. Clinical Psychology: Beyond Psychopathology and Clinical Interventions. *Clinical Psychology: Science and Practice* 2 (1): 28–44.

Adler, A. 1946. *Understanding Human Nature.* New York: Greenburg.

Adler, G., and P. G. Myerson, eds. 1973. *Confrontation in Psychotherapy.* Northvale, N.J.: Jason Aronson, Inc.

Alexander, F. G., and S. T. Selesnick. 1966. *The History of Psychiatry: An Evaluation of Psychiatric Thought and Practice from Prehistoric Times to the Present.* Northvale, N.J.: Jason Aronson, Inc.

Allen, H. 1997. A Capsule History of Psychiatry. *Washington Post,* 7 May, D1.

Ammer, C., and N. T. Sidley. 1982. *The Common Sense Guide to Mental Health Care.* Lexington, Mass.: The Lewis Publishing Company.

Anderson, C. A. 1983a. Abstract and Concrete Data in the Perseverance of Social Theories: When Weak Data Lead to Unshakable Beliefs. *Journal of Experimental Social Psychology* 19: 93–108.

———. 1983b. The Causal Structure of Situations: The Generation of Plausible Causal Attributions as a Function of Type of Event Situation. *Journal of Experimental Social Psychology* 19: 185–203.

Andrews, G. 1983. Psychotherapy Outcome: A Wider View Leads to Different Conclusions. *The Behavioral and Brain Sciences* 6: 285–86.

Arkowitz, H. 1995. Common Factors or Processes of Change in Psychotherapy? *Clinical Psychology: Science and Practice* 2 (1): 94–100.

Armstrong, L. 1993. *And They Call It Help.* Reading, Mass.: Addison-Wesley Publishing Co.

Arnoult, L. , and C. Anderson. 1988. Identifying and Reducing Causal Reasoning Biases in Clinical Practice. In *Reasoning, Inference, and Judgment in Clinical Psychology.* New York: Free Press, 209–32.

BIBLIOGRAPHY

Austad, C. S. 1996. *Is Long-Term Psychotherapy Unethical?* San Francisco: Jossey-Bass Publishers.

Baars, B. J. 1988. *A Cognitive Theory of Consciousness.* Cambridge, Mass.: Cambridge University Press.

Balint, M. 1968. *The Basic Fault.* Evanston, Ill.: Northwestern University Press.

Barringer, F. 1988. In the New Soviet Psyche, a Place Is Made for Freud. *New York Times,* 18 July, A1.

Basch, M. F. 1988. *Understanding Psychotherapy: The Science Behind the Art.* New York: Basic Books.

Bem, D. J. 1967. Self-Perception: An Alternative Interpretation of Cognitive Dissonance Phenomena. *Psychological Review 74* (3): 183–200.

Bergantino, L. 1981. *Psychotherapy, Insight and Style.* Northvale, N.J.: Jason Aronson, Inc.

Bergin, A. E., and H. H. Strupp. 1972. *Changing Frontiers in the Science of Psychotherapy.* Chicago: Aldine Atherton, Inc.

Berne, E. 1961. *Transactional Analysis in Psychotherapy.* New York: Grove Press, Inc.

Bernheimer, C., and C. Kahane, eds. 1985. *In Dora's Case.* New York: Columbia University Press.

———. 1990. *In Dora's Case: Freud—Hysteria—Feminism,* 2d ed. New York: Columbia University Press.

Beutler, L. E.; R. E. Williams; P. J. Wakefield; and S. R. Entwistle. 1995. Bridging Scientist and Practitioner Perspectives in Clinical Psychology. *American Psychologist 50:* (12) 984–94.

Bloom, H. 1986. Freud, the Greatest Modern Writer. *New York Times,* 23 March.

Bodian, S. 1989. A Consumer's Guide to Psychotherapy. *Yoga Journal,* September/October, 50–51.

Bolles, R. C. 1993. *The Story of Psychology: A Thematic History.* Pacific Grove, Calif.: Brooks/Cole Publishing Company.

Boodman, S. 1989. The Mystery of the Chestnut Lodge. *Washington Post Magazine,* 6 October, 16–43.

———. 1992. Advertising for Psychiatric Hospitals: Preying on Parental Fears May End in Unnecessary Treatment for Minors. *Washington Post,* 5 May.

Borch-Jacobsen, M. 1996. *Remembering Anna O.: A Century of Mystification.* Translation by Kirby Olson. New York: Routledge.

Boris, H. 1986. Interpretation: History and Theory. In *Basic Techniques of Psychodynamic Psychotherapy,* edited by M. Nichols and T. Paolino. Northvale, N.J.: Jason Aronson, Inc.

Bowers, K. S. 1987. Revisioning the Unconscious. *Canadian Psychology/Psychologie Canadienne 28* (2): 93–104, 124–32.

Bowers, K. S., and P. Farvolden. 1996. Revisiting a Century-Old Freudian Slip—From Suggestion Disavowed to the Truth Repressed. *Psychological Bulletin 119* (3): 355–80.

Boyer, P., and S. Nissenbaum. 1974. *Salem Possessed.* Cambridge, Mass.: Harvard University Press.

Breggin, P. R. 1992. *Beyond Conflict.* New York: St. Martin's Press.

Breggin, P. R., and G. R. Breggin. 1994. *Talking Back to Prozac.* New York: St. Martin's Press.

Brenner, C. 1955. *An Elementary Textbook of Psychoanalysis.* New York: International Universities Press, Inc.

Brickman, J. 1984. Feminist, Nonsexist, and Traditional Models of Therapy: Implications for Working with Incest. *Women & Therapy* 3 (1): 49–67.

Brill, A. A. 1922. *Psychoanalysis: Its Theories and Practical Application,* 3d ed. Philadelphia: W. B. Saunders Company.

Brody, N. 1983. *Human Motivation, Commentary on Goal-Directed Action.* New York: Academic Press.

Brozek, J., ed. 1984. *Explorations in the History of Psychology in the United States.* London: Associated University Presses.

Bugental, J. F. T. 1987. *The Art of the Psychotherapist.* New York: W. W. Norton and Company.

Buirski, P., ed. 1994. *Comparing Schools of Analytic Therapy.* Northvale, N.J.: Jason Aronson, Inc.

Bulgatz, J. 1992. *Ponzi Schemes Invaders from Mars and More Extraordinary Popular Delusions and the Madness of Crowds.* New York: Harmony Books.

Butler, G., and T. Hope. 1995. *Managing Your Mind: The Mental Fitness Guide.* New York: Oxford University Press.

Byck, R., ed. 1974. *Sigmund Freud: Cocaine Papers.* New York: The Stonehill Publishing Company.

Camp, D. 1994. Child Psychiatry Critics Would Bar Valuable Tools. *Commercial Appeal,* 29 September, 1C.

Campbell, T. W. 1992. Therapeutic Relationships and Iatrogenic Outcomes: The Blame-and-Change Maneuver in Psychotherapy. *Psychotherapy* 29 (3): 474–80.

Canale, A. 1992. *Beyond Depression.* Rockport, Maine: Element Press.

Caplan, A. 1986. With a Friend Like Professor Grunbaum Does Psychoanalysis Need Any Enemies? *Behavioral and Brain Sciences* 9: 228–29.

Caplan, P. J. 1995. *They Say You're Crazy.* Reading, Mass.: Addison-Wesley Publishing Co.

Carlson, R., and B. Shield, eds. 1995. *Handbook for the Soul.* Boston: Little, Brown.

Caws, P. 1986. The Scaffolding of Psychoanalysis. *Behavioral and Brain Sciences* 9 (2): 229–30.

Chessick, R. D. 1980. *Freud Teaches Psychotherapy.* Indianapolis: Hackett Publishing Company.

Chicago Tribune. 1997. APA Convention. 17 August, sec. 2, p. 1.

Chopra, D. 1995. *The Way of the Wizard.* New York: Harmony Books.

Cioffi, F. 1986. Did Freud Rely on the Tally Argument to Meet the Argument of Suggestibility? *Behavioral and Brain Sciences* 9 (2): 230–31.

Cohen, L. J. 1981. Can Human Irrationality Be Experimentally Demonstrated? *Behavioral and Brain Sciences* (4): 317–70.

Cohen, P., and J. Cohen. 1984. The Clinician's Illusion. *Archives of General Psychiatry* 41: 1178–82.

Coles, R. 1995. *The Mind's Fate,* 2d ed. Boston: Little, Brown.

Consumer Reports. 1995. Mental Health: Does Therapy Help? November, 734–39.

Cooper, A. J. 1985. Will Neurobiology Influence Psychoanalysis? *American Journal of Psychiatry 142* (12): 1395–1402.

Cooper, I. S. 1975. *The Victim Is Always the Same.* New York: Harper & Row.

Corday, D. S., and R. R. Bootzin. 1983. Placebo Control Conditions: Tests of Theory or of Effectiveness? *Behavioral and Brain Sciences 6:* 286–87.

Corsini, R. J., and D. Wedding. 1989. *Current Psychotherapies,* 4th ed. Itasca, Ill.: F. E. Peacock Publishers.

Cox, R. 1997. Golden Opportunities for Psychology in the 21st Century. In *American Psychological Association Annual Convention,* 14–17 August, Chicago.

Crews, F. 1986. *Skeptical Engagements.* New York: Oxford University Press.

———. 1995. *The Memory Wars: Freud's Legacy in Dispute.* New York: New York Review of Books.

———. 1996. The Verdict on Freud. *Psychological Science 7* (2): 63–68.

———. 1998 *Unauthorized Freud.* New York: Viking.

Crick, F. 1994. *The Astonishing Hypothesis.* New York: Simon and Schuster.

Dahl, H. 1983. Give Choice a Chance in Psychotherapy Research. *Behavioral and Brain Sciences 6:* 287–88.

Davanloo, H., ed. 1978. *Basic Principles and Techniques in Short-Term Dynamic Psychotherapy.* Northvale, N.J.: Jason Aronson, Inc.

Dawes, R. M. 1994. *House of Cards: Psychology and Psychotherapy Built on Myth.* New York: The Free Press.

Dawes, R. M.; D. Faust; and P. E. Meehl. 1989. Clinical Versus Actuarial Judgment. *Science 243* (March 31): 1668–73.

Dennis, G. 1994. Therapy Under Siege. *New Age Journal,* May/June, 90–97.

Diagnostic and Statistical Manual of Mental Disorders, 4th ed. 1994. Washington, D.C.: American Psychiatric Association.

Dixon, N. F. 1987. Unconscious Reconsidered. *Canadian Psychology/Psychologie Canadienne 28* (2): 118–19.

Douglas, J. H. 1978. Pioneering a Non-Western Psychology. *Science News,* 11 March, 154–58.

Durkin, P. 1993. Trends; Therapy Goes "Green"; Helping People Cope with Worries About the Planet. *Washington Post,* 7 September, B5.

Eagle, M. 1983. Psychotherapy Versus Placebo: An End to Polemics. *Behavioral and Brain Sciences 6:* 288–89.

———. 1986. Psychoanalysis as Hermeneutics. *Behavioral and Brain Sciences 9* (2): 231–32.

———. 1987. Revisioning the Unconscious. *Canadian Psychology/Psychologie Canadienne 28* (2): 113–16.

Eckardt, B. V. 1986. Grunbaum's Challenge to Freud's Logic of Argumentation: A Reconstruction and an Addendum. *Behavioral and Brain Sciences 9* (2): 262–63.

Edelson, M. 1986. The Evidential Value of the Psychoanalyst's Clinical Data. *Behavioral and Brain Sciences 9* (2): 232–34.

Ehrenreich, B., and D. English. 1978. *For Her Own Good.* Garden City, N.Y.: Anchor Press/Doubleday.

Eigen, M. 1986. *The Psychotic Core.* Northvale, N.J.: Jason Aronson, Inc.

Einhorn, H. J. 1986. Accepting Error to Make Less Error. *Journal of Personality Assessment 50* (3): 387–95.

Elkin, I. 1995. Further Differentiation of *Common Factors*. *Clinical Psychology: Science and Practice 2* (1): 75–78.

Elliott, A., and S. Frosh, eds. 1995. *Psychoanalysis in Contexts*. New York: Routledge.

English, O. S., and G. H. J. Pearson. 1937. *Common Neuroses of Children and Adults*. New York: W. W. Norton and Company.

Erdelyi, M. H. 1986. Psychoanalysis Has a Wider Scope Than the Retrospective Discovery of Etiologies. *Behavioral and Brain Sciences 9* (2): 234–35.

Erikson, E. H. 1968. *Identity: Youth and Crisis*. New York: W. W. Norton and Company.

Erwin, E. 1983. Psychotherapy, Placebos, and Wait-List Controls. *Behavioral and Brain Sciences 6*: 289–90.

———. 1986. Defending Freudianism. *Behavioral and Brain Sciences 9* (2): 235–36.

Esterson, A. 1993. *Seductive Mirage*. Chicago and La Salle: Open Court.

Estling, R. 1994. Deep Ecology or Deep Sanity? *Skeptical Inquirer,* 22 September, 539.

Evans, F. J. 1967. Suggestibility in the Normal Waking State. *Psychological Bulletin 67* (2): 114–29.

Eysenck, H. J. 1952. The Effects of Psychotherapy: An Evaluation. *Journal of Consulting Psychology 16*: 319–24.

———. 1983. The Effectiveness of Psychotherapy: The Specter at the Feast. *Behavioral and Brain Sciences 6*: 290.

———. 1986. Failure of Treatment—Failure of Theory? *Behavioral and Brain Sciences 9* (2): 236.

Farrell, B. A. 1986. The Probative Value of the Clinical Data of Psychoanalysis. *Behavioral and Brain Sciences 9* (2): 236–37.

Fenichel, O. 1945. *The Psychoanalytic Theory of Neurosis*. New York: W. W. Norton and Company.

Fine, A., and M. Forbes. 1986. Grunbaum on Freud: Three Grounds for Dissent. *Behavioral and Brain Sciences 9* (2): 237–38.

Fine, R. 1990. *The History of Psychoanalysis*. New York: Continuum.

Fish, J. M. 1983. Enhancing the Therapeutic Respectability of Placebos. *Behavioral and Brain Sciences 6*: 291.

Fiske, D. W. 1970. Planning of Research on Effectiveness of Psychotherapy. *Archives of General Psychiatry 22*: 22–32.

Flanagan, O. J. 1986. Psychoanalysis as a Social Activity. *Behavioral and Brain Sciences 9* (2): 238–39.

Fonagy, P., and M. Target. 1994. The Efficacy of Psychoanalysis for Children with Disruptive Disorders. *Journal of the American Academy of Child Adolescent Psychiatry 33* (1): 45–55.

Foulks, E. F.; J. B. Persons; and R. L. Merkel. 1986. The Effect of Patients' Beliefs About Their Illnesses on Compliance in Psychotherapy. *American Journal of Psychiatry 143* (3): 340–44.

Fox, R. E. 1995. The Rape of Psychotherapy. *Professional Psychology: Research and Practice 26* (2): 147–55.

Frank, J. D. 1972. The Bewildering World of Psychotherapy. *Journal of Social Issues* 28 (4): 27–43.

———. 1974. Therapeutic Components of Psychotherapy. *Journal of Nervous and Mental Disease* 159 (5): 325–42.

———. 1983. The Placebo Is Psychotherapy. *Behavioral and Brain Sciences* 6: 291–92.

Frank, J. D., and J. B. Frank. 1991. *Persuasion and Healing: A Comparative Study of Psychotherapy*, 3d ed. Baltimore: The Johns Hopkins University Press.

Freud, S. 1938. *The Basic Writings of Sigmund Freud*. Translated by A. A. Brill. New York: Random House.

———. 1949. *An Outline of Psychoanalysis*. New York: W. W. Norton & Company.

———. 1951. *Psychopathology of Everyday Life*. Translated by A. A. Brill. New York: New American Library.

———. 1953–74. *The Standard Edition of the Complete Psychological Works of Sigmund Freud*. London: Hogarth Press.

———. 1961. *Civilization and Its Discontents*. Translated by James Strachey. New York: W. W. Norton & Company.

———. 1965. *The Interpretation of Dreams*. Translated by James Strachey. New York: Avon Books.

Ganaway, G. K. 1989. Historical versus Narrative Truth: Clarifying the Role of Exogenous Trauma in the Etiology of MPD and Its Variants. *Dissociation 2* (4): 205–20.

Gardner, H. 1997. *Extraordinary Minds*. New York: Basic Books.

Garfield, S. L. 1983. Does Psychotherapy Work? Yes, No, Maybe. *Behavioral and Brain Sciences* 6: 292–93.

———. 1997. Is Deep-Seated Change a Proper Goal for Psychotherapy? In *American Psychological Association Annual Convention, 14–17 August, Chicago*.

Gaston, L. 1995. Common Factors Exist in Reality But Not in Our Theories. *Clinical Psychology: Science and Practice 2* (1): 83–86.

Gauld, A., and J. Shotter. 1986. Warranting Interpretations. *Behavioral and Brain Sciences 9* (2): 239–40.

Gaylin, W., ed. 1983. *Psychodynamic Understanding of Depression*. Northvale, N.J.: Jason Aronson, Inc.

Geller, J. L., and M. Harris, eds. 1994. *Women of the Asylum*. New York: Anchor Books.

Gendlin, E. T. 1981. *Focusing,* 2d ed. New York: Bantam Books.

Gerstein, D. R.; R. D. Luce; N. J. Smelser; and S. Sperlich, eds. 1988. *The Behavioral and Social Sciences: Achievements and Opportunities*. Washington, D.C.: National Academy Press.

Gilligan, S., and R. Price, ed. 1993. *Therapeutic Conversations*. New York: W. W. Norton & Company.

Glass, G. V; M. L. Smith; and T. I. Miller. 1983. Placebo Effects in Psychotherapy Outcome Research. *Behavioral and Brain Sciences* 6: 293–94.

Goldberg, S. 1991. *When Wish Replaces Thought*. Buffalo, N.Y.: Prometheus Books.

Goldfried, M. R., and M. Merbaum, eds. 1973. *Behavior Change Through Self-Control*. New York: Holt, Rinehart and Winston, Inc.

Gottlieb, A. 1997. Crisis of Consciousness. *Utne Reader,* January/February, 45–48, 106–9.

Gould, S. J. 1981. *The Mismeasure of Man*. New York: W. W. Norton & Company.

Greenberg, R. P. 1983. Revisiting Psychotherapy Outcome: Promise and Problems. *Behavioral and Brain Sciences* 6: 294–95.

———. 1986. The Case Against Freud's Cases. *Behavioral and Brain Sciences* 9 (2): 240–41.

Greenson, R. 1967. *The Technique and Practice of Psychoanalysis*. New York: International University Press.

Gross, M. L. 1978. *The Psychological Society*. New York: Random House.

Gross, P. R., and N. Levitt. 1994. *Higher Superstition*. Baltimore: The Johns Hopkins University Press.

Grunbaum, A. 1986. Precis of *The Foundations of Psychoanalysis: A Philosophical Critique. Behavioral and Brain Sciences* 9: 217–28, 266–84.

Guze, S. B. 1992. *Why Psychiatry Is a Branch of Medicine*. New York: Oxford University Press.

Hale, N. G. 1995a. *Freud and the Americans*. New York: Oxford University Press.

———. 1995b. *The Rise and Crisis of Psychoanalysis in the United States*. New York: Oxford University Press.

Haley, J. 1986. *Uncommon Therapy: The Psychiatric Techniques of Milton H. Erickson*. New York: W. W. Norton & Company.

———. 1996. *Learning and Teaching Therapy*. New York: The Guilford Press.

Hall, C. S. 1954. *A Primer of Freudian Psychology*. New York: Mentor Books.

Hamilton, K. 1996. Need a Life? Get a Coach. *Newsweek,* 5 February, 48.

Hannon, K. 1996. Upset? Try Cybertherapy. *U.S. News and World Report,* 13 May, 81–83.

Hedges, L. V. 1983. Statistical Summaries in Research Integration. *Behavioral and Brain Sciences* 6: 295–96.

Henle, M.; J. Jaynes; and J. J. Sullivan, eds. 1973. *Historical Conceptions of Psychology*. New York: Springer Publishing Company.

Herink, R., ed. 1980. *The Psychotherapy Handbook*. New York: Meridian.

Herman, J. 1993. The False Memory Debate: Social Science or Social Backlash. *Harvard Mental Health Letter* 9: 4–6.

———. 1992. *Trauma and Recovery*. New York: Basic Books.

Herring, M. M. 1985. Debate Over "False-Positive Schizophrenics." *Medical Tribune,* 25 September.

Hicks, R. D. 1991. *In Pursuit of Satan*. Buffalo: Prometheus Books.

Higgins, M. B., ed. 1994. *Beyond Psychology: Letters and Journals, 1934–1939/Wilhelm Reich*. New York: Farrar, Straus, and Giroux.

Hilgard, E. R. 1993. Which Psychologists Prominent in the Second Half of This Century Made Lasting Contributions to Psychological Theory? *Psychological Science* 4 (2): 70–80.

Hill, B. 1994. *The Biophilia Hypothesis*—book review. *New Scientist,* 29 January.

Hill, C. E. 1995. What Are the Mechanisms of Change in the Common Factors? A Reaction to Weinberger. *Clinical Psychology: Science and Practice 2* (1): 87–89.

Hill, S., and J. Goodwin. 1989. Satanism: Similarities Between Patient Accounts and Preinquisition Historical Sources. *Dissociation 2* (1): 39–44.

Hillman, J. 1996. *The Soul's Code: In Search of Character and Calling.* New York: Random House.

Hobson, J. A. 1986. Repressed Infantile Wishes as the Instigators of All Dreams. *Behavioral and Brain Sciences 9* (2): 241–42.

Hoffman, R. 1982. *Science News,* 11 September.

Holender, D. 1987. Is the Unconscious Amenable to Scientific Scrutiny? *Canadian Psychology/Psychologie Canadienne 28* (2): 120–23.

Holt, R. R. 1986. Some Reflections on Testing Psychoanalytic Hypotheses. *Behavioral and Brain Sciences 9* (2): 242–44.

Holzman, P. S. 1994. Hilgard on Psychoanalysis as Science. *Psychological Science 5* (4): 190–91.

———. 1996. On the Trail of the Genetics and Pathophysiology of Schizophrenia. *Psychiatry 59* (May): 117–27.

Hook, S., ed. 1959. *Psychoanalysis, Scientific Method and Philosophy.* New York: Grove Press.

Humphrey, N. 1996. *Leaps of Faith.* New York: Basic Books.

Hunt, M. 1993. *The Story of Psychology.* New York: Anchor Books.

Jaffe, A. 1979. *Apparitions: An Archetypal Approach to Death Dreams and Ghosts.* Irving, Tex.: Spring Publications, Inc.

Japenga, A. 1994. Rewriting the Dictionary of Madness: Is the Diagnostic and Statistical Manual of Mental Disorders a Work of Pure Science or Just a List of Dangerous Labels? *Los Angeles Times Magazine,* 5 June, 18.

Jaroff, L. 1993. Lies of the Mind. *Time,* 29 November, 52–59.

Jaynes, J. 1976. *The Origin of Consciousness in the Breakdown of the Bicameral Mind.* Boston: Houghton Mifflin Company.

Johnson, J., and S. Padilla. 1991. Satanism: Skeptics Abound. *Los Angeles Times,* 23 April, 1.

Johnson, M. K., et al., eds. 1988. Phenomenal Characteristics of Memories for Perceived and Imagined Autobiographical Events. *Journal of Experimental Psychology: General, 117* (4): 371–76.

Jones, E. 1953. *The Life and Work of Sigmund Freud: 1856–1900, The Formative Years and the Great Discoveries.* New York: Basic Books.

———. 1955. *The Life and Work of Sigmund Freud: 1901–1919, Years of Maturity.* New York: Basic Books.

———. 1964. *Essays in Applied Psychoanalysis,* 3d ed. New York: International Universities Press, Inc.

Journal of American Medical Association. 1990. The Future of Psychiatry 264 (19): 2541–48.

Kachele, H. 1986. Validating Psychoanalysis: What Methods for What Task? *Behavioral and Brain Sciences 9* (2): 244–45.

Kadushin, C. 1966. The Friends and Supporters of Psychotherapy: On Social Circles in Urban Life. *American Sociological Review 31*: 786–802.

Kaminer, W. 1992. *I'm Dysfunctional, You're Dysfunctional.* Reading, Menlo Park, and New York: Addison-Wesley Publishing Co.

Kandel, E. R. 1983. From Metapsychology to Molecular Biology: Explorations into the Nature of Anxiety. *American Journal of Psychiatry* 140 (10): 1277–93.

Karasu, T. B. 1986. The Specificity versus Nonspecificity Dilemma: Toward Identifying Therapeutic Change Agents. *American Journal of Psychiatry* 143 (6): 687–95.

Karasu, T. B., and L. Bellak, eds. 1980. *Specialized Techniques for Specific Clinical Problems in Psychotherapy.* Northvale, N.J.: Jason Aronson, Inc.

Kazdin, A. E. 1983. Meta-analysis of Psychotherapy: Criteria for Selecting Investigations. *Behavioral and Brain Sciences* 6: 296.

Kelley, H. H. 1971. Attribution in Social Interaction. In *Attribution: Perceiving the Causes of Behavior,* edited by Edward E. Jones, 1–26. Morristown, N.J.: General Learning Press.

Kernberg, O. F. 1989. *Psychodynamic Psychotherapy of Borderline Patients.* New York: Basic Books.

Kiesler, C. A.; N. A. Cummings; and G. R. VandenBos, eds. 1979. *Psychology and National Health Insurance: A Sourcebook.* Washington, D.C.: American Psychological Association.

Kihlstrom, J. F. 1987. What This Discipline Needs Is a Good Ten-Cent Taxonomy of Consciousness. *Canadian Psychology/Psychologie Canadienne* 28 (2): 116–18.

Kingsbury, S. J. 1995. Where Does Research on the Effectiveness of Psychotherapy Stand Today? *Harvard Mental Health Letter,* September, 8.

Kirk, S. A., and H. Kutchins. 1992. *The Selling of DSM: The Rhetoric of Science in Psychiatry.* New York: Aldine De Gruyter.

Kirkus Reviews. 1992. *The Voice of the Earth*—book review. 1 May.

Kisch, J. 1988. Psychotherapy and Psychopharmacology: Conflict or Confluence. *Psychotherapy in Private Practice* 6 (3): 7–13.

Klaits, J. 1985. *Servants of Satan.* Bloomington: Indiana University Press.

Klerman, G. L. 1983. The Efficacy of Psychotherapy as the Basis for Public Policy. *American Psychologist* 38 (August): 929–34.

———. 1986. The Scientific Tasks Confronting Psychoanalysis. *Behavioral and Brain Sciences* 9 (2): 245.

———. 1990. The Psychiatric Patient's Right to Effective Treatment: Implications of Osheroff v. Chestnut Lodge. *American Journal of Psychiatry* 147 (4): 409–18.

———. 1991. The Osheroff Debate: Finale. *American Journal of Psychiatry* 148 (3): 387–88.

Kline, M. V. 1984. Multiple Personality: Facts and Artifacts in Relation to Hypnotherapy. *International Journal of Clinical and Experimental Hypnosis* 32 (2): 198–209.

Kline, P. 1983. Meta-analysis, Measurement, and Methodological Problems in the Study of Psychotherapy. *Behavioral and Brain Sciences* 6: 296–97.

———. 1986. Grunbaum's Philosophical Critique of Psychoanalysis: Or What I Don't Know Isn't Knowledge. *Behavioral and Brain Sciences* 9 (2): 245–46.

Kluft, R. P. 1987. The Simulation and Dissimulation of Multiple Personality Disorder. *American Journal of Clinical Hypnosis* 30 (2): 104–17.

———. 1988. On Treating the Older Patient with Multiple Personality Disorder: "Race Against Time" or "Make Haste Slowly"? *American Journal of Clinical Hypnosis 30* (4): 257–66.

————. 1989. Reflections on Allegations of Ritual Abuse. *Dissociation 2* (4): 191–93.

Knesper, D. J.; J. R. C. Wheeler; and D. J. Pagnucco. 1984. Mental Health Services Providers' Distribution Across Counties in the United States. *American Psychologist 39* (12): 1424–34.

Koran, L. 1990. Medical Evaluation of Psychiatric Patients. *American Family Physician 41* (4).

Koriat, A.; S. Lichtenstein; and B. Fischhoff. 1980. Reasons for Confidence. *Journal of Experimental Psychology: Human Learning and Memory 6* (2): 107–18.

Kotin, J. 1995. *Getting Started: An Introduction to Dynamic Psychotherapy.* Northvale, N.J.: Jason Aronson, Inc.

Kovel, J. The American Mental Health Industry. In *Critical Psychiatry: The Politics of Mental Health,* edited by D. Ingleby, 72–101. New York: Pantheon Books.

Kramer, P. D. 1993. *Listening to Prozac.* New York: Viking.

————. 1997. *Should You Leave? A Psychiatrist Explores Intimacy and Autonomy—and the Nature of Advice.* New York: Scribner.

Krauthammer, C. 1993. Defining Deviancy Up. *New Republic,* 22 November, 20–25.

Kruglanski, A. W. 1987. The Taming of the Unconscious: If You Can't Beat It, Use It. *Canadian Psychology/Psychologie Canadienne 28* (2): 110–12.

Kuhn, T. S. 1996. *The Structure of Scientific Revolutions,* 3d ed. Chicago: University of Chicago Press.

Kutchins, H., and S. A. Kirk. 1997. *Making Us Crazy.* New York: The Free Press.

Laidlaw, T. A., and C. Malmo. 1990. *Healing Voices.* San Francisco: Jossey-Bass Publishers.

Lambert, M. J.; D. Shapiro; and A. E. Bergin. 1986. The Effectiveness of Psychotherapy. In *Handbook of Psychotherapy and Behavior Change,* edited by S. L. Garfield and A. E. Bergin, 157–211. New York: John Wiley and Sons.

Lanning, K. V. 1989. Satanic, Occult, Ritualistic Crime: A Law Enforcement Perspective. *Police Chief,* October, 62–83.

Lasch, C. 1980. *The Culture of Narcissism.* New York: W. W. Norton & Company.

Lazarus, R. S. 1987. Revisioning the Unconscious. *Canadian Psychology/Psychologie Canadienne 28* (2): 105–6.

Lear, J. 1995. The Shrink Is In. *The New Republic,* 25 December, 18–25.

Lehmann-Haupt, C. 1997. Icon of Psychology Has a Great Fall. *New York Times,* 13 January.

Leibin, V. 1986. Psychoanalysis: Science or Hermeneutics? *Behavioral and Brain Sciences 9* (2): 246–47.

Levitas, G. B, ed. 1965. *The World of Psychoanalysis.* New York: George Braziller.

Lewes, K. 1988. *The Psychoanalytic Theory of Male Homosexuality.* New York: Simon and Schuster.

Lewin, K. 1958. Group Decision and Social Change. In *Readings in Social Psychology,* edited by E. E. Maccoby, T. M. Newcomb, and E. L. Hartley, 197–211. New York: Holt, Rinehart and Winston.

Lipstadt, D. 1993. *Denying the Holocaust.* New York: The Free Press.

Lo, B., and L. Dornbrand. 1984. Letters to the Editor. *New England Journal of Medicine* 311: 1384.

Loeber, R.; K. Keenan; B. B. Lahey; S. M. Green; and C. Thomas. 1993. Evidence for Developmentally Based Diagnosis of Oppositional Defiant Disorder and Conduct Disorder. *Journal of Abnormal Child Psychology* 21 (4): 377.

Lomas, P. 1993. *Cultivating Intuition: An Introduction to Psychotherapy.* Northvale, N.J.: Jason Aronson, Inc.

Luborsky, L. 1986. Evidence to Lessen Professor Grunbaum's Concern About Freud's Clinical Inference Method. *Behavioral and Brain Sciences* 9 (2): 247–49.

———. 1995. Are Common Factors Across Different Psychotherapies the Main Explanation for the Dodo Bird Verdict That "Everyone Has Won So All Shall Have Prizes"? *Clinical Psychology: Science and Practice* 2 (1): 106–9.

MacDonald, H. 1995. SSI Fosters Disabling Dependency. *Wall Street Journal,* 20 January.

Mackay, C. 1996. *Extraordinary Popular Delusions and the Madness of Crowds/Confusion de Confusiones.* New York: John Wiley and Sons.

Macmillan, M. 1997. *Freud Evaluated: The Completed Arc.* Cambridge, Mass.: MIT Press.

Maher, B. 1983. Meta-analysis: We Need Better Analysis. *Behavioral and Brain Sciences* 6: 297–98.

Malcolm, J. 1984. *In the Freud Archives.* New York: Alfred A. Knopf.

Marin, P. 1995. *Freedom and Its Discontents,* 2d ed. South Royalton, Vt.: Steerforth Press.

———. 1996. An American Yearning. *Harper's Magazine,* December, 35–43.

Markowitz, L. 1997. Ten Innovative Therapists Who Do More Than Just Talk. *Utne Reader,* January/February, 57–64.

Marmor, J. 1986. The Question of Causality. *Behavioral and Brain Sciences* 9 (2): 249.

Masling, J. 1986. Psychoanalysis, Case Histories, and Experimental Data. *Behavioral and Brain Sciences* 9 (2): 249–50.

Masson, J. M., ed. 1985. *The Complete Letters of Sigmund Freud to Wilhelm Fliess, 1887–1904.* Cambridge, Mass.: The Belknap Press.

———. 1988. *Against Therapy: Emotional Tyranny and the Myth of Psychological Healing.* New York: Atheneum.

———. 1990. *Final Analysis: The Making and Unmaking of a Psychoanalyst.* Reading, Pa.: Addison-Wesley Publishing Co.

———. 1992. *The Assault on Truth.* New York: HarperPerennial.

McClure, M. B. 1990. *Reclaiming the Heart.* New York: Warner Books.

McHugh, P. 1987a. Psychiatry and Its Scientific Relatives: "A Little More Than Kin and Less Than Kind." *Journal of Nervous and Mental Disease* 175 (10): 579–83.

————. 1987b. William Osher and the New Psychiatry. *Annals of Internal Medicine 107*: 914–18.

————. 1992. Psychiatric Misadventures. *American Scholar 61* (4): 497–510.

————. 1994. Psychotherapy Awry. *American Scholar 63* (1): 17–30.

————. 1995. What's the Story? *American Scholar 64* (2) 191–203.

McHugh, P., and P. Slavney. 1983. *The Perspectives of Psychiatry*. Baltimore: The Johns Hopkins University Press.

Medawar, P. B. 1975. Victims of Psychiatry. *New York Review of Books,* 23 January, 17.

Meehl, P. E. 1960. The Cognitive Activity of the Clinician. *American Psychologist 15* (1): 19–27.

————. 1991. *Selected Philosophical and Methodological Papers*. Minneapolis: University of Minnesota Press.

Mendelsohn, R. 1991. *Leaps: Facing Risks in Offering a Constructive Therapeutic Response When Unusual Measures Are Necessary*. Northvale, N.J.: Jason Aronson, Inc.

Menninger, K. 1958. *Theory of Psychoanalytic Technique*. New York: Basic Books.

————. 1963. *The Vital Balance*. New York: Viking.

Mesic, P. 1992. Presence of Minds. *Chicago Magazine,* September, 101–30.

Miller, A. 1986. *Thou Shalt Not Be Aware*. New York: Meridian.

————. 1990. *Banished Knowledge*. New York: Nan A. Talese/Doubleday.

————. 1993. *Breaking Down the Wall of Silence*. New York: Meridian.

Minsky, T. 1987. Prisoners of Psychotherapy. *New York* magazine, 31 August, 34–40.

Mitchell, S. A., and M. J. Black. 1995. *Freud and Beyond*. New York: Basic Books.

Mithers, C. L. 1994. *Therapy Gone Mad*. Reading, Mass.: Addison-Wesley Publishing Co.

Mohr, D. C. 1995. Negative Outcome in Psychotherapy: A Critical Review. *Clinical Psychology: Science and Practice 2* (1): 1–27.

Molden, P., and I. Gottesman. 1997. At Issue: Genes, Experience, and Chance in Schizophrenia—Positioning for the 21st Century. *Schizophrenia Bulletin 23* (4): 547–61.

Moore, T. 1992. *Care of the Soul*. New York: HarperPerennial.

Moses-Hrushovski, R. 1994. *Deployment: Hiding Behind Power Struggles as a Character Defense*. Northvale, N.J.: Jason Aronson, Inc.

Murphy, G., and A. J. Bachrach, eds. 1954. *An Outline of Abnormal Psychology*. New York: Random House.

New Age Journal. 1992. Is Therapy Turning Us into Children? May/June, 60–65, 136–41.

Nichols, M., and T. Paolino. 1986. *Basic Techniques of Psychodynamic Psychotherapy*. Northvale, N.J.: Jason Aronson, Inc.

Nisbett, R. E., and N. Bellows. 1977. Verbal Reports About Casual Influences on Social Judgments: Private Access versus Public Theories. *Personality and Social Psychology 35* (9): 613–24.

Nisbett, R. E., and L. Ross. 1980. *Human Inference: Strategies and Shortcomings of Social Judgment*. Englewood Cliffs, N.J.: Prentice-Hall, Inc.

Nisbett, R. E., and T. D. Wilson. 1977. Telling More Than We Can Know: Verbal Reports on Mental Processes. *Psychological Review 84* (3): 231–59.

Notturno, M. A., and P. R. McHugh. 1986. Is Freudian Psychoanalytic Theory Really Falsifiable? *Behavioral and Brain Sciences 9* (2): 250–52.

O'Donnell, J. M. 1985. *The Origins of Behaviorism.* New York: New York University Press.

Ofshe, R., and E. Watters. 1993. Making Monsters. *Society 30* (3): 4–16.

———. 1994. *Making Monsters: False Memories, Psychotherapy, and Sexual Hysteria.* New York: Scribner.

O'Hanlon, W. H., and A. L. Hexum, eds. 1990. *An Uncommon Casebook: The Complete Clinical Work of Milton H. Erickson, M.D.* New York: W. W. Norton & Company.

Olfson, M., and H. A. Pincus. 1994. Outpatient Psychotherapy in the United States, II: Patterns of Utilization. *American Journal of Psychiatry 151* (9): 1289–94.

Orne, M. T. 1979. The Use and Misuse of Hypnosis in Court. *International Journal of Clinical and Experimental Hypnosis 27* (4): 311–41.

Orne, M. T., and B. L. Bates. In press. Reflections on Multiple Personality Disorder: A View from the Looking-glass of Hypnosis Past. In *The Mosaic of Contemporary Psychiatry in Perspective.* New York: Springer Verlag.

Ostow, M. 1962. *Drugs in Psychoanalysis and Psychotherapy.* New York: Basic Books.

Pagnini, A. 1986. The Persistence of the "Exegetical Myth." *Behavioral and Brain Sciences 9* (2): 252.

Papolos, D., and J. Papolos. 1992. *Overcoming Depression,* 2d ed. New York: HarperPerennial.

Paul, W. L. 1993. *Therapeutic Communications: Principles and Effective Practice.* New York: Basic Books.

Peck, M. S. 1978. *The Road Less Traveled: A New Psychology of Love, Traditional Values and Spiritual Growth.* New York: Simon and Schuster.

Perrott, L. A. 1996. It's the Paradigm, Stupid! *The Independent Practitioner 16* (4): 193–96.

———. 1997. Re-inventing Your Independent Practice as a Business Psychologist. In *American Psychological Association Annual Convention,* 14–17 August, Chicago.

Perry, S. 1997. Waking Up with the House on Fire. *Utne Reader,* January/February, 53–62.

Perry, S.; A. M. Cooper; and R. Michels. 1987. The Psychodynamic Formulation: Its Purpose, Structure, and Clinical Application. *American Journal of Psychiatry 144* (5): 543–50.

Pers, U. 1995. Touching the Complex Soul of "Elizabeth Frankenstein." *Washington Times,* 23 July, B7.

Pettinati, H. M., ed. 1988. *Hypnosis and Memory.* New York and London: Guilford Press.

Pollock, G. H. 1986. Is There a "Two-Cultures" Model for Psychoanalysis? *Behavioral and Brain Sciences 9* (2): 253–54.

Popper, K. 1986. Predicting Overt Behavior versus Predicting Hidden States. *Behavioral and Brain Sciences 9* (2): 254–55.

Prioleau, L.; M. Murdock; and N. Brody. 1983. An Analysis of Psychotherapy versus Placebo Studies. *Behavioral and Brain Sciences* 6: 275–85, 303–10.

Prochaska, J. O. 1995. Common Problems: Common Solutions. *Clinical Psychology: Science and Practice* 2 (1): 101–5.

Prozan, C. K. 1992. *Feminist Psychoanalytic Psychotherapy.* Northvale, N.J.: Jason Aronson, Inc.

———. 1993. *The Technique of Feminist Psychoanalytic Psychotherapy.* Northvale, N.J.: Jason Aronson, Inc.

Purser, R. E.; C. Park; and A. Montuori. 1995. Limits to Anthropocentrism: Toward an Ecocentric Organization Paradigm? Topic Forum on Ecologically Sustainable Organizations. *Academy of Management Review* 20 (4): 1053.

Putnam, F. W. 1989. *Diagnosis and Treatment of Multiple Personality Disorder.* New York and London: Guilford Press.

———. 1991. The Satanic Ritual Abuse Controversy. *Child Abuse and Neglect* 15: 175–79.

Quinnett, P. G. 1989. The Key to Successful Therapy. *Psychology Today,* April, 46–47.

Rachman, A. 1991. An Oedipally Conflicted Patient. In *Psychotherapy of the Submerged Personality,* edited by A. Wolf and I. Kutash, 217–38. Northvale, N.J.: Jason Aronson, Inc.

Ramirez, D. E. 1994. Toward a Concept of the Counselor as Philosopher/Practitioner: Commentary on Whitaker, Geller, and Webb. *Journal of College Student Psychotherapy* 9 (2): 63–74.

Ratey, J. J., and C. Johnson. 1997. *Shadow Syndromes.* New York: Pantheon Books.

Reich, W. 1951. *Selected Writings: An Introduction to Orgonomy.* New York: Farrar, Straus and Giroux.

———. 1972. *Character Analysis,* 3d ed. Translated by Vincent R. Carfagno. New York: Noonday Press.

Reiser, M. F. 1986. Grunbaum's Critique of Clinical Psychoanalytic Evidence: A Sheep in Wolf's Clothing? *Behavioral and Brain Sciences* 9 (2): 255–56.

Richardson, J. T.; J. Best; and D. G. Bromley. 1991. *The Satanic Scare.* New York: Aldine de Gruyter.

Rieff, D. 1991. Victims, All? *Harper's Magazine,* October, 49–56.

Rind, B., and P. Tromovitch. 1997. *Journal of Sex Research* 34 (3): 237–55.

Roazen, P. 1975. *Freud and His Followers.* New York: Alfred A. Knopf.

Robinson, K. 1994. Book May Create Factory View of Mental Health. *Star Tribune,* 6 November, 1E.

Rogler, L. H.; R. G. Malgady; and W. W. Tryon. 1992. Evaluation of Mental Health. *Journal of Nervous and Mental Disease* 180 (4): 215–22.

Rosenhan, D. L., and M. E. P. Seligman. 1984. *Abnormal Psychology.* New York: W. W. Norton & Company.

Rosenthal, R. 1983. Improving Meta-analytic Procedures for Assessing the Effects of Psychotherapy versus Placebo. *Behavioral and Brain Sciences* 6: 298–99.

Rosenthal, T. L. 1983. Outcome Research: Isn't Sauce for the Goose Sauce for the Gander? *Behavioral and Brain Sciences* 6: 299–300.

Rossi, E. L. 1987. The Psychobiology of Dissociation and Identification. *Canadian Psychology/Psychologie Canadienne* 28 (2): 112–13.

Roszak, T. 1996. The Nature of Sanity, Mental Health and the Outdoors. *Psychology Today,* January, 22.

Ruse, M. 1986. Grunbaum on Psychoanalysis: Where Do We Go from Here? *Behavioral and Brain Sciences* 9 (2): 256–57.

Rutter, V. 1994. A Very Embarrassing Story. *Psychology Today,* March/April, 5, 95.

Sakheim, D. K., and S. E. Devine. 1992. *Out of Darkness.* New York: Lexington Books.

Salter, S., and C. Ness. 1993. Buried Memories, Broken Families. *San Francisco Examiner,* 4–9 April, 1–10.

Sandroff, R. 1989. Is Your Job Driving You Crazy? *Psychology Today,* July/August, 41–45.

Savodnik, I. 1986. Some Gaps in Grunbaum's Critique of Psychoanalysis. *Behavioral and Brain Sciences* 9 (2): 257.

Scharnberg, M. 1993. *The Non-Authentic Nature of Freud's Observations.* Uppsala, Sweden: Uppsala University.

Schwarz, W. 1993. Eco Psychology: Mind Over Matter in a Mad World. *The Guardian,* 20 March, 27.

Sebeok, T. A. 1983. Psychotherapy and Placebo: "Sticks and Stones Will Break My Bones, But Can Words Never Harm Me?" *Behavioral and Brain Sciences* 6: 300.

Seitz, P. F. D. 1966. The Consensus Problem in Psychoanalytic Research. In *Methods of Research in Psychotherapy,* edited by L. A. Gottschalk and A. H. Auerbach, 209–25. New York: Appleton-Century-Crofts.

Seligman, M. E. P. 1995. The Effectiveness of Psychotherapy: The *Consumer Reports* Study. *American Psychologist* 50 (12): 956–74.

Shapiro, D. A. 1983. Refinement, Precision, and Representativeness in Meta-analysis. *Behavioral and Brain Sciences* 6: 300–1.

Shapiro, L. 1993. Rush to Judgment. *Newsweek,* 19 April, 54–60.

Shedler, J.; M. Mayman; and M. Manis. 1993. The Illusion of Mental Health. *American Psychologist* 48 (11): 1117–31.

Shengold, L. 1989. *Soul Murder.* New York: Fawcett Columbine.

Shepherd, M. 1983. Psychotherapy Outcome Research and Parloff's Pony. *Behavioral and Brain Sciences* 6: 301–2.

Shermer, M. 1997. *Why People Believe Weird Things.* New York: W. H. Freeman and Company.

Sherwood, V. R., and C. P. Cohen. 1994. *Psychotherapy of the Quiet Borderline Patient.* Northvale, N.J.: Jason Aronson, Inc.

Shevrin, H. 1986. An Argument for the Evidential Standing of Psychoanalytic Data. *Behavioral and Brain Sciences* 9 (2): 257–59.

Shorter, E. 1997. *A History of Psychiatry: From the Era of the Asylum to the Age of Prozac.* New York: John Wiley and Sons, Inc.

Showalter, E. 1997. *Hystories: Hysterical Epidemics and Modern Media.* New York: Columbia University Press.

Sifford, D. 1987. How a Suit May Change Psychiatric Practice. *Philadelphia Inquirer,* 28 June, sec. I, 1.

BIBLIOGRAPHY

Singer, M. T., and J. Lalich. 1996. *"Crazy" Therapies: What Are They? Do They Work?* San Francisco: Jossey-Bass Publishers.

Skolnick, A. 1978. The Myth of the Vulnerable Child. *Psychology Today,* February, 56–65.

Smith, L. D. 1986. *Behaviorism and Logical Positivism.* Stanford, Calif.: Stanford University Press.

Smith, M. L., and G. V. Glass. 1977. Meta-analysis of Psychotherapy Outcome Studies. *American Psychologist 32* (September): 752–60.

Smith, S. 1995. Applied Ecopsychology—Internet to Nature. *M2 Presswire,* 30 May.

Spence, D. P. 1982. *Narrative Truth and Historical Truth.* New York: W. W. Norton & Company.

———. 1983. Therapeutic Effectiveness: What Domain Is Being Studied? *Behavioral and Brain Sciences 6*: 302.

———. 1986. Are Free Associations Necessarily Contaminated? *Behavioral and Brain Sciences 9* (2): 259.

———. 1987. More Than a Metaphor? *Canadian Psychology/Psychologie Canadienne 28* (2): 108–10.

Spitzer, R. L., ed. 1994. *Case Book: A Learning Companion to the Diagnostic and Statistical Manual of Mental Disorders,* 4th ed. Washington, D.C.: American Psychiatric Press.

Spock, B. 1961. *Dr. Spock Talks with Mothers.* Cambridge, Mass.: The Riverside Press.

Stafford-Clark, D. 1965. *What Freud Really Said.* New York: Schocken Books.

Starr, P. 1982. *The Social Transformation of American Medicine.* New York: Basic Books.

Steinem, G. 1992. *Revolution from Within.* Boston: Little, Brown.

Stone, A. A. 1984. The New Paradox of Psychiatric Malpractice. *New England Journal of Medicine 311*: 1384.

———. 1995. Where Will Psychoanalysis Survive? Address to American Academy of Psychoanalysis, 9 December.

Storr, A. 1986. Human Understanding and Scientific Validation. *Behavioral and Brain Sciences 9* (2): 259–60.

Strupp, H. H. 1986. Transference: One of Freud's Basic Discoveries. *Behavioral and Brain Sciences 9* (2): 260.

———. 1995. The Psychotherapist's Skills Revisited. *Clinical Psychology: Science and Practice 2* (1): 70–74.

Sulloway, F. J. 1992. *Freud, Biologist of the Mind,* 2d ed. Cambridge, Mass.: Harvard University Press.

Tavris, C. 1992. *The Mismeasure of Woman.* New York: Touchstone.

Taylor, R. L. 1982. *Mind or Body: Distinguishing Psychological from Organic Disorders.* New York: McGraw-Hill.

Terr, L. 1990. *Too Scared to Cry.* New York: Basic Books.

———. 1994. *Unchained Memories, True Stories of Traumatic Memories Lost and Found.* New York: HarperCollins.

———. 1991. Childhood Traumas: An Outline and Overview. *American Journal of Psychiatry 148* (1): 10–20.

Tetlock, P. E. 1994. The Psychology of Futurology and the Future of Psychology. *Journal of the American Psychological Society 5* (1): 1–4.

Thompson, C.; M. Mazer; and E. Witenberg, eds. 1995. *An Outline of Psycho-analysis*. New York: Random House.

Thornton, E. M. 1983. *The Freudian Fallacy*. Garden City, N.Y.: The Dial Press.

Time, 1979. Psychiatry on the Couch. 2 April, 74–82.

Torrenzano, S. 1995. The Academic Journey of a Body-Centered Psychothera-pist. *Massage Therapy Journal*, Spring, 31–36.

Torrey, E. F. 1972. *The Mind Game: Witchdoctors and Psychiatrists*. New York: Emerson Hall.

———. 1974. *The Death of Psychiatry*. Radnor, Pa.: Chilton Book Company.

Toumey, C. 1997. *Scientific American* 276 (1): 96–100.

Tversky, A., and D. Kahneman. 1974. Judgment Under Uncertainty: Heuristics and Biases. *Science* 185: 1124–31.

Ursano, R. J., and R. E. Hales. 1986. A Review of Brief Individual Psychother-apies. *American Journal of Psychiatry* 143 (12): 1507–17.

U.S. Department of Health and Human Services. 1995. *United States Health 1994*. Washington, D.C.: Government Printing Office. DHHs Pub. No. (PHS) 95–1232.

Valenstein, E. S. 1986. *Great and Desperate Cures*. New York: Basic Books.

Vaughan, S. C. 1997. *The Talking Cure*. New York: G. P. Putnam's Sons.

Victor, J. S. 1993. *Satanic Panic*. Chicago and La Salle: Open Court.

Wachtel, P. L. 1973. Psychodynamics, Behavior Therapy, and the Implacable Experimenter: An Inquiry into the Consistency of Personality. *Journal of Abnormal Psychology* 82 (2): 324–34.

———. 1986. Early Freud, Late Freud, Conflict and Intentionality. *Behavioral and Brain Sciences* 9 (2): 263–64.

———. 1987. "The Unconscious" and Unconscious Processes. *Canadian Psy-chology/Psycholgie Canadienne* 28 (2): 107–8.

———. 1993. *Therapeutic Conversation: Principles and Effective Practice*. New York: Guilford Publications, Inc.

Wagstaf, G. F. 1981. *Hypnosis, Compliance and Belief*. New York: St. Martin's Press.

Walker, S. 1996. *A Dose of Sanity: Mind, Medicine, and Misdiagnosis*. New York: John Wiley and Sons, Inc.

Walsh, M. R., ed. 1987. *The Psychology of Women*. New Haven, Conn.: Yale University Press.

Watters, E. 1991. The Devil in Mr. Ingram. *Mother Jones*, July/August, 30–33.

———. 1993. Doors of Memory. *Mother Jones*, January/February, 24–29.

Wax, M. L. 1986. Psychoanalysis: Conventional Wisdom, Self-Knowledge, or Inexact Science. *Behavioral and Brain Sciences* 9 (2): 264–65.

Webster, R. 1995. *Why Freud Was Wrong*. New York: Basic Books.

Weeks, L. 1996. Sometimes a Show Is More Than a Show. *San Francisco Chronicle*, 4 March.

Weinberg, G. 1984. *The Heart of Psychotherapy*. New York: St. Martin's Grif-fin.

Weinberger, J. 1995. Common Factors Aren't So Common: The Common Fac-tors Dilemma. *Clinical Psychology: Science and Practice* 2 (1): 45–69.

Weiss, J. 1990. Unconscious Mental Functioning. *Scientific American*, March, 103–9.

BIBLIOGRAPHY

White, S. H. 1994. Hilgard's Vision of Psychology's History. *Psychological Science* 5 (4): 192–93.

Wilson, G. T. 1983. Limitations of Meta-analysis and the Lack of Evidence That Psychotherapy Works. *Behavioral and Brain Sciences* 6: 302–3.

Wolberg, L. R. 1988. *The Technique of Psychotherapy (Part One)*, 4th ed. Northvale, N.J.: Jason Aronson, Inc.

———. 1995. *The Technique of Psychotherapy (Part Two)*, 4th ed. Northvale, N.J.: Jason Aronson, Inc.

Wolf, A., and I. Kutash. 1991. *Psychotherapy of the Submerged Personality.* Northvale, N.J.: Jason Aronson, Inc.

Wood, G. 1978. The Knew-It-All-Along Effect. *Journal of Experimental Psychology* 4 (2): 345–53.

Woolfolk, R. L. 1986. Hermeneutics and Psychoanalysis. *Behavioral and Brain Sciences* 9 (2): 265–66.

———. 1998. *The Cure of Souls: Science, Values, and Psychotherapy.* San Francisco: Jossey-Bass Publishers.

Young, A. 1995. *The Harmony of Illusions: Inventing Post-Traumatic Stress Disorder.* Princeton, N.J.: Princeton University Press.

Young, J. H. 1967. *The Medical Messiahs.* Princeton, N.J.: Princeton University Press.

Zuckerman, M.; D. M. Kuhlman; J. Joireman; P. Teta; and M. Kraft. 1993. A Comparison of Three Structural Models for Personality: The Big Three, the Big Five, and the Alternative Five. *Journal of Personality and Social Psychology* 65 (4): 757-68.

Index

Adams, Samuel Hopkins, 230
Alexander, Franz, 82, 83
Alexander, Norman, 197, 203
Allen, Henry, 211
Almeida, Rhea, 151
American Academy of Psychoanalysis, 64
American Medical Association, 79
American Psychiatric Association, 73, 74, 79, 219
American Psychoanalytic Association, 73, 78, 79, 80–81, 82
American Psychological Association (APA), 90, 227, 236, 247–49
convention of, 29–36, 167
American Psychological Society, 53, 231
"American Yearning, An" (Marin), 125
Anderson, Craig, 166, 167
And They Call It Help (Armstrong), 219
antidepressant drugs, 47–48, 96–99, 215, 222, 227, 243
anxiety, 35, 39, 40, 95, 134, 138–39, 140, 172, 195, 215, 223, 225, 226
Armstrong, Louise, 219
Arnoult, Lynn, 166, 167
Art of the Psychotherapist, The (Bugental), 143, 145, 157
assumptive systems, 133–34, 136–37, 140–41, 228
asthma, 82–83, 93, 178
asylums, mental, 77, 82

attention deficit/hyperactivity disorder, 220–21
Austad, Carol Shaw, 235–36
autism, 225

Basic Techniques of Psychodynamic Psychotherapy (Nichols and Paolino), 145, 148
behavioral therapy, 21, 29, 90, 93, 125
belief-building process, 13, 17, 19–20, 27, 49–50, 70, 159–92
causal theories in, 166–70, 187–88
cultural influence in, 187–92
patient confirmation in, 17, 19–20, 38, 39, 40, 42–43, 50, 120, 125–27, 134–40, 147, 158, 159–70, 171–79, 181–82, 187, 188, 234–35
see also interpretations; transference
Bem, Darryl, 197, 202, 203
Beyond Depression (Canale), 153
biomedical approach, 20–22, 23–25, 37, 41, 42–48, 90, 91–92, 99, 125, 142, 152, 208, 211–31, 243–46
accountability of, 44
advances in, 44–45, 213–14, 224–25, 228
diagnosis in, 215–23, 225
environmental factors in, 223–24, 243
mental complexity and, 43–44, 47, 245–46

277